CHEYENNE GARDEN GOSSIP

Locals Share Secrets for High Plains Gardening Success

BARB GORGES

YUCCA ROAD PRESS

CHEYENNE, WYOMING

Also by Barb Gorges:

Quilt Care, Construction and Use Advice

Cheyenne Birds by the Month (with photographer Pete Arnold)

Dear Book: The 1916-1920 Diary of Gertrude Oehler Witte

All photos are by the author with exceptions listed on the Photo Credits page.

Much of this book was previously published in the Wyoming Tribune Eagle, 2012-2021, but has been adapted and updated.

No remuneration has been received by the author from companies whose products are mentioned in this book.

Published in 2021 by Yucca Road Press
3417 Yucca Road
Cheyenne, Wyoming 82001

Printed by Frederic Printing, Aurora, Colorado. 1st printing

Book design by Chris Hoffmeister, Western Sky Design

ISBN 978-0-9992945-6-7

DEDICATED TO MARK
AND ALL THE CHEYENNE GARDENERS,
PAST, PRESENT AND FUTURE.

TABLE OF CONTENTS

The Shane Smith Grand Conservatory is the central feature of the Cheyenne Botanic Gardens.

FOREWORD

This is a book that speaks to you directly, by not only the author, Barb Gorges, but many accomplished gardeners on the High Plains* in Southeast Wyoming. To be a successful gardener here is no easy task. In fact, I believe it is the most challenging garden climate in the lower 48 states.

Why is gardening here such a challenge? Let's look at Cheyenne, which is indicative of much of the High Plains. It has the highest average number of hailstorms per year in the nation, between 8 and 11. Cheyenne is the fourth windiest city in the nation with a daily average wind speed of 13 miles per hour. This means for every calm day you must have a 26-miles-per-hour day to make that average work. Cheyenne also has unpredictable spring and fall frosts. This kills fruit blossoms in spring and can turn a garden brown even in early September.

Plants grow at night. The warmer it is at night, the faster they grow. Because of Cheyenne's 6,000-foot elevation, it has cool summer nights, staying mostly in the 40s and 50s. Gardens grow much faster when most of the nights are in the upper 50s to mid-60s. This is why that 65-day tomato still takes 80 days to produce.

Finally, Cheyenne often has many winter days with little or no snow cover. There are years when Cheyenne has fewer days with snow on the ground than other lower altitude Front Range towns. This lack of snow cover combined with the relentless wind desiccates plants. That is why you often must drag out the hose in winter to water your trees, shrubs and perennials to keep them alive and in maximum health. Whew! Gardeners on the High Plains deserve a medal for their harvests and beautiful flowers.

Because of the challenging climate, Cheyenne and High Plains gardeners must do things differently. To have a successful garden in this climate you often need different scheduling and different varieties, and you must develop creative hail-protection strategies. On top of all that, it helps to become an accomplished weather watcher.

In this book, Barb has put together a diverse and experienced group of expert gardeners, who first appeared in her regular writings for the Wyoming Tribune Eagle in her excellent Cheyenne Garden Gossip column and blog. Barb also offers up her own great tips from her extensive gardening experiences.

This book has a wide breadth of gardening and landscaping subjects. Besides the traditional flowers and vegetables, Barb discusses how to successfully grow habitat gardens, rain gardens, xeriscapes, ground covers, fruit trees, worm farms, hoop house gardens, straw bales gardens and more. Both newbies and experienced gardeners are sure to find enlightening information.

While the High Plains are an exceptional challenge, this book will help you even the odds in your garden's favor. Go get your hands dirty!

Best Regardens!
Shane Smith
Founder and Director Emeritus of the Cheyenne Botanic Gardens

*Horticulturists generally consider that the heart of the High Plains includes southeastern Wyoming, northeastern Colorado, western Nebraska and western Kansas.

Look for Shane Smith's snippets of wisdom throughout the book. They are a distillation of 40 years of gardening experience in Cheyenne, at work and home.

Penstemons are showy wildflowers often found in gardens: Rocky Mountain Penstemon, *Penstemon strictus (left) in the Gorges garden and* Sidebells Penstemon, *Penstemon secundiflorus (right) at Belvoir Ranch (before wind turbines were installed).*

PREFACE

I am a descendant of farmers. Though I never gardened growing up, I had a window full of houseplants by high school. I went off to the University of Wisconsin – Stevens Point to study natural resource management, which is about growing trees and wild animals. I minored in writing and worked on the campus weekly.

Volunteer and bottom-rung jobs took me to national parks, forests and rangelands in Colorado, Utah, South Dakota, Montana and Wyoming and eventually back to school at the University of Wyoming to study range management.

Another back-to-school episode, some years after being a naturalist-in-training in New York City, was earning my certification in elementary education. I learned that if someone doesn't understand what you are saying, it is your job to understand what they do know and work from there.

After my husband, young boys and I moved to Cheyenne, Wyoming, I started planting perennials familiar to me, natives of the Great Plains and Rocky Mountains, like penstemon and prairie coneflower.

After a dozen years as the monthly bird columnist for the Wyoming Tribune Eagle (my husband Mark and I are active Audubon members), I asked if I might also write a monthly garden column, contingent on taking the local Master Gardener training.

I was lucky to join the group of seasoned gardeners willing to share their knowledge. The director of the Cheyenne Botanic Gardens, Shane Smith, now retired, was also supportive as were other local professionals.

There should be a locally-written garden newspaper column for every town, especially in the Rocky Mountain states where growing conditions can change in 20 miles or less. A book for local gardeners means readers might accumulate local wisdom in less time than without a guide. This book is an adaptation and update of garden columns I wrote from 2012 through 2021.

Cheyenne gardeners like to say this is a tough place to garden, but my philosophy is that any place can be tough if you don't understand how to choose the right plant for the right place. And sometimes you must make the right place yourself.

What I've learned about gardeners is that they can't resist a challenge. There is always a new variety or newly rediscovered heirloom that might work here. Can cuttings from the groundcover in the backyard be propagated and transplanted to grow in the front yard? Why not give it a try?

If you are already a gardener, I hope this book gives you new ideas. If you want to be a gardener, I hope this book provides inspiration as well as guidance that will improve your chance of success.

Barb Gorges
May 2021

New to Cheyenne but not to gardening, Sandra Cox grew vegetables successfully her first year here.

INTRODUCTION

A TRANSPLANTED GARDENER BLOOMS IN CHEYENNE

There's only one thing that beats Sandra Cox's love of gardening: It's love for her family.

In July 2017, she gave up gardening in the Hudson Valley of New York state to move to Cheyenne at the invitation of her son and his family. She left behind a newly planted orchard and everything she knew about gardening there to start over at her new home.

When Sandra arrived, no one had watered her new yard for some months, and our clay soil required a pickax to plant the calla lilies she brought with her. But with care and mulch, by the end of the season, time to dig them back up, she was pleased to see a healthy population of earthworms.

Sandra's garden in New York was in the same Zone 5 USDA Plant Hardiness Zone (coldest temperature rating) as Cheyenne. But there are six major differences:

1. Cheyenne has alkaline soils rather than acidic, so adding lime or wood ash is a no-no.

2. Cheyenne has a shorter growing season at 6,000 feet. Sandra has learned she will have to start her peppers and eggplant indoors earlier and put them outside, with protection, earlier.

3. Cheyenne has 12-15 inches of precipitation annually, one-third of New York's. Watering is necessary much more often here. She's thinking about installing an irrigation system.

4. Cheyenne has hail. Although the tomato plants this summer made a comeback, the tomatoes themselves were scarred. Sandra's planning to protect them with wire cages next year.

5. Cheyenne has different soil — clayey instead of sandy.

6. Cheyenne has wind. Sandra found floating row covers blow away and she needed mulch to keep the soil from drying out.

Although she arrived mid-summer 2017, Sandra went to work establishing a vegetable garden. "I disturb the soil as little as possible to avoid disrupting the earthworms because they do all the work for you," she explained.

Instead, she spread leaves over the abandoned lawn, laid down a layer of cardboard from the packing boxes from her move, then covered them with wood chips from the city compost facility. To keep the chips from blowing away, she laid wire fencing over them and pegged it down.

On warm days over the winter when there was no snow on the ground, she watered to keep the cardboard moist and composting. In the spring, she removed the fencing and planted directly into this mulch.

Sandra researches the best varieties to plant in our climate. Her first fall, she planted grapes and an apple and a plum tree. Last spring, she planted pear, peach and sweet cherry trees. The cherries did very well.

In the north-facing front yard, Sandra has planted shrubs for privacy and perennials for pollinators and pleasure. The city's street tree planting program, Rooted in Cheyenne, came out and planted a burr oak and a linden. A huge spruce tree shades the house on hot summer afternoons.

One day last fall, she called and asked if we'd come harvest some kale and Swiss chard since she had too much. What an oasis of lush green! And her giant sunflowers were at least 12 feet high. A sunny yard helps, but much of her success can be attributed to her dedication to compost — she composts everything, and her chickens help break it down.

Sandra hasn't used fertilizer yet — other than fish emulsion and well-aged chicken manure. She's planning to do a soil test this next year to see if she has any deficiencies, but her plants didn't seem to show any signs.

Pests are not a problem so far. Sandra thinks it is only a matter of time before the pests catch up with her. Already she's concerned about the big spruce tree being attacked by the ips beetle. It has killed other spruces in her neighborhood, she thinks. The city forester recommended winter watering — good for all her newly planted trees and shrubs, but also good for older trees for which drought stress makes them more susceptible to pests.

Unlike New York, which normally has constant winter snow cover,

Cheyenne has snowless weeks plus days when the temperatures are above freezing — good days for watering trees.

Sandra remembers that growing up on the family farm was a constant delight, from taking care of the goats to eating apples while high up in the branches, to joining her parents and five siblings in the field after dinner to weed, joke around and enjoy each other's company. Her siblings still enjoy gardening and farming, as does her son, who has a degree in horticulture. Her granddaughters have caught the family enthusiasm as well.

"Bloom where you're planted" is an old axiom that doesn't just mean, "make the best of a situation." For Sandra, it means with a little studying up, she can joyfully grow a garden anywhere, even here.

GARDEN GALLERY

Tava Collins asked for her neighbors' permission before hanging flowers on the side of their garage.

Jutta Arkan has created a cottage-style, flower-filled border.

Bonnie Harper's flower garden is a series of terraces.

Karen Pannell's husband, Fred, built on her vision of found objects as planters.

Garden plots are available to the public through the Cheyenne Botanic Gardens.

Behind the Cheyenne Botanic Gardens' propagation greenhouse is this photogenic bridge.

Claire and Bud Davis created this sheltered garden close to their house on the prairie.

Pat Scott fills her townhouse's tiny backyard almost entirely with her favorite annuals.

Bea Dersham's small, cul-de-sac-restricted front yard is all garden.

Mitchell Chapman's front garden is enjoyed by passersby.

Three bumblebees are attracted to Lila Howell's scabiosa, or pincushion flower, in her perennial bed in June.

In May, Kim Parker's front garden sparkles with daffodils, pink species tulips, pale yellow primrose and flashy 'Peppermint Stick' tulips.

PART 1

GROWING BASICS

The raised bed for growing vegetables in the Gorges' backyard is located to catch the most sun.

CHAPTER 1:
GARDEN LOCATION

FIND SUN, SOIL AND WATER

Is this the year you've decided you'll spend more time on flowers and vegetables and make that boring expanse of lawn more colorful and edible? Here's how to start.

Find the sun

Find where the sun shines on your yard and where the shadows are. This is the very first and most important step you must take. If you didn't notice last growing season, you can estimate.

See where the shadows of trees fall during the day. Find the sunny, south-facing side of your house.

For vegetables you want the sunniest location possible, at least six hours of full, summer sun. Do you have overgrown trees and shrubs that need pruning or any that are dying and in need of removal, which will make it sunnier? However, a little shade by late afternoon keeps veggie leaves from temporarily wilting.

Keep vegetable gardens close to the house so it is easier to step out, pull the occasional weed and pick the ripe tomatoes.

Flowers aren't as picky about sun because there are kinds suited to different light levels: sun, part sun, part shade and full shade. If you desire to grow a certain kind, google its light requirements.

Block the wind

In most residential neighborhoods there are enough obstacles, houses and landscaping to blunt the wind. But if you are out on the prairie, you might want to put delicate plants in the lee of the barn or first plant a board fence or windbreak to the north and west.

Get the dirt

Soil is anything a plant can stick a root into.

Good soil for vegetables (and other annuals) has lots of microorganisms that help feed the roots. Most vegetables are big feeders. They use lots of nutrients, so you'll want to dig in compost the first year and then add layers of leaf/plant/kitchen compost mulch after that as needed. No need to dig more than 0 to 2 inches again in future years.

If you use chemical fertilizer instead, follow the directions. Too much nitrogen gives you leaves and no fruit, and too much of any fertilizer gives you sick or dead plants. And remember, Cheyenne has alkaline soils so do not add alkaline amendments like lime and wood ash.

Perennial plants rated for our USDA Plant Hardiness Zone 5 or colder (Zones 3 and 4), especially native plants, are quite happy with whatever soil is available. If you are trying to grow flowers in the equivalent of pottery clay, gravel pit or sandbox, you might look for native species adapted to those kinds of soil. Or consider growing your plants in a raised bed or container you can fill with better soil.

Water carefully

Here in the West, water is a precious commodity, so save money by not throwing it everywhere. If you have a sprinkler system, make sure it isn't watering pavement.

The new era of home landscaping encourages us to replace our lawns with native perennials because they use less water. Native plants also provide food for birds, bees and butterflies, and habitat for beneficial insects.

The Cheyenne Board of Public Utilities, our water department, installed a demonstration garden at its headquarters to demonstrate how to have a beautiful landscape with less water.

But you will need to water a new perennial garden regularly until it gets established, and at other times, so figure out how far you want to lug the hose or stretch a drip irrigation system.

Once established, a native perennial garden not only takes less water than a lawn, but it doesn't require the purchase of fertilizers, pesticides or gasoline for the mower, or time spent using them. Instead, your time can be spent admiring flowers rather than mowing. However, if you convert a large lawn to a meadow or native prairie, you might want to mow it once a year.

Vegetables are water hogs. The fruits we harvest, especially tomatoes and cucumbers, are mostly water. Unless you like to contemplate life while watering by hand, check out drip irrigation (Chapter 12). You can even put a timer on the system.

Sprinklers, on the other hand, waste a lot of water, especially when it evaporates in the heat and wind before it can get to the plants.

If you abstain from watering between 9 a.m. and 5 p.m., you'll lose less to evaporation.

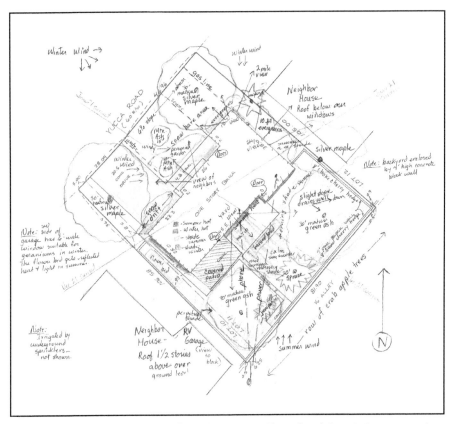

Get a diagram of your property from the county. Then sketch in existing vegetation, views and wind and sun directions.

Tyler Mason shows how wide bed-style gardening is characterized by mulched paths.

CHAPTER 2: **SITE PREP**

IT'S ALL ABOUT DIRT

Once you've selected a garden site, curb your enthusiasm in the spring until the soil is thawed and not muddy before getting out your shovel. Digging in wet soil destroys its structure.

In the spring of 2012, Mark, my husband — who is a Laramie County Master Gardener — and I established a new vegetable garden and instead of removing lawn, we had a spruce tree that needed to be removed and the largest roots dug up.

Revealing the dirt

Digging up turf with a sharp spade is hard work. One advantage is it will keep you from making your garden too large in the first year. If you are careful, you can use the spade-sized chunks to fill in bare spots elsewhere in the lawn or knock the dirt off them and compost the remains.

Or, if you plan, as my friend Sandra Cox did (see Introduction), cover the lawn in cardboard and mulch over the winter, keeping it moist.

Another option is to stake clear plastic over the turf for a few weeks, allowing the intense heat of the sun to kill off the grass and weeds.

Conventional herbicides should only be used in the residential landscape under the recommendation and guidance of the Laramie County Extension office or the Laramie County Conservation District.

Caution: Check for underground utilities before digging in your yard.

All it takes is a simple call to 811. The call and visit are free.

Fixing the dirt

Every gardener believes that his or her soil could stand improvement. I believe enough compost added over time can redeem almost every soil type.

Cheyenne's default soil is clay-like, making it difficult for plant roots to grow and draw water. Local gardeners overcome this by digging in compost at the beginning — partially decayed plant material — sometimes to a depth of about one or two feet. Mark did just that for our new garden, using the leaves from our trees that served as protective mulch for my perennials over the winter. Adding more to the top few inches every year eventually makes for loose and fluffy soil.

"Cheyenne has pretty well-balanced soil. The only clay I found was if you dig a foot or two down in some parts of the city…or where a contractor stripped off the original topsoil."—Shane

Compost is available commercially in bales. It's also available from the City of Cheyenne's compost facility. Or you can compost kitchen waste (plant-based materials only) (Chapter 9).

Be sure the compost doesn't include vegetation treated with herbicides or it might kill your plants. If you are gardening organically, make sure your compost ingredients were grown organically also.

Livestock manure use in a vegetable garden growing food for human consumption is tricky because of potential pathogens. Never use manure from cats, dogs or pigs. If you raise livestock, consult with the UW Extension office or the Laramie County Conservation District to learn how to age it and apply it safely.

"Horse manure is usually the weediest. I had better luck with cow, goat, or chicken manure." —Shane

My experience is that composted leaves and grass will improve soil structure — and encourage the soil microorganism community to flourish, acting as a low dose of fertilizer. Our veggies grow just fine on that diet.

If your plants have failed to thrive in the past or you are curious about the fertility of your soil, you could have it analyzed by experts who can tell you what kinds of amendments might be needed, and how much (Chapter 17).

Remember, our soil here, with few exceptions, is alkaline, not acidic as it is back east, so don't add wood ash and limestone.

Digging the dirt

If you do a good job of digging a new garden, you shouldn't have to do it again. Obviously, perennial gardens don't get rototilled every year. Mine receives a top dressing of leaf litter annually because I don't sweep the soil surface clean (another instance of my gardening by "neglect"). Many perennials are natives that grow in less than perfect dirt anyway.

Keep it small if this is your first time gardening. This vegetable patch uses a modified wide bed layout.

You don't have to dig the vegetable patch or annual beds each year either. I've taken the advice of Eliot Coleman, an organic market gardener in Maine and author of the book *Four-Season Harvest* and others. After the initial dig, he amends only the top few inches each year. That way soil structure isn't destroyed. Also, the less you disturb the soil, the fewer weed seeds sprout.

"I tell people to either not rototill or only do it lightly and not very deep. However, one exception is if you plant your garden near a tree. If I didn't chop the roots out to a pretty good depth each spring, I would have to water that garden daily if not twice a day because the tree was stealing all the water." — Shane

Wide bed method

Shane Smith, Cheyenne Botanic Gardens director, now retired, is also a soil protectionist. He is a proponent of wide beds rather than planting vegetables in traditional rows. Plants are set in short cross rows or staggered, depending on the space they need.

Somewhat like establishing raised beds, minus the boards to contain the soil, each bed is as wide as you can comfortably reach, maybe 3 feet. A 2-foot-wide footpath between beds means you never walk on the beds themselves, preserving the fluffiness of their soil (roots need the air), and you never have to waste time and money improving the soil of the pathways.

See Cheyenne Botanic Gardens website, Resources tab, "Gardening Tips" for more information on wide bed gardening.

PEPPER
Mini Belle Mix

BEET
Chioggia
Beta vulgaris

$2.99
1.5 grams)

**COOL SEASON
55 DAYS**
Sow in
early spring or
late summer

HEIRLOOM
*The candy-
stripe beet.
When cut,
beautiful red
and white
interior rings
are revealed.
They look like
peppermints!*

Botanical

TOMATO
Oregon Spring

TOMATO BUSH
Silvery Fir Tree
lycopersicon lycopersicum

$2.39
30 seeds

**WARM SEASON
58 DAYS** from
transplanting
after last chance
of spring frost
Determinate type

HEIRLOOM
*Compact size,
silvery foliage,
and red
tomatoes
that look like
dangling holiday
ornaments.
Pretty in a
container!*

Botanical

A seed packet is colorful, but it also has important information for growing those particular seeds.

CHAPTER 3: **SEED CHOICE**

NORTHERN, SHORT SEASON VARIETIES BEST

Why grow from seeds?

"It is so much fun to grow your own stuff," said Barb Sahl, who teaches some of the Laramie County Master Gardener classes.

Plus, you can grow varieties that might not be available at local nurseries. Best of all, you can time their growth so that they are the optimum size for transplanting to the garden.

Can I call myself a gardener if I buy blooming bedding plants and keep them alive until frost?

Possibly. But my real test is whether I can start something from seed indoors. February is not too early to make plans.

My inspiration is the pep talk

Kathy Shreve and Barb Sahl, Laramie County Master Gardeners, gave at the Master Gardeners' class. It looks so simple: fluorescent shop light, sterile seed-starting medium and pots, proper watering, a little air circulation and fresh seed.

Seed. There's the sticky spot. Some plants I like don't do well in Cheyenne or would need more sun than my shady yard offers.

This is my experiment for the coming growing season: raise from seed at least one easy annual flower and a fast tomato.

Why all the bother? Because just as I can bake my own bread, even though it's much easier to buy a loaf at the bakery, I want to see if I can grow something from scratch.

Seeds

There are several seed companies out there that cater to our unique gardening needs.

I was already familiar with Maine's Pinetree Garden Seeds. This company offers a reasonable climate match. I ordered from them years ago and Kathy does today.

Shane mentioned three seed catalogs recently that match other aspects of our challenging growing conditions.

For high altitude, try Seeds Trust in Littleton, Colorado. For drought-hardy plants, High Country Gardens in Santa Fe, New Mexico, offers recommendations on xeric gardening and both plants and seeds. For a comprehensive flower and vegetable catalog, check Johnny's Selected Seeds, in Maine.

"I also like Seeds N' Such and Territorial Seeds. Adaptive Seeds has a goal of taking F1 hybrids and turning them back into high yielding open pollinated seeds." — Shane

You can also check local garden centers, but do read the seed packets carefully.

Planting strategy

For my summer project, Catherine Wissner, University of Wyoming Extension horticulturist, recommended I start with a cherry tomato plant. The fastest tomato I could find, maturing in 55 days, is called 'Gold Nugget,' which produces yellow cherry tomatoes.

Local gardeners who want to grow tomatoes without greenhouses or other protection should look for tomatoes that mature in 55 to 60 days, she said. This means with luck, you'll harvest your first tomato 69 to 80 days after May 25 — that is, between Aug. 2 and 13. The average first frost date looms barely more than a month later, about Sept. 20.

Why all the extra time? Vegetable seed packets and catalogs will tell you how many days it takes for seeds to germinate and how long until harvest time. However, here you need to extend those time frames by many days, Catherine said.

"Days until harvest...it is like EPA mileage figures: your results may vary..." — Shane

When she starts vegetables indoors, Catherine first adds another 14-20 days after germination to allow plants to grow to transplant size.

She then adds another 14 to 20 days after transplanting outdoors. That accounts for transplant shock. At that point, she starts counting the stated days to maturity.

For my annual flower, Catherine recommended cosmos, which produces brightly colored flowers.

The cosmos I've chosen, a dwarf variety in a mix of shades of pink, germinates in seven to 10 days. Maturity is at least 75 days for some cosmos varieties, so if I want flowering plants to put out in May, seeding indoors the first of March might not be too soon to start. But because even dwarf cosmos could be 2 feet tall at flowering, they'd get too big for my setup, so I'll wait a bit.

Both the flowers and the tomato will need "full sun," at least six hours per day. I'll have to think about where to fit them in my shady yard, or which tree to cut down.

It's easy to see why buying well-developed plants from the nurseries is so popular when, for instance, some varieties of tomatoes are rated at 120 days to maturity, the number of days between seed germination and the first fruit is harvested.

Harvest ripe flower seeds before they self-sow — or the birds eat them.

SEED PLANTING TIME CALCULATIONS

The USDA Plant Hardiness Zone Map shows Cheyenne in Zone 5b, meaning our maximum cold temperatures are -15 to -10 degrees Fahrenheit. Because of our 6,000-foot elevation and northern latitude, we also have a short growing season.

Cheyenne's average first frost-free date is May 25 — that's considered a safe time to get your plants in the ground.

After that, the growing season is only 90 to 110 days long before the average first frost date.

You can see why season extenders like Wall O' Water, hoop houses or high tunnels — modern, lightweight greenhouses — are popular here. They can push the planting date earlier by weeks, as well as extend the growing season in the fall.

Using Catherine's formula, catalog or seed packet-printed days to maturity plus 14-20 days to get to transplant size, I figured for my first attempt at growing from seed I needed to plant my vegetable and annual flower seeds four to six weeks before May 25, in early April.

My number of days from transplanted to first fruit harvested were about a week or two longer than what was printed on the seed packages stated below. But every year is different.

Beans, bush, 'Bountiful' - 46 days

Beets, 'Early Wonder' - 50 days

Cabbage, 'Red Express' - 63 days

Carrots, 'Parisian' - 55 days

Cucumber, 'Marketmore' - 60 days

Cucumber, 'Sweeter Yet' - 48 days

Eggplant, 'Fairy Tale' - 50 days

Eggplant, 'Orient Express' - 58 days

Peppers, sweet, 'Lunch Box Red' - 55 days (to green)

Squash, summer, 'Yellow Crookneck' - 42 days

Tomato, 'Silvery Fir Tree' - 58 days

Tomato, yellow cherry, 'Gold Nugget' - 55 days

Tomato, 'Early Girl' - 52 days

"I really like 'First Lady' tomatoes." — Shane

Teenage tomatoes are started in a bathtub temporarily set up with shelves and lights.

CHAPTER 4:
SEEDS INDOORS

GET EARLY START FOR OUR SHORT GROWING SEASON

In my quest to cultivate an early tomato from seed, as well as an annual flower, the dwarf cosmos, by March I found I'd accumulated 16 packets of other seed. I sorted them by when they needed to be started indoors.

But some plants do best when seeded directly into the garden. I have five packets of sunflowers on standby, along with seeds for lettuce and radishes. Some local gardeners like to direct sow cucumbers and squash because they are finicky about transplanting. Corn is always direct-sown.

I've done the calculations: number of days that seeds require to germinate as given on the seed packet, plus two weeks for growing to transplant size by May 25, the average last frost date. I marked a spare calendar with the planting dates for each vegetable or flower.

The earliest is marine heliotrope 'Peruvianum,' very tiny seeds, which I started March 1. I'm not familiar with this annual — it showed up instead of a marigold I ordered, but I'm curious.

There are three factors important to seed starting success, says Shane Smith, retired Cheyenne

Botanic Gardens director. They are using sterile soil, sterile pots and planting seeds to a depth twice the width of the seed.

Soil

Don't bother using soil out of your garden because there are too many pathogens and weed seeds. Always buy fresh "soil-less" potting soil, which is light and fluffy and usually sterile. If you have time, leave it out in subfreezing weather for a couple of weeks to kill any insects.

Cheyenne Botanic Gardens horticulturist Jessica Friis has had good results with the compressed bricks of coco coir (coir pith or coco peat) — the pulverized husks of coconuts. Just add water and poof! Ecologically, it is better to be using a waste product instead of mining peat from wild bogs, which is not considered a renewable resource.

You can make your own soil-less seedling mix using University of Wyoming Extension horticulturist Catherine Wissner's recipe: 3 parts milled sphagnum (peat moss), 2 parts perlite and 1 part good quality potting soil.

"I have had good luck with other seed starting mixes rather than potting mixes. Often they have fertilizer in them, which can burn young seedlings. Heavily fertilizing seedlings can increase 'damping off.'" — Shane

I tried a bag of "Seed Starting Jiffy-Mix," but it dries out too quickly. It sets seed starting up for failure, Catherine said.

I don't need a lot of seed-starting mix. Once the seedlings have several true leaves, not just those first two "seed leaves," I can move them into larger pots with regular, cheaper potting soil.

Pots

Laramie County Master Gardener Kathy Shreve and I use the Self-Watering Seed Starter from Lee Valley. They also have one about the size of an egg carton, the Windowsill Seed Starter. Both have little planting cells.

Because the seedlings require only a few weeks before they need repotting, I have been able to start all my small seeds in shifts in this watering system. More robust seed varieties do well in other containers covered with plastic wrap until they sprout.

I scavenge for my other containers, washing and sterilizing plastic pots from plant sales and nursery purchases, as well as whatever stores throw out. It's appalling how much plastic waste the horticultural industry produces.

Any container you can sanitize can be reused — Styrofoam cups, tall drink cups (especially for tomatoes), yogurt cups — just be sure to poke a lot of holes in the bottom for drainage. Jessica has used old cake pans to start seeds. Without adding holes, she waters carefully. Clean pots and then soak them in a 10% bleach solution for a minimum of 10 minutes, then rinse.

There are pots made from compressed fibers of various kinds. The idea is that you can plant the pot and all right into the garden and the roots will grow right through the walls. My experience is that the roots stay in the pot. It is better to tear it away when transplanting and throw the pot in the compost pile.

Paper pots

I have the "PotMaker," a little wooden cylinder that you roll a strip of freshly-read newspaper around several times. The paper needs to extend beyond the bottom edge so that it can be folded underneath. Crimp the fold well.

Gently pull the paper cup shape off the cylinder and fill it with potting soil. If handled carefully or rather, not handled after setting in a plastic tray, these little pots will hold up until the plant is ready for transplanting outdoors. While newspaper is degradable, I prefer to remove it (if there aren't too many roots already growing through it).

You could use any cylindrical object to make the size pot of your choice, up to the size of a wine bottle. Wrap the paper around two to three times, but not so tightly you can't slip it off. And use a freshly read newspaper — nothing that's been sitting out for weeks accumulating disease spores.

Depth

The rule of (the green) thumb is plant no deeper than twice the width of the seed, not the length or thickness, Shane says. Seeds have evolved to sprout with just heat and moisture, though a few need light, too, but for buried seed, if they don't

Clockwise from lower left: heat mat, Self-Watering Seed Starter, potting soil, paper pot maker, fluorescent light.

reach sunlight before they use up the energy stored within the seed, you'll never see them.

In the Master Gardener classroom, Kathy demonstrated how to pick up a very tiny seed: Use the end of a dampened toothpick to touch the seed, and then brush the seed onto the surface of the growing medium.

Moisture

Pots need to have drainage holes in the bottom. While you are waiting for seeds to germinate, the growing medium can't get too soggy or too dry.

I was particularly intrigued with Kathy's Seed Starter from Lee Valley. It is a miniature, self-contained greenhouse with a tray of planting cells, a clear plastic dome lid used to keep moisture in until the seeds sprout and a water reservoir below that should only need filling every few days.

The ends of a porous mat hang down into the reservoir and capillary action brings moisture across the mat placed under the planting cells where the soilless planting medium wicks it up to the plants. A less fancy method is to gently spritz the soil surface when necessary and lay plastic wrap over it until sprouts show.

Cheyenne gardener and beekeeper Verena Booth said she sprouts difficult seeds the way, for example, alfalfa is sprouted for salads using a jar, as explained on the Wikihow website, and then she pots them up.

Another method of seed germination is folding seeds in a wet paper towel placed in a plastic bag. It worked for me.

Light

The only sunny windowsill at our house is already full, so I'm using a 4-foot-long fluorescent shop light suspended over the workbench downstairs. One with special grow light bulbs would be nice. Windowsills are rarely bright enough and ours would be a poor choice anyway because we have low-e glass, which keeps out a part of the spectrum and makes my houseplants leggy.

However, Laramie County Master Gardener Barb Sahl and Kathy agree that cool-white fluorescent bulbs work fine for starting plants. The blue spectrum is perfect for seedlings. Keep the light close to the seedlings, 1 to 2 inches above. Kathy gives her seedlings light 16 hours a day.

Barb leaves her lights on 24/7, a technique endorsed by Leslie Halleck, author of *Gardening Under Lights*, not for tomatoes, but for other seedlings for their first two to three weeks.

Air

Damping off disease breaks a lot of hearts. One day the brave little seedlings are vigorously reaching for light and the next they are lying flat — rotted off at the soil surface. Sterile soil helps prevent this. Kathy and Barb also use moving air, a preventative that seeds started outdoors get naturally. But it's too cold to open a window, so try a fan set on low and place it across the room. The other benefit of subjecting seedlings to a breeze is they grow stronger stems.

"Damping off is a general descriptor of many seedling diseases. Old seed can be more susceptible. I have successfully fought off the beginnings of damping off by sprinkling some cinnamon on the soil surface, as it is a natural fungicide." — Shane

Heat

Heat, especially for plants of tropical origin — tomatoes, eggplant, melons, cucumbers and peppers — is necessary to germinate their seeds. The cost of plugging in a heat mat I bought through a garden supply store to put under a flat of seedlings is probably less than turning up our household thermostat to 80 degrees Fahrenheit. Once the seedlings sprout, turn off the heat mat.

Fertilizer

Most seed-starting and regular potting soils have fertilizer added, so let the little plants chew on that a few weeks before giving them anything more — and then figure half strength of whatever the directions recommend.

Success!

Don't worry if by the end of May your plants aren't blooming and aren't as mature-looking as the ones at the store. Blooming plants sell better, but often their roots are pot-bound in those tiny containers and the plants, especially flowers, might not really recover to grow much the rest of the summer.

You can make sure your starts aren't pot-bound and are at just the right stage to jump into the garden and keep growing.

LIGHTING FOR ROBUST SEEDLINGS

There's a misconception that windowsills work great for starting vegetable seeds. After all, millions of houseplants can't be wrong. But houseplant origins are typically the shady understory of tropical forests. Vegetables prefer full sun. Also, many windows are now treated to improve energy efficiency (lowering heat transference) by blocking parts of the spectrum. Greenhouses work better than windows because they give plants direct light from more directions for more hours per day.

Without a greenhouse — glass or hoop house — we're talking supplemental lighting. On a recent trip to my nearest big box hardware store, I found all kinds of grow light bulbs that will fit in a lamp but are not adequate for more than a couple pots. The store also had ordinary 4-foot-long fluorescent shop lights that fit perfectly over two flats of seedlings and will produce decent growth, whether you find full-spectrum bulbs or special grow light bulbs.

But LED lights are taking over. At the same store, I found 4-foot LED shop lights. The bulbs are integrated with the fixture and come in a variety of light levels, 3,200 to 10,000 lumens, with a range of prices to match, $15 to $75.

There are also LED bulbs, both regular and grow lights, that will replace the bulbs in your T8 or T12 fluorescent fixtures, but they won't be quite as energy efficient as the integrated ones.

You'll notice LED bulbs can be about four times more expensive than normal fluorescents, but they cost less than half as much to run and are supposed to last longer.

Then there are the industrial LED grow lights that emphasize blue and red lighting — the important part of the spectrum for growing plants. They come with industrial prices as well. Choosing one gets quite technical. Check out the Colorado cannabis grow suppliers for advice.

However, the few weeks of light our tomato seedlings need hardly justifies industrial lighting.

Light set-up

Because you want to keep the light around a couple inches above the tops of the seedlings, you need to be able to adjust the distance as they grow. Too close and seedlings dry out. Too far and they get spindly. Hang the shop light using the chains that come with it, shortening as needed. Joe Lamp'l, host of PBS's "Growing a Greener World," suggests using ratchet pulleys instead.

Or, rather than move the light, you can stack boxes under the flats to bring them up to the light and remove the boxes to adjust the distance as the plants grow.

How do you hang the shop light? You can hang it from the ceiling over a table, especially somewhere like an unfinished basement room.

A set of adjustable utility shelves works well if there is a way you can attach your light fixtures to the underside of the shelves and adjust them. Keep in mind the distance between shelves must accommodate seedling height at six or eight weeks plus a couple inches of space and the light fixture depth.

Mark and I put freestanding utility shelves in our unused bathtub. For the top shelf we put an expandable shower curtain rod over it and hang the shop light from it.

Plugging it in

Some shop lights can be strung together. Otherwise, if you have multiple lights, you are looking at a power strip, giving you a handy way to flip them on and off all at once. Or plug the power strip into a timer. Lamp'l's latest home research shows 16 hours of light per day is about right — seedlings need to sleep too.

Indoor-grown seedlings are "hardened off" for a few hours a day outdoors before transplanting.

CHAPTER 5: **SEEDS/ SEEDLINGS OUTDOORS**

DIRECT SOW SEEDS AND TRANSPLANT SEEDLINGS

Cheyenne's spring weather is unpredictable. Make sure you have your old sheets at the ready to cover your plants on a cold night. Or try a product called floating row cover, which is spun polyester fabric available at many garden centers. You'll need a few rocks to hold it down.

Direct sowing seeds

Read the seed packet directions to find out how deep and when seeds need to be planted directly in the garden. Try making a wide bed vegetable garden (Chapter 2) to avoid compacting the soil.

Don't hesitate to thin seedlings as recommended, because crowding will decrease your yield, as a friend discovered when she harvested the skinniest carrots she'd ever seen.

I collected seeds from last year's flowers: marigold, feverfew, penstemon and gaillardia. Because the seeds didn't cost me anything, I can sprinkle them generously this spring where I've pulled the winter leaf mulch away around the fading tulips.

I will water the seeds well and crumble a thin layer of old leaves over them for shade. My soil does not have a tidy, smooth surface so enough seeds always find the right spot to take root.

Timing transplanting

There are plenty of flowers and vegetables that weather a little frost — tulips, daffodils, crocus and other early bulbs and early perennials. Mature pansies can be planted as early as April 15 and they bloom all summer.

Among the vegetables, the cole crops such as cabbage, broccoli and cauliflower do fine with a bit of frost, either seeded directly or as transplants that were started even earlier indoors. No wonder cabbage-based dishes are a feature of ethnic cooking in cold, northern, short-growing-season countries.

By May 25 it should be safe to transplant everything else and sow seeds for plants that don't need a head start, such as marigolds, squash and pumpkins, or those that dislike being transplanted, such as sunflowers and nasturtiums.

There is a 10% chance of frost until June 8 so some Cheyennites wait until then to transplant the heat lovers: tomatoes, peppers and eggplant.

Keep old sheets at the ready for protecting new plants on frosty nights.

Hardening off

If you buy plants that were on display outdoors, they are ready for planting.

But if they were indoors or you grew your own, give them an opportunity to gradually adapt to sun and wind, a process known as hardening off. Put the plants outside for a couple hours one day where the sun and wind aren't too strong, and a couple hours longer the next day, increasing exposure over several days, making sure plants don't wilt.

"At the Cheyenne Botanic Gardens, we grew around 50,000 bedding plants (in the greenhouse) so hardening off wasn't an option. We gave them a slightly higher dose of liquid fertilizer about a week to five days prior to setting out, and a very thorough watering prior to planting." — Shane

Transplanting techniques for annuals and vegetables

Jessica Friis, Cheyenne Botanic Gardens horticulturist, recommends that for annual flowers and vegetables, break up the soil crust first, 6-8 inches deep and add compost. If the soil seems tough, water it and give it a day or two before transplanting.

Another option is to dig into an established annual bed only to make holes for putting in the plants and then mulching them with compost.

"Water plants really well before planting, getting them soaking wet," Jessica said. When you dig a hole for a plant, she recommends making it twice the width of the root ball, so the roots have an easy time growing.

Make sure your hole is deep enough the roots don't fold back on themselves.

"We bury plants a little deep, up to the bottom set of leaves," said Jessica. "It gives a little extra protection."

On tomato plants, you can even

These vegetables were started in the Self-watering Seed Starter, then potted up in newspaper pots. The pots were removed before transplanting in the garden.

bury the second set of leaves.

Hold small, delicate plants by the root ball over the hole at the proper height and fill in around it with dirt. Larger, sturdier plants can be held by the stem close to the root ball.

For plants that are root-bound, Jessica said there is a debate about whether to "tear" the roots first.

"Try to loosen them up without breaking them," she said.

When pulling annuals out in the fall, she said it is easy to see that roots that circled round and round in their pots before planting never grew any further out all summer — and neither did the plant tops.

If not root-bound, keep the root mass intact as much as possible to lessen transplant shock. Otherwise, a plant must re-establish all those little root hairs before the green part can start growing again.

For seedlings in peat pots, the pots don't decay much in the soil here and can inhibit growth. Break off the bottoms and sides if the roots haven't penetrated them yet. And if they have, leave the pot whole except don't leave the rim of the pot sticking above ground — tear it off.

Transplanting perennials

For perennials, planting bare-root works well because the roots stretch out more quickly into their new space. Gently clean off all the potting soil on the roots and swish them in a bucket of water before planting. This works for trees and shrubs as well.

"We first learned of (bare-root planting for herbaceous plants) from our crevice garden designer, Kenton Seth. Now I am trying it on everything and am having great results. Be sure to gently rinse the soil off the roots and swish them around in a bucket of water. Also be sure the prepared hole is wet. You are never too old to learn something new. As Thomas Jefferson said, 'I am an old man but I am a young gardener'" — Shane

Spacing

In Cheyenne, we should space annual flowers more closely than recommended, Jessica said. Since we have such a short growing season, flowers won't otherwise fill in the garden completely until nearly the week before the average first frost (Sept. 20), so planters at the Children's Village are packed thick.

"Wave petunias really fill a space. The best filler of all waves is the 'Silver Wave.' One plant can cover 4 to 6 square feet, even in Cheyenne." — Shane

Fertilizing

"We use a slow release fertilizer, like Osmacote, applying it once a month," Jessica said. "Or you can use a liquid fertilizer every week to two weeks."

She fertilizes closely-packed planters every week. However, many perennials, especially natives, require little fertilizing other than decomposing mulch.

Mulch

Don't forget a layer of mulch for all your plants. Two to three inches of bits of semi-decomposed plant material, including leaves and grass clippings, will keep the soil from drying out too quickly. It also will shade out the weeds. However, don't leave mulch touching plant stems.

Water again

And finally, water well each day for several days, until plants are established, but water carefully so plants don't become mud-bedraggled. There is no such thing as a set watering schedule for the rest of the growing season. You must see how fast your soil dries out. Plants in containers might need water every day in the heat of summer.

Rabbits

Do you have trouble with rabbits snacking on your new plants? Jessica has found that a short, rabbit-proof wire fence works better than deterrents that must be reapplied frequently.

JESSICA'S SHOPPING TIPS

"Ideally, you'd want smaller plants that aren't root-bound. It's hard to find that. Find some that haven't bloomed yet. Make sure they have been well watered, and the soil feels moist," Jessica said.

There shouldn't be roots poking out of the drainage holes. If you take the plant out of the pot, you don't want to see roots spiraling around and around. Instead of removing the plant from the pot to check, you can squeeze the thin plastic pots of small plants. They should have some give. Root-bound pots full of roots don't give much.

If given the choice between a small plant of one kind of annual and a larger plant of the same kind, remember it will take the larger plant longer to recover from transplanting and the smaller plant will nearly catch up in size in that time. You might want to save money and buy the smaller plant to begin with — unless it too is rootbound.

"Count the plants in the 4- and 6-packs. All too often there will be one empty cell. I also keep an eye out for where there are two plants in one cell pot. That's a bonus."— Shane

When picking out perennial plants that will grow well here, look for those marked "Plant Select." This is a breeding program partnership between Colorado State University, Denver Botanic Gardens and growers. This label is an indication that the variety will perform well in Colorado, which generally means it will also thrive in Cheyenne. You can find them in area nurseries.

"Many of the Plant Select offerings came from the old Cheyenne Horticulture Field Station." — Shane

Winter-sown perennial flower seeds like cold and snow, and protection from predators.

CHAPTER 6:
WINTER SOWING

PLANT SEEDS OUTDOORS IN WINTER IN COVERED CONTAINERS

When I asked her for tips on starting perennial seeds, Laramie County Master Gardener Michelle Bohanan said, "winter sowing." I soon discovered it is an increasingly popular concept and practice.

Winter sowing is what our native and other temperate zone plants do naturally. After they set seed, the flowers and fruits dry. Within months or years, they either shatter and release the seeds, a messy bird picks at them, or the wind blows them. You might shred a few dried flower heads yourself from time to time.

The seeds eventually land on the ground where they are subjected to moisture and cold. That, and the cycles of freezing and thawing, eventually break the seed coat, which is necessary if it is tougher than the strength of the seedling. Giving seeds a cold treatment is known as stratification.

Surprisingly, many seeds require light to germinate. Day length, or cumulative solar warmth, tells them when it is safe to sprout.

With our occasional spring snow-storms, it's good that not all seeds, even of the same variety or species,

Winter sown seedlings sprouting the first week in May will be ready in a few weeks to be transplanted to a protected place in the garden or into individual small pots.

her winter sowing by seeding in shallow, covered containers she set out in her garden. In spring, there was no need to harden off the seedlings because they were already acclimated to the outdoors. She merely transferred them into her garden. Another benefit? No need for grow lights or heat mats. She's been spreading the word since.

How to winter sow

I visited Michelle on a nasty day in January with half a foot of snow on the ground. I brought along a translucent plastic gallon milk jug and a little packet of arctic aster seed I'd received in a seed exchange.

With a pair of heavy-duty scissors, Michelle punctured the jug just below the handle and cut all the way around, creating a 4-inch high pot and a separate cover. She put in about 3 inches of her favorite commercial potting soil, already moistened.

Next, she spilled a couple dozen seeds onto a plastic container lid and with a toothpick, sorted through them, kicking out any unfertilized seeds. They look lighter because they don't have the germ of the seed needed for germination.

Like many small seeds, these require light, so Michelle gently pressed 16 into the soil in a 4 x 4 grid but didn't bury them. Then she forced the upper half of the milk jug, upright, into the bottom half to protect the seeds, leaving off the jug's cap.

In our drier climate, Michelle has had, over seven years, good results

require the same exact amount of light and heat. If the first up are frozen out, the slower germinating fill in behind.

Of course, the plants that have winter sowing down to a fine art are the weeds.

The problem with merely sprinkling seed over your flower bed is that seed is expensive, and you don't know how hungry your local birds and mice are going to be.

It occurred to New York state gardener Trudi Davidoff to safeguard without making additional openings for drainage in the bottom of the jug. However, I found I had to puncture the bottoms after the snow on top of my jugs began to melt or the contents would begin to float.

Many kinds of recycled containers can be used. The bottom needs to be at least 3 inches deep for the soil and the top needs to clear the soil surface by at least 2 inches. The top also needs to be clear or translucent. You provide adequate ventilation and drainage openings as needed.

On the jug in permanent marker Michelle wrote the name, source and number of seeds and the date of planting.

Back at home, I put the milk jug in a snowdrift on the northeast side of our back fence.

Michelle already had 35 jugs going and figured she was only 25% of the way through her winter sowing plans.

Timing and location

Since then, I've had good results starting jugs in January, February and the beginning of March.

But figuring out where to put your jugs is also important. If placed along the south-facing wall of your house, some seedlings sprout too soon. Along a north-facing wall may delay them. I leave mine in snowdrifts in the shadow of the back wall with about an hour of sun a day until mid-April and then move them to a sunnier location. These mini-greenhouses are easy to move, so just experiment.

Maintenance

While seeds left lying on the ground require no help from us, ones in containers do.

Michelle's milk jugs have the opening at the top, plus the gaps where the upper part of the jug is pressed into the bottom, which allow for some snow and rain to seep in and some heat to escape when it warms up in the spring.

However, she does check her jugs regularly to make sure they don't dry out, especially the ones under cover of her hoop house. She can tell by the lighter color of the soil (although this doesn't work for all potting soils), or she can lift the jug and tell by the weight if it needs watering.

When the weather gets warm, to keep seedlings from baking, it is necessary to pull the top off during the day, partially or wholly.

What to grow

Try native perennials from our northern temperate climate, Zone 5 or colder, especially if you are turning your lawn into bird, butterfly and bee-friendly habitat. Popular flowers include varieties of pentemon, coreopsis, milkweed, coneflower and gaillardia.

Try cold-tolerant vegetables from the cabbage family, herbs and flowering annuals, but probably not slow-starting annuals like petunias. It would take all summer for them to finally bloom.

The seeds of tropical plants, like tomatoes, eggplants and peppers, might also get started too late to produce before first fall frost.

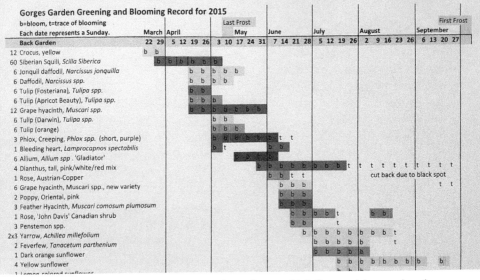

Record-keeping takes many forms. This chart shows which flowers bloomed and when, and what color.

CHAPTER 7:
RECORD KEEPING

USE JOURNALS, NOTECARDS, SPREADSHEETS

Along with her garden journal noting weather and garden improvements, Laramie County Master Gardener Wendy Douglass has a method for tracking her new perennials. She makes a 5x7-inch index card for each, attaching the tag from the nursery, recording where the plant was bought, the date and location planted and any helpful horticultural notes.

Wendy also marks each new plant in the garden with a palm-sized, flattish rock on which she writes the plant's name and date planted using oil-based Sharpie markers. In spring, these rocks might become little gravestones for plants that don't make it through the winter, but at least they aren't forgotten. And their cards are moved to the "Deceased" file.

Catherine Wissner, University of Wyoming Extension horticulturist, tracks the productivity of the vegetables growing in her high tunnel greenhouse by weighing nearly everything. She jots notes in the field all season long, and during the winter, she adds them to a simple record-keeping system she has devised using Excel.

I like the Excel idea because it is

easy to insert new information and add pages. My computer is better organized than the binders I have tried to use in the past. Plus, I can insert digital photos.

My tomato records

As a record-keeping example, here are my notes for the tomatoes. Almost all were plants I grew from seed and transplanted or direct seeded between May 24-27.

Indeterminate tomatoes continue growing and flowering all season. Determinate tomato types reach a mature size and fruits ripen about the same time.

"Maturity" means number of days between transplanting or direct seeding in the garden until the first fruit is harvested — according to the seed companies.

Under "Harvested" are my actual days to maturity as well as the numbers and weights of fruits harvested as of Sept. 8.

Gorges tomatoes 2012:

Started three of the four from seed and planted 1 each in containers with potting soil amended with leaf compost. Needed fish emulsion fertilizer every week or two.

-- "Gold Nugget" yellow cherry, determinate, Pinetree Garden Seeds. Maturity: 55 days. Harvested: 60 days onward, 137 fruits, 3 lbs. so far. From seed.

-- "Large Red Cherry," indeterminate, American Seed Company. Maturity: 55-60 days. Harvested: 70 days onward, 65 fruit, 3 lbs. so far. A substantial cage would work better than tying it to a stake.

-- "Silvery Fir Tree" heirloom, determinate, from Master Gardener sale. Maturity: 58 days. Harvested: 75 days onward, 41 fruit, 8.5 lbs. so far. Tastes fine.

-- "Early Girl" hybrid, indeterminate, Ferry-Morse seed company. Maturity: 52 days. Harvested: 83 days onward, 23 fruit, 7.5 lbs. so far. Needs substantial cage for support. Luckily, tomatoes were hard and green at the time of the hailstorms and only sustained a few scars.

Season analysis

Slugs got most of the beans and infested the cucumbers and squash, but daily examination, beer traps and watering less cut them down from 36 on the worst day to only a few each day.

Other problems, such as the fungus on the pumpkin, powdery mildew on the squash leaves, leaf miners on the beet leaves, and cabbage worms on the cabbage, will all benefit from crop rotation. With my garden only measuring 14 by 14 feet, too small to rotate within, I was thinking about the next year planting the kinds of vegetables I hadn't tried yet or maybe planting more containers in a different part of the yard.

I think damage from hail made my plants more susceptible to disease and pests.

I had no weeds, unless you count the cherry tomato that popped up among the beets, or the sunflowers planted by the birds, which welcomed bees.

My leaf mulch and intensive

style of gardening prevented weeds, though I need to be more careful not to provide damp and shady slug habitat.

Having harvested 60 pounds of produce as of Sept. 8 from my shady garden, with maybe another 10 pounds of tomatoes still ripening, and given the two hailstorms, I was happy with my first year of vegetable production. I will continue to keep a lookout for more short-season vegetable varieties.

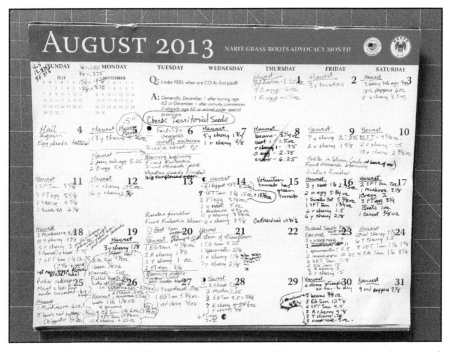

Free calendars are handy for jotting garden notes. This one was used to also record the vegetable harvest.

PART 2

GARDEN CARE

Tilling the garden destroys the community of microorganisms that would otherwise aid the gardener.

CHAPTER 8:
SOIL MICROBE CARE

HELP LITTLE CRITTERS TAKE CARE OF YOUR GARDEN

There are a billion microbes in a teaspoon of healthy soil. The interactions of the whole community of microbes are a giant web of who eats whom and who feeds whom, said Jeff Lowenfels, Alaskan garden columnist and author who spoke in Cheyenne in 2017.

Basically, decaying plant material feeds microbes and in turn, microbe "excrement" feeds plant roots.

Microbes include nematodes, bacteria, fungi and protozoa. There are some bad actors, but generally, everything balances, and plants grow.

For example, prairies and forests have self-sustaining soil microbial communities — no synthetic, chemical fertilizers or pesticides are required.

But when European farmers landed in the New World, they opened things up with the plow and have continued to plow ever since. Regular plowing (or hoeing or rototilling) disrupts the soil microbes. They can't do their jobs.

Farmers repaired damage somewhat with applications of manure and compost. But then came the 20th century's inventive use of nerve gas left over from World War I as insecticide, and leftover nitrogen-based bomb-making materials from World

War II became the perfect fertilizer.

Except that it wasn't healthy for the microbes.

Synthetic fertilizers starve the microbes in a way and pesticides kill off beneficial organisms, causing the need for a never-ending cycle of synthetic fertilizer and pesticide application. This is great if you own stock in the large chemical companies, but bad when you understand the side effects including health issues for animals and humans — especially farmers, because the chemicals get into drinking water and food.

Lowenfels happily dispensed advice on garden chemicals for years until someone sent him two electron microscope photos, one of a fungus that had trapped a root-eating nematode, and the other of a nematode happily chomping a tomato root unimpeded.

In the first photo, the plant was secreting a substance that attracted the fungus, which in turn attacked the nematode. In the second photo, the fungus was missing due to the use of synthetic fertilizers and pesticides.

After his conversion, Lowenfels wrote three books. He said the essential one is *Teaming with Microbes, The Organic Gardener's Guide to the Soil Food Web*, coauthored with Wayne Lewis. You'll notice the play on words in the title — healthy soil is teeming with microbes, and you'll be teaming with them.

Put away the rototiller

First, put away your rototiller. It's not even recommended for ripping up your lawn to make a pollinator garden because it leaves a lot of grass that will resprout. Annual rototilling is detrimental to the soil microbe community. Ron Godin, recently retired extension agronomist in western Colorado who spoke in Cheyenne also in 2017, said this advice translates to farming as well.

It will take time to undo the cultural tradition of breaking soil down into a fine, clump-less and smooth expanse of dirt. But there are two reasons for disturbing the soil as little as possible, even in a vegetable garden.

First, every time you dig into soil, you bring up weed seeds, most of which require light to germinate. You just made more work for yourself. Cut weeds off at the soil surface rather than digging them (except thistle).

Second, microbes feeding your plants and fending off bad stuff can't function if you break them up. Keeping them intact means less work for you, less fertilizer spreading and less watering because healthy soil holds water better. Pesticides are a last resort for serious problems. Re-inoculate your soil with microbes soon after.

In windy Cheyenne, there's also a third benefit to not tilling your soil into fine dust: microbes "glue" things together and the resulting clumpy soil doesn't blow away.

To plant seeds or transplants, make an opening just large enough. The roots will find their way without the soil being "fluffed." Healthy soil has lots of air spaces already. Then mulch.

Godin's rule is 100% cover, 100% of the time. Cover for large gardens or farms could be annual cover crops later mowed to form mulch. In small gardens use leaves and grass clippings.

Replace chemical fertilizers

In the years chemical fertilizers have been around, studies show fruits and vegetables have dropped in nutritional value. It's due to the missing micronutrients soil microbes used to pull from decomposing plant material and mineral soils. Synthetic fertilizer is incomplete.

Traditionally, organic gardeners dig compost into the soil, but Lowenfels says digging breaks up the soil community. Better to side-dress plants, leaving the compost (or plant-based mulch) on the soil surface where microbes will get at it and break it down. It works on the prairie and in the forest — there are no 100-year-old piles of dead grass, leaves or pine needles.

Lowenfels said there are three different groups of plants in your yard. Perennial flowers, shrubs and trees want their nitrogen in the form provided by fungally dominated soils. The compost that promotes this is the brown stuff (mixed with a little green): dry leaves, bark, wood chips, twigs, branches — like the forest floor.

Annuals, including vegetables, prefer their nitrogen produced by bacterially dominated soil. This is green stuff (with a little brown), grass clippings, freshly picked weeds (without seeds) and fruit and vegetable kitchen scraps.

The prairie, like your lawn, falls in between. It appreciates finely shredded brown fall leaves and thin layers of green grass clippings.

Brew compost tea

Compost tea, which is compost soaked in water, is another way to inoculate your garden with microbes and feed them too. If compost and compost tea smell ugly, that's anaerobic activity. You need aerobic activity — more air.

Lowenfels gives directions for making a bucket into "a simple actively aerated compost tea brewer using aquarium pumps and air stones." Fertilizing your plants, and yes, your houseplants too, is as easy as watering them.

While chemical companies made their fortunes keeping our soils addicted to their products, new companies are offering to aid us in bringing our soils back to health. They are building better compost tea brewers. Labs can estimate your microbe population. Our local independent garden centers will sell you mycorrhizal fungi in powdered form you mix with water.

This new era of catering to microbes has gone mainstream. Lowenfels reported that at the 2016 Garden Writers of America conference, none of the tradeshow vendors was pushing synthetic fertilizers or pesticides.

Since 1982, my husband, Mark, and I have cared for our lawn and garden without a rototiller or synthetic fertilizers and pesticides. We mulch the garden and use natural lawn fertilizers. I look forward to adapting Lowenfels's ideas to step it up.

Mark Gorges' cedar compost bin has removable front slats, perforated pipe for air and wire sides.

CHAPTER 9:
COMPOST MAKING

KEEP COMPOSTING SIMPLE

"Compost, 3. A mixture of various ingredients for fertilizing or enriching land." (This definition first recorded in print in 1258 A.D.)—The Compact Edition of the Oxford English Dictionary.

It wasn't long after agriculture was invented, I'm sure, that someone began talking about composting. Maybe it even predated agriculture, when someone simply noticed the plants growing next to refuse piles were larger than the rest.

Today, composting methods can vary, but they ultimately accomplish the same thing: providing a nutrient-dense soil for your plants.

Styles of composting

There are the free-form methods of composting where, like jazz, we are inspired to experiment with what's available. Whatever goes into the piles eventually decays.

Then there are the methods requiring careful construction, like classical music: a particular size and construction of bin, proper proportions of green and brown materials, and a certain amount of moisture and manipulation to maximize the speed of decomposition.

And of course, rather than make their own music, many folks opt for the radio, sending yard waste to the city's compost facility. And, hopefully, everyone is also picking up finished compost to use in their gardens.

Benefits of composting

Whatever kind of composting you choose, keep in mind the benefits of applying composted material to your yard:

- Compost provides nutrients, same as chemical fertilizers, plus more micronutrients.

- Compost has microorganisms that help plants absorb nutrients.

- Compost releases nutrients slowly so that plant growth is healthier.

- Compost helps the soil hold water.

- Composting by using leaves and grass clippings as mulch means you don't have to buy other mulching materials. If your yard doesn't produce enough stuff to compost, visit the city compost facility or ask neighbors.

At the most primitive level, composting can be accomplished with tools you already have for yard and garden maintenance, and with not much more effort than disposing of yard waste.

The science of composting

Over time, Mother Nature rots nearly every once-living thing. Still, there are a few principles to keep in mind for best results.

Several sources say the optimal size of a pile is a cubic yard, 3 x 3 x 3 feet. Using some kind of container — a bin, trashcan or fencing — holds it together.

Composting requires the right amount of moisture. With our dry climate, you might need to add water sometimes.

Composting requires oxygen, otherwise you might get the odor of anaerobic decomposition. Holes in the side of the bin or wire mesh sides help. So, does turning the pile so that the stuff in the center trades places with the outer part.

Introducing good microbes speeds the process and is as easy as adding a little dirt — even soil clinging to weed roots might be enough.

Mixing green stuff, like grass clippings, with brown stuff, like dried leaves, with the addition of regular turning, can make the compost "cook" hot, possibly hot enough to kill weed seeds and diseases. But like me and Mark, my husband, most folks I talked to don't manage their compost at that level — not enough to reach that sanitizing heat level.

What not to compost

We are primarily discussing composting yard and garden waste and so everything is a candidate. However, here are exceptions:

- No seeds of weeds. Add weeds to compost before they go to seed.

- No weeds that sprout easily from little segments of roots, like Canada thistle, bindweed and creeping bellflower (Creeping bellflower has lavender bell-shaped flowers and is common in Cheyenne).

- No diseased plants.

- No woody stuff unless it is chipped into small pieces. If it doesn't decompose in one batch, sift it out and add it to the next, or put it under your shrubs and trees as wood mulch.

- Nothing that has been treated with herbicides within two months. Same goes for pesticides, especially if it is intended for the organic vegetable garden.

- Manure is best avoided by the home gardener, especially for root crops, said Chris Hilgert, Wyoming Master Gardener program coordinator. It must be from a grazing animal — not from cats, dogs or people. It could be full of seeds. It could be full of salts, which our soils do not need. It could be full of medications. It could be too hot — too strong — and burn your plants if it hasn't aged enough. It could be from animals that ate plants treated with herbicides. If you have livestock, consult with the Extension office or the Conservation District for instruction.

- No meat, no dairy, no grease, no oils, no salt, no processed food with unpronounceable ingredients. Maybe eggshells. To be safe, just stick to fruits and vegetables — including coffee grounds.

"My number one tip for creating compost: Stop using your sink disposal. Put tape over the switch. Get a good kitchen compost container with a tight lid and start using it." — Shane

- And no wood ash. Gardening books written by easterners forget that places like Cheyenne already have alkaline soils and wood ash will make it worse. However, biochar might be worth investigating. Biochar is charcoal produced by pyrolysis of plant matter.

Methods

Years ago, Mark and I bought a system that is essentially a sheet of heavy green plastic with several stakes that fit into a set of slots in the sides to form it into a barrel shape 3 feet high and 8 feet around (2.5-foot diameter). We throw stuff in and when we need some compost, perhaps months later in the spring, we dig out the stuff at the bottom.

We have four large trees that shed plenty of crispy curled brown leaves in the fall. Some of those we layer in the vegetable garden after frost to decompose. Some I use in the perennial flower bed for winter insulation — thinning them out in the spring if necessary.

We bag up the rest of the leaves to keep them from blowing away, saving them for spring when we dig more of them into the vegetable garden, use them as mulch or add them to the bin between layers of lawn clippings — though clippings are often used as mulch as well.

I visited Laramie County Master Gardener Maggie McKenzie to see her composting experiments.

Her husband, Don, built a nice three-bin system. One bin is for collecting, one for cooking and one is available for spreading.

She is also having success with "lasagna gardening:" To start a new garden bed, lay down a thick layer of wet newspapers or wet cardboard. The Wyoming Tribune Eagle is printed with soy-based ink and is safe to use.

Top that with a 2-to-3 inch layer of peat, then a 4-to-8-inch layer of yard waste, then more peat, then more yard waste, until you have built up 18 to 24 inches. As it ages, it will shrink. Letting it overwinter is best.

Maggie's lasagna is for vegetables and is set up inside a raised bed frame, which keeps the wind from taking it apart. For annual upkeep, just add more layers. It is supposed to be ideal for starting and maintaining any kind of garden.

Maggie is also trying a variation of lasagna gardening that includes logs and other woody debris. Known as a hugelkultur bed, the woody layer is placed on top of the wet newspaper or cardboard.

The decomposing wood provides a steady supply of nutrients and holds moisture. Don finished the mounds nicely with retaining walls of sandstone.

COMPOSTING BASICS

1. Collect organic matter: fruits, veggies and yard waste. You can also add coffee grounds and compostable tea bags.
2. Find or build a container. The optimal size is about a cubic yard: 3 x 3 x 3 feet. The sides can be made of wire mesh or solid material.
3. Composting requires the right amount of moisture, so water might need to be added if it seems dry.
4. The mixture needs oxygen, either through the holes in the bin or by turning the pile. This will also reduce the odor. Healthy compost does not smell bad.
5. Adding good microbes can speed the process. Don't worry, it's as easy as adding a little dirt.

The result: Microorganisms from the soil eat the waste and break it down to its simplest parts. What remains is a fiber-rich, carbon-containing humus filled with nutrients plants love. Compost is a soil conditioner, mulch and fertilizer all wrapped into one. It is a natural fertilizer for flower beds, vegetable gardening and farming.

See Cheyenne Botanic Gardens website, Resources tab, "Gardening Tips" for more information on composting.

John Heller shows off a handful of red wigglers used in worm composting.

WORM COMPOSTING

Have you ever seen a girl handle a worm without expressing squeamishness or a boy hold a worm without trying to scare a girl? I have.

At the Boys and Girls Club of Cheyenne, there is a worm composting bin. The kids, self-proclaimed worm farmers, gave me a tour of their livestock. Taking off the lid, they moved the partially composted material to one side with a hand-sized rake and didn't hesitate to plunge their hands in to wrangle a red wiggler or two and bring them out for inspection.

After I'd been introduced to the worms and enlightened about their biology, the worms were carefully returned to the bin. The kids washed their hands and then dried them with paper towels.

Laramie County Master Gardener Maggie McKenzie, a volunteer at the club who works under Carlos Gonzales, youth development professional (when I visited in 2018), oversees the worm farm. She reminded the kids to throw the paper towels in the bin for the worms to process. The worm castings (worm poop) will go into the club's garden outside as soon as it is warm enough. It will be great fertilizer for the vegetables which are grown organically — without chemicals.

Three months before, I witnessed Maggie and two other Master Gardeners, Susie and John Heller, give this batch of compost its start.

Bins

Vermicomposting, composting with worms, is simple. You can build your own bin using a well-washed 5-gallon bucket that has a lid. John said at home they have used the plastic buckets kitty litter comes in.

Punch holes in the sides 4 inches up from the bottom edge for aeration. Punch another few in the bottom for drainage of the worm urine. It's valuable natural fertilizer you'll also want to collect.

The Hellers donated a fancy bin to the club. It comes in removable layers, like a layer cake. The worms start off in the lowest one and as compost is finished in that layer, bedding material and food are added to the next layer up. The worms migrate to it through its mesh bottom. This leaves the compost in the first layer to be harvested.

Bedding and food

The Hellers start with a sheet of black ink newspaper (no color) laid in the bottom of the bin. For bedding they shred or tear newspaper into 1-inch-wide strips, moisten it like a wrung-out sponge, and then crumple it into a 1-inch layer.

Next, 2 to 3 inches of food are placed on top. Kitchen scraps are best, but not meat, dairy or grease. Susie said to think about what nutrients are needed in the garden. We have a lot of calcium in our soil, so she leaves out eggshells. The smaller the scraps of food are, the faster the worms will digest them. The Hellers sometimes dice theirs.

A little sand is needed because worms, like chickens, have a crop and a little rough sand in their crop helps them break up and digest tough fibers.

Some things are too hard for worm digestion, like avocado pits. Seeds from tomatoes and other fruits pass through unscathed and will sprout. The worms are not fond of citrus fruits. However, the worms will eat Starbucks coffee filters and tea bags, said Susie.

Worms

The Hellers added a pound of worms to the new bin, which they ordered for about $6 from the Wyoming Worm Wrangler. Red wigglers, smaller and redder and more active than garden-variety earthworms, work best. The worms placed on top soon crawled below to get away from the light.

The lid was placed firmly on top of the bin. It's important to keep the worms in the dark, said Susie. And if there isn't at least a little light outside the bin 24 hours a day, the worms will come out to explore.

Temperature is important too. If it drops below 45 degrees Fahrenheit, the worms will go into hibernation. If it gets above 80 or 90 degrees Fahrenheit, the worms in the bin will die. In nature they can crawl deeper in the soil to stay cool, said Susie.

Maintenance

Maggie brings in a produce bag of kitchen scraps about every week to 10 days, "I usually add some paper at the same time — newspaper and paper towels — which helps keep odors down if I overload the worms."

The worm bin should smell like clean dirt. If it gets a rotten smell, add more newspaper — or old brown tree leaves if you have them. Maggie's one worm failure though, was from letting the bin dry out too much.

Harvest

If you use a one-bucket system, in three to six months you'll have a bucket of worm castings to spread on your garden. At that point you'll want to sort out the worms and save them for your next batch.

Here's how: Push all the worm-laden compost to one side and put fresh scraps on the other side. The worms will move to the greener pasture on their own in a few weeks. If all went well, they've been reproducing, laying little white eggs.

As the Boys and Girls Club kids will tell you, it's fun to be a worm farmer. There's nothing quite like the gentle, cool touch of a hard-working, compost-making, red wiggler when it gets a break from the bin to explore the palm of your hand.

Dry leaf mulch suppresses weeds, conserves moisture, fertilizes soil and diminishes hail bounce.

CHAPTER 10: **MULCHING**

MOTHER NATURE USES MULCH, SO SHOULD WE

My front yard perennials grow so closely together they are a living mulch. They nearly completely shade out weeds.

Elsewhere, I let fallen leaves cover the bare ground all winter. In spring I thin out the leaves to give small spring-blooming bulbs and self-seeding flowers a hand. Later, I put some of the leaves back, along with lawn clippings.

Be sure your lawn hasn't recently had weed killer applied before using your clippings or they will kill your plants. Over the course of the growing season, as the mulch breaks down, you'll have to add

to it. Straw and pine needles are also recommended by experienced gardeners here.

"One of my favorite mulches is pine needles. No, it won't make our soils too acidic as most people believe. Also, it won't blow away and lasts a good while." — Shane

I am not fond of sheets of plastic or weed barrier cloth covered by rock or bark mulch around landscape plantings. I worked on a college grounds crew one summer and discovered the weeds punctured the plastic. All kinds of dirt and detritus, including weed seeds, blew in around the rocks requiring me to sort it out.

If you like rocks, make a rock garden (Chapter 44). It will be less labor intensive than redoing rock mulch every year to keep it looking nice. Plus, vegetation cools the local environment in summer.

Plant-based mulch does several things besides shading out weeds. It also:

- Slows evaporation of soil moisture (saving money on watering)

- Decomposes and adds to the nutrients in the soil

- Keeps beneficial organisms and earthworms cool and happy

- Keeps the soil surface from forming a crust that can repel water

- Keeps plants from getting splattered with mud during hard rain

- Keeps hail from bouncing and creating more damage

- Keeps dry soil from blowing — though you might have to figure out how to keep the mulch itself from blowing away until your plants are big enough to offer wind protection.

"To my knowledge, I was the first one to propose that bouncing hail caused damage after watching hundreds of hailstorms eat my Cheyenne gardens. After much observation, I did see a difference between mulched and unmulched damage." — Shane

If you find slugs under your mulch, maybe you need to water less often. Remove some of the mulch for a while to let things dry out. Avoid mulch touching plant stems.

Straw mulch, like that from Devon Henry's chicken coop, works well for vegetable gardens. Wood chips are best for mulching around woody plants.

Rock and gravel mulch are difficult to keep looking nice. Never use weed barrier cloth under mulch, especially around trees and shrubs.

Are dandelions growing in a mountain meadow at 10,000 feet still weeds?

CHAPTER 11: **WEEDING**

DON'T LET WEEDS STEAL FROM YOUR PLANTS

"A year of weeds leads to seven years of hoeing." — Folk saying recounted in "Sustainable Horticulture for Wyoming," University of Wyoming Cooperative Extension Service.

The penstemon in my perennial flower garden is creeping into the lawn. The grass is creeping into the flowers. Technically, that means both penstemon and grass are weeds — out-of-place plants.

Besides growing where they are unwanted, most weeds are aggressive, crowding out preferred plants and even reducing the productivity of vegetables. Often native to Europe or Asia, coming here accidentally or intentionally, they seem to outpace even native plants, excelling where ground is disturbed.

Unfortunately, weeds aren't usually considered as edible as our vegetables or as beautiful as our flowers.

Tyler Mason, former Cheyenne Botanic Gardens horticulturist (he left to earn his Ph.D. at Colorado State University in organic agriculture) practices integrated pest management, opting for the least toxic, but effective, methods to control weeds.

Know your adversaries

The two biggest weed pests in gardens here are field bindweed and Canada thistle. Both develop extensive roots.

Creeping bellflower, *Campanula rapunculoides*, with stalks

INTEGRATED PEST MANAGEMENT

"Best practices for managing weeds that are hard to kill:
"I think that the IPM approach is best because you use a combination of cultural, mechanical, physical, biological and chemical approaches. Step one is proper identification of the weed. Step two is to consider digging, pulling, mowing, grazing, biological control and other options first and chemical options as a last resort."

— Chris Hilgert, University of Wyoming Extension
Master Gardener Coordinator

of multiple lavender bell-shaped flowers, runs a close third because it spreads too well.

"Creeping bellflower has plans for world domination and has roots that can go down 2 feet deep and up to 1 inch in diameter." — Shane

Also on Tyler's list are dandelion, curly dock, crabgrass, plantain and common groundsel.

Dalmation toadflax, *Linaria dalmatica*, is a serious problem in our area grasslands and around rural homes.

The book *Weeds of the West* is a great field guide to weeds in gardens, cropland and rangeland.

Or check your unknown plant against Wyoming's official noxious weeds list. Visit the U.S. Department of Agriculture's plant website and click on the "Invasive and Noxious Weeds" link to find Wyoming's list with links to photos of the species. The site also has a plant identification key.

Beware of Trojan horses

Manure is great fertilizer, Tyler said, but not if it still has viable seeds when not thoroughly composted. Sometimes, weed seeds come with plants you bring home.

Don't stir things up

There are hundreds of seeds lying dormant in the soil just waiting for a bit of sunlight. Tilling the vegetable patch brings them to the surface.

No-till gardening is becoming more popular (Chapter 8). Once a bed is built, the soil and its microorganisms can finally do their thing, improving soil structure and fertility. Compost and other amendments are added as top-dressing.

In the Botanic Gardens' community garden Tyler is using wide-bed gardening in his plot this year instead of the traditional rows. Each bed is a berm about 6 inches high by 2 to 3 feet across, running the length of his garden. Access paths on either side are well-mulched with straw, reducing the area needing to be weeded.

By not stepping on the berm

and compressing it, the soil holds more water.

"Be effective with your water," Tyler said. Water right where you need it. Same with fertilizer — don't broadcast it over the garden, otherwise the excess will feed the weeds.

A stirrup hoe is useful for weeding if you haven't mulched your vegetable garden yet. It's designed to cut weeds off a quarter-inch below the soil surface.

Get them early

If your garden has any bare soil, you are bound to see weed seedlings. Pull them right away. Even thistle and bindweed are easy to pull, roots and all, when they are less than 2 inches tall. To disrupt seedlings while you are in a standing position, use a stirrup hoe like Tyler does, pulling it through the top quarter-inch of soil to sever the roots.

How do you know which is a weed seedling and which is a vegetable seedling? Plant seeds in a pattern. Or give your garden an advantage over weeds by transplanting starts rather than direct seeding.

Keep them in the dark

Black plastic sheeting, with holes cut for inserting vegetables, is a way to mulch them. Used with drip irrigation and soluble fertilizers, it can be pricey.

Weed barrier cloth is often used for landscape plantings. But it can make it harder for the roots of desired plants planted within it to get water and nutrients. Within a year, dirt blows in on top and weeds sprout anyway.

Rock mulch is popular these days, but it doesn't contribute nutrients the way a mulch of organic materials can, like bark.

In flower and veggie gardens, Tyler recommends materials that compost quickly and can be turned under (if you are a traditionalist), such as grass clippings, tree leaves, straw (not hay with seeds). Take care they are not from diseased plants. Also, make sure they were not sprayed recently with herbicides. Weeds that poke through mulch are easier to pull because the soil surface has not been baked by the sun.

Another way to keep weed seeds in the dark is to grow more densely — keep the ground shaded. Maintaining a healthy lawn cut about 3 inches high will shade out weeds, Tyler said.

Behead them

It is amazing how many seeds one weed can produce. The Master Gardener manual says dandelions have 15,000 seeds per plant.

Don't let weeds flower. If you don't have time to remove them, deadhead them by hand or mower. Our Golden Retriever eats our unsprayed dandelion heads when I point them out to her.

"There are other weeds that can produce up to 80,000 seeds per plant. Never walk past a weed." — Shane

Dig them out

Tyler is fond of the hori hori knife, a traditional Japanese garden tool that looks like a narrow, pointed hand trowel with a sawtooth edge on one side. This is a good tool for weeds that breach the mulch, are too big for the stirrup hoe, or that have roots about as deep as the hori hori is long. However, noxious weeds like bindweed will multiply if pieces of root are left behind.

"The Garrett Wade Professional Gardener's Digging Tool, which is like a hori hori on steroids, is the best one on the market because its handle is off-set and provides leverage. They are so incredibly heavy duty — a bit expensive — but last a lifetime." — Shane

Overgraze them

When I was a range management student, I learned that cattle prefer forbs (wildflowers) over grass. They will nibble these "ice cream plants" to death if left in a pasture too long.

If you have bindweed in your garden, keep removing the green leafy parts as often as you can and eventually the plants should starve to death. At least they won't spread or go to seed.

Don't mow the thistles! It encourages rhizomes — underground stems — to spread and pop up more plants. Catherine Wissner, University of Wyoming Extension horticulturist, said to spray the individual plants when they are blooming or after the first frost. These non-native thistles are a tough, invasive plant that requires tough measures.

If you have an overgrazed pasture full of weeds, especially noxious weeds, please consult the Laramie County Conservation District.

Poison the invincible

There might be a situation that justifies using herbicides. But first, you must find the right one for your weed, so you must be able to identify it.

Different herbicides work in different ways. You must follow the directions exactly as to formula strength, timing and weather conditions for safety as well as effectiveness. This is true whether you use an herbicide approved for organic growing like Suppress, one Tyler recommends, or a conventional herbicide.

"The Suppress label recommends that it works best on weeds 6" or less. It is basically an acid, like vinegar." — Shane

Keep in mind that some herbicides will volatize — turn to toxic gases — when temperatures are more than 85 degrees Fahrenheit and then will blow onto non-target plants, the neighbors, your pets or yourself, Tyler said. He doesn't recommend broadcast spraying or using feed and weed products. It can lead to toxic runoff, which pollutes surface and groundwater. Spot treat instead.

People want to exceed the herbicide label recommendations, but if too strong, the herbicide can burn the top of the plant, not allowing the plant to transfer the toxin to its roots. It re-sprouts instead of dying.

Finally, be sure to deadhead weeds before spraying so that bees and butterflies won't be poisoned by poisoned flowers, Tyler said.

Draw the line

I heard that a concrete curb poured around the edge of a flower bed can be breached by grass, my most abundant "weed."

I'm trying this solution instead: edging a bed with flagstones flush with the lawn. The lawnmower can run two wheels along them and no string trimming is necessary. However, in the spring, or whenever grass shows up between the stones, I can upend them and take a shovel to the white root-like grass stems, known as rhizomes, and cut them back.

I learned another edging solution from Herb Schaal, the landscape architect of the Paul Smith Children's Village at the Cheyenne Botanic Gardens. He has his own beautiful gardens and lawn in Bellevue, Colorado.

Herb digs a trench between lawn and garden about 6-8 inches wide and deeper than the grass roots grow. Then he fills the trench with mulch to keep people from breaking ankles and so that the lawn mower wheels can run on it and no edge trimming is required. He cleans roots out of the trenches once a year and refills them.

The advantage of these methods over concrete curbing: I can change the size and shape of my flower beds whenever I like.

Gardening is about discrimination, discouraging some plants and favoring others. Vigilance is important. But is there a gardener who doesn't enjoy, within moderation, an excuse to spend time out in the garden?

WEED PHILOSOPHY

"...a rose by any other name would smell as sweet?"
— *William Shakespeare*

"A weed by any other name can be the exuberant flower you fell in love with and planted three years ago."
— *Barb Gorges*

Non-native Sweet William is weedy but native Western Tiger Swallowtails love it.

There is no official horticultural definition of what a weed is. In everyday usage though, a weed is a plant out of place that is disrupting management goals.

This spring I realized my perennial flower beds needed renovation, weeding, editing, improving, whatever you want to call it — kind of a Marie Kondo tidying up. Volunteer Sweet William, *Dianthus barbatus*, is taking over the herb bed. Even though me and the swallowtail butterflies love its multiple shades of pink, it is crowding out other plants and about to become a weed.

I rarely have traditional, ugly weeds like kochia because they won't find enough bare, sunny spots. But because the beds were carved out of the lawn, grass is my biggest weed. The yarrow patch might require digging up and trying to sort out the grass roots. Or I could start over, replacing it with a shovelful of uninfected yarrow from somewhere else in the yard.

Many of the plants in my perennial beds are gifts from either plants or birds dropping seeds. Because individual perennial plants can't last forever, I've learned to remove mulch in the spring and let unidentifiable seedlings grow up enough that I can tell whether they are friend or foe. I know that a columbine that sprouts on its own in a shady spot on pure clay left from construction will grow better than anything I can plant, other than another columbine.

Our mountain ash trees produce a plethora of seedlings every year. I pull them because otherwise they would become a forest. The trees were originally bird gifts, from fruit plucked from the tree across the street.

We once had aspen trees that had to be cut down — they aren't long lived away from the mountains. The lawn exploded in aspen sprouts wherever the roots ran underneath. Spraying them with something mildly toxic left brown spots in the lawn around each undying sprout. However, by clipping back each sprout regularly, in two years the roots finally lost their fight and that was that.

After months of winter dormancy, I realized oregano was taking over a bed. Why should I be surprised? It's a mint and all mints have spreading reputations.

I vaguely remember a few years ago looking around for spare plants after enlarging this bed. The oregano in the herb bed needed thinning and bees like the flowers so I planted some along with another mint, bee balm (monarda or horsemint). But the oregano took over half the bed when I wasn't looking, and the bee balm was barely hanging on. Other plants were in hiding, hungering for water and sunlight, which the oregano refused to share.

Maybe I should have harvested the oregano and dried it. Instead, I added most of it to the compost bin. The remainder standing in that bed will make green filler, and later, cut flowers, for bouquets this summer.

Then there are the hollyhocks. Years ago, I tried to grow them in the alley, but a neighbor mistook the first year's leaf rosettes for weeds and mowed them while trying to be neighborly. I then encouraged hollyhocks to grow elsewhere and this year they are finally forming a herd. But then I realized they had surrounded my hardly-ever-blooming peonies. So, I moved a few hollyhocks and discovered how vigorous their root systems are. We will see next year if the peonies appreciate less competition.

There's a saying about transplanted perennial plants, "The first year they sleep, the second year they creep and the third year they leap." This is the third year for cutleaf coneflowers given to me by a friend thinning her garden. They seem to be living by that maxim's timeline so I might have some to share with other friends next year.

My new weed philosophy: Sometimes you must take a shovel to plants before they become weeds.

Clockwise from top left: punch gun, ¼-inch tubing, emitters, loop stakes and barbed couplings.

CHAPTER 12:
DRIP IRRIGATING

SAVE TIME AND SAVE WATER (AND MONEY)

Imagine the twist of a flipper at your faucet or a timer automatically turning on the water to your whole garden. It travels out via tubing with little emitters at each plant, or thin tubing with an emitter on the end taking it to farther plants, or through soaker hose tubing. The plastic tubing is covered by mulch, which also suppresses weeds. This "drip irrigation" can use 30-50 percent less water than sprinklers. It makes sense to concentrate water where the plants are.

Mark and I installed drip irrigation for our vegetables and flowers at the back of the yard, including a raised bed, hooking it up to our outside faucet. One advantage to drip is you can avoid water on your tomato plant leaves, but that is not as much a problem in our dry climate as elsewhere.

Drip irrigation on a timer still needs to be adjusted for unusual wet or dry spells, but it is a huge convenience for us — and our pet sitter when we travel.

All the plastic components are still in good shape after eight years in the garden because they are away from sunlight, mostly under mulch, especially in winter. The few holes have been easy to mend. In winter we remove the mechanical parts attached to the faucet and store them inside.

Drip installation

Installing drip is easy enough. However, it took a few extra trips to the store, once because we forgot to buy an end cap — and two extra trips because the clerk accidently let us go home with underground sprinkler tubing, which does not work with drip emitters — it is too thick.

Actual installation, including 25 emitters at the ends of 25 spaghetti tubes, took about as long as driving round trip to the store four times — just over two hours.

It is best if the tubing and fittings are all from the same company, but you'll use general plumbing materials to get from the typical ¾-inch-diameter home outside faucet to the recommended ½-inch-diameter drip tubing for home use.

To give you an idea of cost, here is my shopping list circa 2012, in order of installation from the faucet:

- $3 – **Vacuum breaker** (3/4-inch), a simple backflow preventer keeps water in the hose or drip tubing from getting sucked back into your household water supply.

- $11 – **Y-connector** (3/4-inch), allows you to hook up the drip system and a hose at the same time at the same faucet and turn them on independently.

- $5 – **Water pressure regulator** (3/4-inch), to prevent blowing up your drip tubing when you turn the water on.

- $10 – **Y-filter** (3/4-inch). There are other types, but all keep sediment in the water from clogging emitters.

- $6 – **Length of PVC pipe, cement, converter to ½-inch tubing, etc.** We had the PVC pipe extend to ground level and then attach to the drip tubing.

- $0.80 – **½-inch elbow fitting.** The tubing is so flexible we didn't need more than one elbow. There are also T-fittings so that you can have the tubing branch off, down each row of vegetables or to each raised bed. The fittings are forced onto the ends of the tubing — no tool required.

- $10 – **½-inch tubing**, 100 feet, cuts easily with pruners

- $1.50 – **Bag of 10 ½-inch loop stakes** to hold the tubing in place.

- $10 – **Punch gun**, makes the right size holes in the ½-inch tubing to fit the emitters or barbed couplings attaching the ¼-inch tubing.

- $2 – **Bag of 25 ¼-inch barbed couplings** to pop into the holes in the ½-inch tubing to connect the ¼-inch-diameter tubing. Each hole corresponds to a plant you want to water. These barbs are not needed if you run your ½-inch tubing right next to each plant and put an emitter in each hole.

- $7 – **¼-inch tubing**, 100 feet, cuts easily with pruners. I used plain tubing, but there's also

GALLONS PER HOUR CALCULATIONS

Which emitters you chose, 1 or 2 gallons per hour, depends on how much water pressure you have, how quickly your ground soaks up water and how long you want to leave the system on during each watering. You can mix them in the same system if some plants need more water than others.

If your faucet flows at 100 gallons per hour, you could, theoretically, use up to 100 1-gallon or 50 2-gallon per hour emitters.

How much water does your faucet produce per hour? Figure out how many seconds it takes for it to fill a 1-gallon container.

Take that many seconds and divide them into the number of seconds in an hour (3,600). If it takes 10 seconds to fill, divide 10 into 3,600 seconds in an hour and you have the rate of 360 gallons per hour.

tubing with holes every so many inches and tubing of a porous material — soaker tubing.

- $4 – **Bag of 10 emitters**, either 1 gallon per hour or 2, to pop into the holes on the ½-inch tubing. Or, if you use plain ¼-inch tubing extensions, you pop them into the ends of those tubes. You can also install little sprinklers that spray instead of emitters, which only drip, but that defeats the idea of saving water by keeping it from becoming airborne and evaporating. See how to calculate gallons per hour in "gallons per Hour Calculations."

- $2 – **Bag of "goof plugs"** in case you have punched a hole you don't want and need to plug it.

- $1.50 – **Bag of 10 ¼-inch loop stakes** for holding the ¼-inch tubing in place.

- $1 – **end cap, ½-inch**. If you don't have this on the far end of your ½-inch tubing, you just have a holey hose!

We already had some Teflon tape and a wrench for all the plumbing connections, so I didn't count them.

Because I set up my system for 25 plants, I had to buy multiple packages of emitters, barbs and loop stakes. My total was $90 back then. But remember, I've saved water and time for the past eight years.

These antelope, living at F.E. Warren Air Force Base, often come into town to graze gardens.

CHAPTER 13: **PESTS**

SHARE LESS OF YOUR GARDEN WITH WILDLIFE

Summer in the garden looks so idyllic from afar — especially back last winter when you were dreaming about it. And then a couple weeks after the last frost, the annoying summer visitors show up, the garden pests.

I asked Catherine Wissner, University of Wyoming Extension horticulturist for Laramie County, what pests people call about most. Her top three are ants, yellowjacket wasps and weeds.

Integrated pest management is the best way to deal with animal pests. This means using methods with a minimum impact on human health, the environment and non-target organisms.

Methods include growing the right plant in the right place, checking plants regularly, identifying pests correctly and trying physical and biological control methods before reaching for chemicals.

When it comes to garden pests, we humans, the big-brained species, should be able to outsmart a small, hungry critter. Right?

Ants

We had little brown ants making themselves at home along the cracks in our patio. We followed Catherine's suggestion to put a sugar substitute, aspartame (one brand is NutraSweet), on top of every mound. Between that and caulking the cracks, we cut down on the numbers. But will aspartame work on bigger ants?

"Aspartame only works for the tiny sugar ants," Catherine said. "For the bigger ants you can buy ant traps at the grocery store. They seem to work and there are no poisons for pets to get into."

Yellowjackets

Yellowjacket wasps, though yellow and black, have hard and shiny-looking exoskeletons compared to furry honeybees and bumblebees.

Yellowjackets like the meat and sugary foods served at picnics and they can be aggressive in late summer. But Catherine notes their ill effects on the beneficial garden insects as well.

"All wasps are predacious and go after caterpillars, grasshoppers and sometimes spiders as a food source for their larvae. If you are trying to develop a butterfly garden, then they are a problem," she said.

Catherine recommends yellowjacket traps sold at hardware stores: "The best one I found is a hexagonal green sticky trap that hangs. It also catches flies. Late April is the best time to put out traps (to catch the queens)."

To picnic safely in our yard, we have used the yellow plastic traps with the refillable attractant (which is toxic to pets). We hang them out of reach and 20 feet away from pets, food and people. The brand we use has a wasp identification chart and so far, we've caught prairie and western yellowjackets.

Keep Benadryl or similar antihistamine on hand if someone gets stung and starts to swell.

Eventually, we screened in our patio, screening out the yellow jackets and mosquitoes and made it a "catio" from which our two cats can safely watch birds. I think they've also taken care of the ants.

Aphids

It's hard to see tiny green (or other color) aphids, but easy to see the damage they cause sucking on plant leaves, making them curl or grow misshapen.

Prevention is the best cure for aphid and many other insect infestations. Catherine said, "They are a good indicator of plants and the soil system being off balance. Too much fertilizer and not enough water typically invites bugs."

In other words, a stressed plant is a target for hungry insects who, like wolves, go for the sick and weak, stressing them further.

Besides adjusting fertilizer and water amounts, you can knock aphids off with a stream of water. If the leaves are sticky with aphid "honeydew" you might want to prune them away before the stickiness attracts other insects and fungus. And you can try treating the leaves with neem oil.

Beneficial insects

Some beneficial insects leave behind a bit of cosmetic damage. The leafcutter bee cuts little half circles out of the edges of oval leaves until they resemble prickly holly leaves. The material is for building its nest. It doesn't usually hurt the plant and as Catherine said, "They are important in the garden and pollinate a wide variety of vegetables, fruits and flowers."

Slugs

It's surprising to find slugs in Cheyenne, with average precipitation of only 15 inches a year. I didn't have any until a few years ago.

I asked Catherine her favorite remedy for slugs. "Chickens," she said.

If that isn't an option, beer traps have worked well for me in the vegetable garden. I sink a 6-ounce yogurt container in the ground up to its rim and fill it halfway with cheap beer, though I hear expensive beer works better. The slugs are attracted to the yeast, dive in and drown. The next morning, I remove the slugs by pouring out the traps through an old kitchen strainer held over a bowl. Then I pour the beer back in the traps. The beer can be reused several days.

For slugs in the flower garden, it is easier to change the habitat—thinning out the vegetation and removing the leaf mulch for a while, giving the birds a chance to find any slugs I didn't already pick off. "More air, less moisture," said Catherine.

Deer and antelope

You might think deer and antelope are only a problem for the folks living on acreage outside of town, but the antelope on F.E. Warren Air Force Base walk into the west side neighborhoods in late winter looking for snacks.

Both deer and antelope are browsers, fond of shrubbery, but they will occasionally pick on less woody plants. While many plant catalogs will mark certain plants as deer resistant — most catalogs don't have customers with antelope problems, Catherine pointed out — that isn't a

CHICKEN MULTI-TASKERS

A flock of chickens can remove pests, turn over compost and fertilize the garden.

Chickens are allowed within city limits. However, on the City of Cheyenne website, city codes for animal care and control list restrictions for keeping chickens.

Chickens consider garden pests tasty snacks. They like to rummage around in the compost pile, helping to aerate it. Chicken manure can become garden fertilizer. And you might be able to harvest eggs and meat to go with your vegetables.

Sandra Cox's chickens eat grasshoppers and other pests.

"We used to herd turkeys through our original community gardens on Whitney Road. We had a gigantic infestation of grasshoppers and the turkeys wiped them out. We ended up with two 30-pound turkeys." — Shane

guarantee they won't get eaten.

Various substances are recommended as repellents but need to be reapplied frequently and after rain. Or you can build a cage to protect an important plant.

There's only one solution for growing vegetables in deer-filled neighborhoods, Catherine said, "Tall double fencing." The idea behind a fence inside a fence is that deer are hesitant to jump a fence into a space if there isn't enough room to take a running jump back out.

Birds

While Mark and I invite birds to our yard for the many pleasures and benefits they provide, if we want to harvest our chokecherries or grow other fruit, we could put up netting at the right time — before the fruit begins ripening because birds like it greener than we do. But, Catherine said, "It needs to be monitored several times a day as birds have a tendency to get tangled up in the netting."

Tree squirrels

Like the birds, you need to either fence them out or beat them to the harvest.

Ground squirrels, pocket gophers and prairie dogs

These rodents are more likely to be a menace to rural gardens. Try protecting trees and other plants with chicken wire and repellents. Consult the Extension office or the Laramie County Conservation District for how to safely use the last resorts of traps and poisons.

Rabbits

Fencing is the best option to manage marauding rabbits.

In the unfenced front yard, I don't grow any flowers that are lush and delicious, like pansies. Instead, the rabbits nibble our grass. One garden blogger I read suggested growing clover in your lawn, a rabbit favorite, as a distraction. It also provides nitrogen for lawns, a key nutrient.

My friend Florence Brown has certain plants she guards with the prunings from her rosebushes. The thorny mulch can keep rabbits away as well as dogs and cats.

"I had some luck with rabbit repellents, but fencing is best." — Shane

Thrips etch designs noticeable on the top of the leaf. They are the tiny white flies in this photo of the bottom side of the leaf.

Rabbits always seem to eat your most prized plants. Fencing can be the best protection.

CHAPTER 14: **RABBITS**

HELP RABBITS CONTROL TASTE FOR GOURMET GREENS

"Flopsy, Mopsy and Cotton-tail, who were good little bunnies, went down the lane to gather blackberries. But Peter, who was very naughty, ran straight to Mr. McGregor's garden, and squeezed under the gate!"

— *The Tale of Peter Rabbit*
by Beatrix Potter

It must have been Peter Rabbit I caught snipping my green tulip buds the morning of May 1 as they lay helpless in a patch of melting snow. I saw him through a window and ran out in my bare feet to shoo him away. Then I walked the dog back and forth a few times to leave her scent.

I picked up the six tulip buds, each left with a 4 to 6-inch stem and put them in a vase inside. I'm happy to say they ripened and opened. The other buds, left unscathed, recovered from the snow, stood up again and also bloomed.

The tulip vandal couldn't have been my regular rabbit, the one sitting in the front yard almost every day. My garden beds have never been attacked before. Well, except the time I tried pansies in the whiskey barrel planter and the rabbits jumped in and ate them all. Otherwise, I grow only hardy perennials in the front yard.

The backyard has Peter Rabbit's favorite vegetables, but there are three rabbit deterrents: the raised beds (higher than the old whiskey barrel), the dog, and the concrete block wall. The gates have vertical bars in the lower half less than 2 inches apart.

But I was shocked when the 900 seedlings and assorted mature plants we planted in the spring in the Habitat Hero demonstration garden at the Cheyenne Botanic Gardens were nearly completely obliterated by rabbits.

The following fall we planted a couple hundred bulbs and the rabbits didn't dig up very many before we fenced the garden in March with wood stakes and chicken wire. It kept the rabbits out and allowed plants to make a comeback. Later, we put in a better looking fence.

It is ironic we are establishing wildlife habitat yet fencing out rabbits. There is plenty for rabbits to eat in the rest of Lions Park. They are prolific, but only live two years, providing they are the 15% making adulthood. The Lions Park rabbits feed the resident Cooper's hawks.

Laramie County Master Gardener Kim Parker said her solution is dogs and fencing, "At our house, we have successfully used low, 18-inch fencing to keep the bunnies out while my garden establishes, then we take it down and 'let them eat cake.'

"Most of the year, I don't think they eat hardly anything (at least not that I notice), although I notice that in the winter they nibble on some grass and grape hyacinth leaves. Weird. They also have spots in our buffalograss lawn where they like to rest, but the dog keeps them from lingering long."

Also, Kim said, "Perhaps using plants that they don't want to eat helps, or that are vigorous enough that it doesn't matter if they get eaten, like grape hyacinth or fall asters for example."

The *Wyoming Master Gardener Handbook* mentions rabbit repellents to spread around or spray on your plants, but they are only effective until it rains. Be careful what you spray on vegetables you'll eat. Ultrasonic devices are ineffective. Eliminating access to hiding spots, like nearby brushy areas is important.

Fencing is the only surefire cure. For cottontails, the handbook recommends 30 inches high and for jackrabbits (hares), 36 inches, preferably something like chicken wire with small openings. If rabbits gnaw on your trees and shrubs, wrap pieces of quarter-inch hardware cloth around trunks, 30-36 inches high.

For the Habitat Hero garden at the Cheyenne Botanic Gardens, much of the fence is up against the sidewalk so rabbits can't dig their way in. Otherwise, you need to allow for an extra 12 inches of fencing beyond the height you want: 6 inches at the bottom bent at a 90-degree angle to the outside of the garden and then bury that flange 6 inches deep.

Remember, if you decide to have a rabbit for dinner, you must follow the Wyoming Game and Fish Department hunting and trapping regulations.

Pete Michael's "Hailbusters" protect plants from being shredded as this rhubarb was.

CHAPTER 15:
HAIL PROTECTION

"HAIL BUSTERS" KEEP ICY VANDALS AT BAY

After three hailstorms decimated gardens in various parts of Cheyenne, I wanted to see how one man uses what he calls "Hail Busters."

Pete Michael also busted bad guys for a living. As the Wyoming attorney general, he was the state's chief law enforcement officer at the time I visited but is now retired.

He's perfected a system for keeping hail behind bars. Well, bouncing off half-inch hardware cloth, anyway.

One popular hail protection device used around town is what I think of as the "duck and cover" method.

At the sound of the first hailstone on the roof, Jan Nelson-Schroll said she ducks outside and covers her garden with a tarp or blanket, hopefully not getting injured herself.

One variation is to install a series of poles in the middle of the garden ahead of time so that the weight of the covering and the hail doesn't flatten the plants.

Another variation is the one my husband, Mark, used to use. When he grew our tomatoes in containers, he would run out and drag them under the patio roof.

The problem is that you might not be home when hail hits. Or you might not be quick enough, or the tomatoes have gotten too big to lug around. Thus, in our garden we had scars on the tomato stems, shredded rhubarb leaves and a puddle of rose petals.

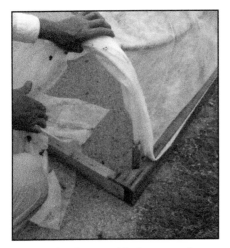

Pete Michael's portable low tunnel offers hail protection and can be removed for harvesting.

Low tunnel

The first contraption Pete showed me that he'd built was essentially a "low tunnel," often used for season extension.

His is a 16-foot long portable wooden frame 3 feet wide that sits on the ground. Plastic tubing meant for circulating water in radiant floor heating makes 2-foot high hoops spanning the width at 18-inch intervals. The ends of the hoops fit into attached 6-inch lengths of electrical conduit pipe.

The whole thing is like a covered wagon with white polyester floating row cover (he uses Agribon) stretched tight and kept in place with strips of lathe nailed over it

around the wooden frame. The long loose ends are pulled together and staked out to keep the wind from lifting the frame.

Pete is growing fancy squash that profited from the extra heat of being covered. And they were protected from the hail July 13 — though the cover material is now shot with holes.

Hail Busters

It's the Hail Busters though, that keep hail away and give Pete peace of mind. Pete is a serious vegetable grower. He says he's tried growing just about every vegetable imaginable. His backyard is filled with raised beds 3 feet wide (same width as the hardware cloth comes) by either 6 or 8 feet long.

Each bed has a hail busting wooden frame made with one-by-twos in the same dimensions as the raised bed. The frame is screened with the half-inch hardware cloth, wire screen with half-inch openings. It stops a lot of hail or at least slows it down so it is less damaging.

He built everything with salvaged lumber, but he did say having to buy a roll of the hardware cloth was a bit pricey.

I have seen other gardens built with screen roofs. The difference here is that the roofs, the Hail Busters, can be set at different heights depending on plant growth.

The tomato cages in one raised bed are sturdy enough that the screen lays on top of them.

In other beds, several stakes planted in the bed support the screen. When it's time to tend the plants, the screen can be set aside.

A lot of hail comes sideways, but these beds are close together, offering some protection.

"The best solution was hardware cloth mounted above the wide beds at about 5 feet or so. Be sure and bend the edges so the cut ends don't catch on your clothes or scratch your skin." — Shane

Multi-purpose

Hail protection turns out to be only one use for these screens.

Two raised beds become cold frames in the fall. Their screen tops, built with more substantial 2-by-4s, are hinged to the raised beds on one side, then covered with salvaged clear plastic. Pete finds much of his salvaged materials just from being observant walking to and from work.

Early in the growing season, when birds might otherwise steal the seeds he just planted, Pete can lay the regular screens directly on the raised bed frames.

When tender seedlings emerge, the screens keep the rabbits out. And when starting cool season lettuce in August, the screening itself, or some added floating row cover, can give them necessary shade.

In the fall, floating row cover — or blankets — are easily supported to protect vegetables on freezing nights, extending the growing season.

Flowers and hail

Growing vegetables under cover is one thing, but no one who admires flowers would want to look at them through Hail Busters unless they were growing a valuable crop for market or seed.

Pete does grow flowers, without cover, including a magnificent stretch of hollyhocks in the middle of a vegetable bed located between the sidewalk and street. They were a little worn looking from the hail two weeks before, as were the thick bunches of Shasta daisies growing around the house. The big beds of penstemons at the front gate had gone to seed.

Mark Gorges inserted 4-inch plastic pipes in the corners of his raised bed (before filling it) so that the 2 x 4 hail guard supports can be removed at the end of the season.

His secret is to grow perennials. Annuals, which people plant at the beginning of the season and which are supposed to bloom continually until they die in the first frost, are easily wiped out by hail. They will revive faster if you give them some liquid fertilizer once a week afterwards, Shane Smith, now retired director of the Cheyenne Botanic Gardens, told me.

"I found that petunias were the best annual flower to come back from a hailstorm." — Shane

But, Pete said, perennials bloom in waves — if you are strategic. Say your penstemons are at their peak when the hail comes and knocks off all their flowers (their stems tend to be tougher than your average annual). After the storm, you can decide whether they look bad enough to cut back or if they just need a bit of trimming, leaving them with plenty of green to continue photosynthesizing, storing energy for next year.

But coming up behind the penstemons might be your daisies. At the time of the storm, their buds were small enough to be missed by the icy missiles.

And if you choose perennials with skinny leaves, they aren't as much of a target for hail.

SUCCESSION PLANTING

Pete Michael said, "Knowing your succession crops, and having seed on hand, can relieve a lot of stress over hail. If a crop of lettuce gets hammered and it is long in the tooth anyway, then compost it and start something else.

"If it is early June to July 4, try planting the empty bed with bush beans. Even with good hail protection and thus no need to clear out a crop, I'm constantly removing a crop that is past prime and planting something new. In some beds, I get three crops in a year."

Even though it was early November when I last heard from him, Pete reported, "I have nice kale, cilantro and spinach that I covered before the last storm and I will cover again on Sunday. With proper crop selection, Cheyenne has a plenty long growing season, except for some southern crops, like okra, that need warm, humid nights."

A tiling or trenching shovel is one of Kathy Shreve's favorite tools for fitting in more flowers.

CHAPTER 16: **TOOLS**

MASTER GARDENERS LIST MUST-HAVE GARDEN GEAR

Gardening smart and using the best tools for you and your garden situation means gardening can be less of a chore and more fun, leaving you with time to enjoy your results.

I asked Laramie County Master Gardeners which tools they consider essential for gardening. I also investigated best garden tool maintenance practices.

My hypothesis was tools for digging, cutting, watering, hauling and composting would be at the top of the list.

Surprisingly, only one person, Mike Heath, listed a power tool, a rototiller for tilling vegetable beds.

For his 4,000 square-foot garden and his gardening method, he thinks it is necessary.

Apparently, most of the Master Gardeners responding have gardens small enough to use only hand tools, just love gardening by hand, or are in the no-till or minimal till camp (Chapter 8).

"Curved handled garden trowels are incredible. They give you leverage you never knew you had. You can't beat the circle hoe. I also like the cobra head cultivator. Have you ever heard of ratchet pruners? They increase your hand strength by many times." — Shane

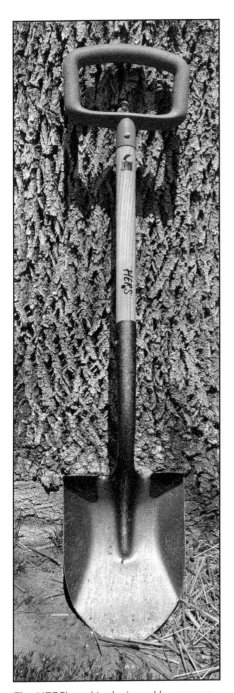

The HERShovel is designed by women to fit women more ergonomically. It comes in three sizes.

Hori hori

Outside of the rototiller, all the other favorite tools mentioned were split evenly between digging and cutting.

One tool does both: the hori hori.

A Japanese tool, the hori hori is "a cross between a knife and a trowel and I use it for everything," wrote Salli Halpern.

Wanda Manley said, "This is my 'go-to' tool … great for fluffing soil, transplanting, making furrows, etc. Does not rust."

Rosalind Schliske said, "In the last couple of years, my new favorite garden tool is a soil knife." The "knife" she mentions seems to be a modern hori hori, with a composite handle instead of wood.

The hori hori's 7-inch cutting blade, serrated on one side, is formed into a shallow length-wise V-shape. It can be used to cut and scoop out a small planting hole and makes a fabulous weed remover.

Susan Jones swears by a hand weeder sold under the Corona brand. It also has a serrated edge, but a molded plastic, more ergonomic handle and a V-shaped notch in the tip of the blade that helps pop out weeds with taproots, like dandelions.

Shovels

Only Kathy Shreve and Mike mentioned shovels on their lists. Kathy finds a tiling or trenching shovel to be most useful. The flat-edged, straight and narrow blade is perfect for inserting new plants into her established perennial beds. The weight of the wooden handle adds to

TOOL MAINTENANCE

No matter what digging and cutting tools you invest in, maintaining them will save you time, money and effort.

Jim Stallard had been in the seasonal tool sharpening business for 16 years when I met him in Fort Collins, Colorado.

Jim has seen it all, including dirt left on metal long enough that the moisture from it caused rust. He uses a wire brush to clean off dirt before putting away tools. More of us need to think about providing a convenient place to store tools out of the weather — and then train ourselves to put our tools away.

Jim uses silicone spray lubricant on the metal parts of tools — it's especially nice on the blades of pruners and loppers because it doesn't cause them to bind up or rust the way some products do.

Keeping tools sharp — even the blades on shovels and hand spades — makes gardening work easier. You can check online for tips on how to do it yourself, but there is nothing like letting a professional like Jim put a fresh edge on a tool at the beginning of the season.

its heft, she said, giving her a little extra oomph as she digs in.

Shovels and spades (the distinction between them is not clear) come in a wide variety of blade and handle options. It takes some experience to match one with what fits your hands, height, strength and type of digging you need to do. The same is true of hand trowels or hand spades. In our clay-type soils, go for better quality tools that won't snap as soon as you encounter a tough situation.

Pruners

One favorite cutting tool was mentioned by both Kathy and Wanda by brand name: Felco hand pruners. I finally have a pair myself, after years of being frustrated by cheaper pruners falling apart. Plus, Felco has replaceable parts and accessories available at area garden centers.

Felco pruners are bypass-type cutting tools, meaning the two halves slide by each other as they cut, like scissors, rather than the anvil-type, where one side is a blade and the other side is a flat surface.

Hand pruners might not be the best at snipping chives — you'd want scissors for that, but they do work fine for cutting flowers and are tough enough for cutting pumpkins off the vine, not to mention doing a little tree and shrub pruning.

Loppers

Once your trees and shrubs get beyond hand pruner size, it's time to look for loppers.

Both Bud Davis and Kathy swear

Essential tools: dandelion digger, hori hori, trowel, folding pruning saw, pruners, loppers.

by their ratcheting loppers, which can handle more than my pair, rated only for a maximum branch diameter of 1.25 inches. Kathy prefers the Fiskars brand while Bud got both of his pairs, a bypass for green wood and an anvil-type for dead wood, from Garrett-Wade. His loppers even have telescoping handles to help reach farther or get more leverage.

The other essentials

One can make do with old buckets and wheelbarrows for hauling and make compost with just a simple pile of plant debris. Watering can be as complex as drip irrigation (see Chapter 12) or as simple as a hose. I was hoping someone could recommend a hose that never kinks. That would indeed be a tool that makes the work easier.

However, it was Richard Steele, a Laramie County Master Gardener intern at the time of the survey, who said, "The best tool … is having access to the knowledge of the Master Gardeners."

PART 3

VEGETABLES, FRUITS, HERBS

Short-season varieties increase your chance of harvesting vegetables before the first frost.

CHAPTER 17:
VEGETABLE GARDENING

QUICK REVIEW: HOW TO BE A VEGETABLE GARDENER IN CHEYENNE

If you've gardened elsewhere in the country, there are three things you need to know about vegetable gardening in Cheyenne: use drip irrigation, prepare hail protection (Chapter 15) and never add lime to our alkaline soils.

If you've never gardened before, well, it's mostly about choosing the right vegetables for our climate and season length, giving plants the right amount of water, and mulching.

Step 1 – Find a spot for a vegetable bed or containers.

It should be sunny for at least six hours a day, preferably morning, and be relatively level and within reach of a hose or a drip irrigation system (Chapter 12).

Keep the veggies close to your back door so that it is easy to saunter out every day to admire them and pull a couple little weeds.

If the site currently doesn't even grow weeds well, it could be subsoil left behind by the builders. The soil can be amended and over time, become productive. But for success this season, think raised bed or containers (Chapters 37 and 38).

Also, if this is your first attempt at vegetable gardening, keep the size of the bed reasonable, maybe 4 feet wide (what you can reach across from either side) by 6 or 8 feet long.

"Try to stay away from trees even if they are to the north. All too often their roots will invade your beds." — Shane

Step 2 – Prepare the bed.

I have never used a rototiller. I prefer the (husband with) shovel method. Digging by hand will keep you from creating a bed bigger than you can manage, especially if this is your first garden. There are other methods if you plan ahead (Chapter 2).

If you have any compostable material, like last year's tree leaves, lawn mowings not treated with pesticides, vegetable debris from the kitchen or any old plant materials that don't include weed seeds or invasive roots or diseases, you can dig that in.

Dedicated gardeners will send soil samples out for analysis on exactly what the soil needs for growing vegetables. If your veggies show signs of malnutrition, think about doing that later in the season (Chapter 18).

Some gardeners work their soil until it's as fine and chunk-free as cocoa powder, but that isn't necessary — in fact, it's hard on the soil microbes that can help you (Chapter 8).

Step 3 – Shop for seeds.

If you know any successful gardeners in our area, see if they will gift you some seeds. Otherwise, you need to read the seed packets carefully. Keep in mind our average last day of frost is around May 25 and our average first day of frost is mid-September. It's a short season. You need to look for short-season vegetables (Chapter 3).

Each packet will tell you how many days from seed germination until maturity (harvest). Remember, some seeds take a week or more to germinate. Look for vegetable varieties that are in the range of 45 to 70 days. You can try starting tomatoes indoors (Chapter 4) or growing them with a season extender like a hoop house or row cover (Chapter 40).

Each packet will have more seeds than you can use in one season. Store them in an air-tight container in the refrigerator.

Meanwhile, look for tomatoes, eggplants, cucumbers and peppers ready to transplant.

Easy-to-grow-from seed directly sown in the garden are the squashes, beans, kale, chard and leaf lettuces (not head lettuce) (Chapter 5).

Step 4 – Plant seeds and transplant plants.

Follow the seed packet directions on when and how to sow seed. Make sure your soil is moist already.

For transplanting, normally you put the plant in the soil so it sits at the same height as it did in the pot. However, if it's a tomato that looks a little leggy, you can bury a few inches of its stem (Chapter 5).

Step 5 – Mulch.

We use old tree leaves and

pesticide-free grass clippings at our house. Straw is good, but not hay or anything with seeds. An inch or two of mulch will keep down the weeds and keep the soil from drying out too fast (Chapter 10).

Step 6 – Water.

Catherine Wissner, University of Wyoming Extension horticulturist, said consistency is most important. Once the plants are established, you can let the top inch of soil dry out (test it with your finger) in between thorough waterings, but if you are not consistent with providing enough water, you will not get good yields.

If you seem to have impenetrable clay soils, try watering for a couple minutes, then water elsewhere and then come back 15 minutes later and see if the soil will absorb the rest of the water it needs.

Step 7 – Fertilize.

Seedlings don't need fertilizer for a few weeks, but vegetables are soon hungry. Organic gardeners use compost — like your mulch as it decays, or "teas" made from soaking compost. Read up first. Avoid all manure, Catherine recommended. It tends to be salty (bad for our soils), full of weed seeds and may harbor pathogens. Avoid chemical fertilizers with too much nitrogen too — nitrogen grows great leaves but little if any fruit. Do not use weed and feed products — they will kill your veggies.

Step 8 – Weed.

If you mulch and don't overwater, you shouldn't have much of a weed problem. Visit your veggies every day. Pull by hand or use a dandelion digger (no hoe) on any little green interlopers. It's much easier than waiting until the weeds grow roots to Earth's core and shed seeds across the continent (Chapter 11).

Step 8 – Protect.

Everything is out to get your veggies before you can harvest them: frost, wind, hail, antelope, rabbits, insects, diseases. There are preventative and non-chemical actions you can take. (Chapter 13).

Step 9 – Harvest.

I remember the first summer I grew vegetables. I told my husband, a veteran vegetable grower, that I wanted to try growing them myself from start to finish. I did, and those vegetables had the most incredible flavor.

KATHY'S VEGETABLE TIPS
The details of success from Kathy Shreve

I spent an early summer evening in the garden with Kathy Shreve, a Laramie County Master Gardener, reviewing what to know about local vegetable gardening.

Timing

Wait until the end of May or later to transplant tender veggies such as tomatoes, eggplants and cucumbers, or put them under a season-extending cover like a low tunnel (Chapters 15 and 40). You can also plant them in containers you can scoot in and out of the garage.

While peas, cabbage types, lettuces and other greens can be planted earlier than the end of May, most vegetable seeds planted directly in the garden prefer warmer soil temperatures. Measure with a soil thermometer found at garden centers.

Kathy said we can plant as late as June 20. Plant fast growing crops as late as July if you want a fall harvest (Chapter 15 tip on succession planting).

Transplanting

If the plant was not outside in the sun when you bought it, it will need hardening off. Start with the plant in the shade for two or three hours. Then day by day increase the amount of time it spends in direct sun in increments of an hour or two. Keep it well watered.

When transplanting, Kathy advises digging a hole for your plant, filling it with water, then letting it drain before planting.

To remove a plant from a plastic pot, turn it upside down with the stem between your forefinger and middle finger. Squeeze the pot to loosen the soil and shake it very, very gently.

If there are a lot of roots, you can gently tease them apart a bit before putting the plant in the hole.

Hold the plant by the root mass so that it will sit in the hole with the soil at the same level of the stem as it was in the pot. Fill soil in around the roots, then tamp the soil gently.

However, tomatoes can be planted deeper because any part of their stem that is underground will sprout roots, the more the better. In fact, Kathy said to pinch off all but the top three or four leaves and bury the bare stem.

Lastly, keep plants well-watered, not soggy, while they get established. Wait a couple weeks before adding fertilizer to avoid burning the plants.

Mulch

Kathy mulches 2 to 3 inches deep with certified weed-free straw available at local feed stores. Besides keeping the soil from drying too fast and shading out weeds, mulch keeps rain and overhead watering from spattering dirt onto plants, which could spread disease. It can also keep hail from bouncing and inflicting damage twice.

Direct sowing

Root crops like carrots and beets don't transplant well, so you are better off starting them from seed.

Because Cheyenne is dry, Kathy plants in a little trench a couple inches deep. That way, when moisture comes, it will collect down where the plants are.

Seed packets tell you how deep to plant. Lay the seed in the bottom of the trench and sprinkle that much dirt on them. Then Kathy waters well, but gently, so she doesn't wash out the seeds. Keep the soil surface moist until the seeds germinate.

Lightly mulch when the seedlings are visible, adding more as the plants get bigger.

Mark rows with popsicle sticks or plastic knives left from picnics.

Water

Once plants are established, let the top 1-2 inches of soil dry out between waterings. Test by sticking your finger in the soil. Water deeply.

Kathy waters every other day using soaker hose and drip irrigation systems, except when it rains. She originally tested her system for 30 minutes to see if water made it to the root depth and decided on 40 minutes.

Water in the morning, or at least make sure leaves are dry before dark.

Bugs

Never use pesticides until you identify your problem (try Google or the Extension office), and then try the least toxic method first.

More is not better. Never apply more than the directions indicate (Chapters 11 and 13).

Slugs indicate a garden is too wet. Kathy said to roll newspaper to make 1 to 2-inch-diameter tunnels. Place rolls on the ground around affected plants in the evening. By sunrise, the slugs will be inside the rolls to get away from the light and you can dispose of them, rolls and all.

Fertilizer

Kathy likes slow-release products, which are less likely to burn the plants, as are the natural fertilizers. Additionally, compost tea is a good soil conditioner.

More is not better. Kathy uses half of what is directed until she sees how the plants respond.

Over-fertilization of fruit-producing vegetables like tomatoes often keeps them from producing the flowers that become the fruit. Kathy said they need to be stressed a little bit because it gets them thinking about preservation of the species and producing seed, rather than just enjoying life and producing leaves.

"Just leaves" is OK if you are growing leafy vegetables such as lettuce, kale, spinach and chard.

Trellis and cage

If you are growing vining vegetables, getting them off the ground means fruits stay cleaner and don't rot, and they are easier to find and pick. Use old chain link gates, bed springs, or anything else — be creative (Chapter 50).

Hog panels make sturdy tomato cages 5 feet high and 2.5 feet in diameter for larger, indeterminate varieties, with chicken wire over the top for hail protection. Otherwise, use jute twine to loosely tie the stem to a bamboo stake.

Add flowers

Adding annual flowers like alyssum, marigolds and sunflowers, or herbs including dill and oregano, attracts pollinators and beneficial insects to your garden.

Get a soil sampling bottle from the conservation district, follow directions and mail to CSU.

CHAPTER 18: **SOIL TESTING FOR FOOD CROPS**

GET THE DIRT ON WHAT YOUR SOIL NEEDS

Do you really know what nutrients your lawn and garden need and how much?

You could be adding too much of a good thing. Besides wasting your money, consider the bigger picture.

If the fertilizer has more nitrogen than your lawn needs, the excess washes into the groundwater, wasting your money and polluting someone's future drinking water.

Excess phosphorus washing into local streams and ponds causes algal blooms, suffocating aquatic life.

It's not always obvious when your plants need more or less supplementary food. In extreme cases, you'll see yellowed leaves or stunted growth in malnourished plants. Too much nitrogen, for example, could spur the plant into producing an overabundance of leaves but no blossoms — no flowers, no fruit.

Test your soil. Sampling is easy. Unlike my Soils 101 class in college, I didn't have to dig a 5-foot-deep pit. I sent in samples from the top 6 inches of the areas I wanted the soil testing lab to examine.

What a soil test tells you

Soil texture will tell you something about its fertility.

Is your soil sandy? If so, water (and dissolved nutrients) will percolate through it quickly.

Is your soil clayey like so much of Cheyenne's? Water moves through it slowly. The lab can recommend how much water and what rate you should apply it to your garden or lawn.

Testing for electrical conductivity tells you how salty your soil is, which can affect the availability of nutrients to plants. Some soils are naturally salty, but sometimes they become that way because too much fertilizer has been added over time, or the irrigation water is salty — comparatively speaking.

Knowing a soil's pH will help you understand how easily some nutrients can be taken up by plants. It will also tell you what plants might not grow well.

The Cheyenne area typically has alkaline soil. That is why soil amendment advice for the acidic soils of the eastern U.S., such as adding lime or wood ash, can be counterproductive here. Acid-loving plants, such as blueberries and rhododendron, will not grow here unless you plant them in a container in which you can acidify the soil.

The percentage of organic matter in your soil should match your garden plans. It is possible to add too much compost or manure for the plants you want to grow.

Get a soil-testing kit

Home testing kits sold in stores are not usually designed for our alkaline soils and will not be precise enough.

Colorado State University's Soil, Water and Plant Testing Laboratory in Fort Collins is one of the few remaining labs of this kind at land grant universities. Being in our "neighborhood," the folks at the CSU lab will understand our soils better than those farther away. They have developed testing specifically for the home gardener.

Follow the directions

The routine garden and landscape soil test cost $35 in 2021. When your kit arrives, follow the directions precisely. CSU asked me to dig a perfect cylinder 6 inches deep — five to 15 times in random places in my garden or lawn.

I was able to borrow a soil probe from the Laramie County Conservation District. A soil probe is a nifty little tool, a stainless steel pipe about an inch in diameter and 3 or 4 feet long, with a crossbar handle. You punch it into the ground 6 inches and pull out your sample, which you then dump out the side vent.

Well, almost. In my vegetable garden I had trouble keeping the soil in the tube until I was ready to dump it in my plastic dishpan. It needed a little moisture.

Twirling the probe didn't get me more than an inch into one spot in my front lawn. I hit solid clay near the house — probably left by the builders 50 years ago. I needed a sharp tool to dig the clay out of the probe.

I sampled both the vegetable garden and the front lawn areas. I took enough sub-samples of the lawn to make 2 cups' worth of dirt and mixed them together in the dishpan, doing the same in a separate dishpan for the vegetable garden sub-samples.

The directions said to break up clods and remove organic matter. I picked out as many roots as I could, and a few worms. I spread the dirt (excuse me, soil) out in the bottom of the pans and, by the next day, both samples were dry enough. Don't use the oven — it will stink up the house and distort your nitrogen readings.

The paperwork asks what's been growing in the tested area, what fertilizers have been used and how much it is irrigated. They also want to know what you plan to grow so they can make recommendations.

No good or bad soil

There is no good or bad soil. It just depends on what you want to grow and whether your soil currently is capable.

In a way, my perennial flower bed performs its own suitability exam. I plant a new type of perennial and if it doesn't thrive, I know I should remember that experience, write it in a journal and try something else the next year.

But now that I'm growing vegetables, which can deplete soil nutrients, and we have a lawn that isn't quite thick enough to shade out the dandelions, I'm curious to see what a soil test can tell me.

Results

My soil test results came by email from Colorado State University's Soil, Water and Plant Testing Laboratory.

As I opened the attachment, it reminded me of getting my cholesterol numbers from the health fair. Both tests document my progress in healthy living — or making healthy soil — within the limits of genetics — or bedrock.

pH balance

My front lawn's pH was high at 7.4, but my vegetable garden was 7.2, within the preferred range of 6 to 7.2.

I have alkaline soil, which is typical for this region. Most plants will still grow fine, except for acid-loving species. Because acidification treatments cost money and are not long lasting, we Westerners should instead take advantage of alkaline-loving plants.

Soil texture

Local gardeners talk about Cheyenne's clay soil texture, so I was surprised my vegetable garden tested as sandy loam and the front yard as sandy clay loam.

"Loam" describes the perfect combination of sand, silt and clay particles for horticulture and agriculture: just enough sand for good drainage, just enough silt and clay to hold water and nutrients.

The modifier "sandy" means water will drain more quickly. This explains why I needed to water the veggies so often last summer. With "clay" in the lawn's soil texture description, it means it holds water well, but percolation is slower. That means when you water, apply it slowly.

Organic material

In my vegetable garden, organic material tested at 3.9%. This isn't bad for an area that was first cultivated a year ago and amended with leaf compost.

The recommendation is to increase this category to 5% over the next two or three years by adding 2 to 3 inches of plant-based compost or 1 inch of animal-based compost in spring or fall, incorporating it into the top 6 to 8 inches of soil.

The front lawn, which I would love to convert to a flower garden, came in at 4%. Though I can improve that, less is fine for native, drought-resistant plants I would choose.

Without organic matter, soil would be nothing but weathered rock. Yes, you get many nutrients from minerals, but organic material feeds the soil microorganisms that feed your plants. The process also improves soil structure, which improves water permeability and absorption (think lower water bill). There can be as many as a billion microorganisms in a quarter teaspoon of topsoil. They are the real engines of plant growth.

Remember where organic material comes from? Plant and animal matter. It's a cycle as old as life.

Fertilizer history

Sometime during the 20th century, chemists determined plants could grow with nutrients from chemically processed mineral salts.

Today, it is common knowledge that highly processed fertilizers don't feed microorganisms the way organic (plant and animal-based) fertilizers do. And sometimes they leave behind a buildup of salty residue that is hard on plants.

Unfortunately, the big fertilizer companies have become so influential that it is not always easy to pursue what we now call organic gardening and farming — back to the future, as I think of it, because organic growers use Grandpa's pre-chemical farming knowledge augmented by new discoveries about organic materials.

Fertilizers

The vegetation of natural landscapes is the result of perfect nutrient cycling. However, gardens and lawns are more intensively grown and the natural nutrient cycle often needs our help.

But reports show we over-fertilize, polluting groundwater and surface water with the excess, and waste our money.

As I read labels on various bags and bottles, I realized perhaps the reason we over-fertilize is because many of us have trouble understanding the labels. We calculate fertilizer amounts as best we can — and then throw in a little extra for good luck.

Instead, we should err on the side of less. I confess to being stingy. In the days I only grew perennial flowers, I never fertilized with anything other than decomposing leaf mulch. We seldom fertilize our lawn, and only with one of the slow release organic fertilizers.

But now, thanks to my soil

test, I have actual numbers to strike a balance between stingy and overgenerous.

N is for Nitrate (Nitrogen)

Both my lawn and vegetable garden were low in nitrogen. Nitrogen is one of the three major nutrients, the one responsible for stems and leaves. But if you put too much on in one year, it interferes with producing flower and fruit buds and the excess disappears before the next growing season.

P is for Phosphorus

Surprisingly, in my vegetable garden, this came in high. But the lawn needs some. Phosphorus gives plants strong roots, resistance to disease and good fruit development.

K is for Potassium

Again, the vegetable garden came in high, and the analysis recommends adding a bit to the front yard — if I convert it to flowers. Plants need potassium for successful blooming — for flowers and fruiting vegetables like tomatoes.

"Most Cheyenne soils have adequate potassium so never pay more to get a higher level of it." — Shane

Other results

Electrical conductivity: In both areas of my yard, electrical conductivity was low, a good thing, meaning no salty, plant-killing soil.

Lime: Rated medium, OK for growing plants.

Why a local store sells lime is beyond me. With very, very few exceptions, adding lime to Wyoming soils will only increase alkalinity, perhaps to toxic levels.

Micronutrients: Zinc, iron, manganese, copper and boron are all necessary for healthy plants but, as in my yard, they are seldom deficient here.

"Iron deficiency (leaves turning yellow with green veins — chlorosis, or turning completely yellow or dying) is incredibly common in our landscapes and gardens. I have since learned that not all iron chelate treatments are the same. Some perform better in our alkaline soils. The absolute best are those with the active ingredient EDDHA. It worked noticeably better in Cheyenne." — Shane

See Cheyenne Botanic Gardens website, Resources tab, "Gardening Tips" for more information on iron deficiency.

Recommendations

All processed fertilizers, whether they are chemically manufactured or lightly processed organic — meaning carbon-based, not necessarily organic as in growing method — have their N-P-K percentages listed on the label such as "5-10-5." The plants don't care where these nutrients come from. But organic-based fertilizers release nutrients more slowly, provide some of that important organic material and

When you send in your soil sample, be clear about what you plan to grow: corn, cornflowers or cactus, like this plains prickly pear.

micronutrients, and they can be safer around children and pets.

Needing just nitrogen for the vegetable garden, the soil test results recommended urea or ammonium sulfate, or one of three more organic choices: blood meal, corn gluten meal or alfalfa meal pellets — for that last item, think rabbit food.

The lawn needs three times as much nitrogen and phosphorus, by weight, as it does potassium. None of the "balanced" fertilizers containing all three really came close to these proportions, so I also looked at the individual recommendations for phosphorus and potassium. For phosphorus it was either bone meal (organic) or triplesuperphosphate (chemical). For potassium, potassium chloride or composted manure.

Calculations

My soil test result sheets explained how to figure out how much of the unconventional fertilizers I needed — after all, alfalfa pellets don't come with nitrogen-phosphorus-potassium analysis.

For my 100 square foot garden I only need a pound of 30% nitrogen fertilizer — 15 pounds of alfalfa pellets that will provide organic material as well. Perhaps my leaf compost can substitute for some of that.

Spreading

I think I can spread fertilizer over my tiny garden evenly by hand, but for the lawn, if I don't convert it to garden this year, one of those spreaders for which you can adjust the rate would be better.

On the other hand, a mature

lawn doesn't need fertilizing until late summer. But when we mow, we should start leaving our clippings on the lawn to decompose. They will not become thatch — other issues cause thatch build-up.

The next test

In four or five years we can do another soil test and see how we've progressed toward our goals.

Caveats

Always read fertilizer directions thoroughly — and follow them for best results, and for your own health.

Think twice about using manure. It must be from vegetarian animals, weed seed free and old enough it won't burn plants.

"I'm not big on manure. Too many weeds and too salty. However, I do like composted chicken manure in small amounts early in the season." — Shane

Be aware of how much salt comes with the fertilizer of your choice.

Organic materials from your own yard — unless sprayed with pesticides or diseased — are not yard waste. They're treasures.

There are many fertilizer sources I haven't discussed that are worth looking into, such as fish emulsion and cover crops that become green manure, among others.

"I am a big believer in using fish emulsion in the first half of the growing season. It is not only a fertilizer but also is a stimulant and acts like a fungicide. I get great results and much less disease. Unfortunately, even the 'low odor' formulas stink for around 24 hours, so never apply prior to having guests in your yard." — Shane

Don't hesitate to ask for advice from the conservation district, the extension office or the botanic gardens.

Rusty Brinkman grows heirloom vegetables organically to sell at one of Cheyenne's farmers markets.

CHAPTER 19:
HEIRLOOM VEGGIES

LOCAL CHEF GROWS FOR TASTE AND VARIETY

At the Laramie County Fair, I was checking out the blue-ribbon vegetable winners and one name kept popping up over and over: Rusty Brinkman.

I met Rusty and his partner Vally Gollogly one summer at a lunch they catered at their home just outside Cheyenne — a garden-to-table treat.

This spring, Rusty added a high tunnel and a half-dozen chickens. The greenhouse-like high tunnel will let him grow vegetables that need a longer growing season than Cheyenne allows. The chickens keep the insect pest numbers down, but at the cost of a little pecking damage. They seem to like yellow vegetables so Rusty throws a little vegetation over the yellow squashes to protect them.

His backyard garden is sizeable, but he also helps garden another 4,000 square feet over at his uncle's, where he has a real greenhouse to get seedlings started in spring.

A couple years ago when he and Vally had an abundance of dill, they thought it would be fun to offer the excess at the Tuesday Farmers Market. Now they are regulars, under the Mooo's Market banner. Vally specializes in prepping the flowers and herbs, Rusty the veggies.

Their booth has a certain flair, a certain presentation. That might be because Rusty's day job is owner of Crow Creek Catering. As a chef, the Cheyenne native has plied his trade in Denver, New York and the Colorado governor's mansion. He knows presentation is an important part of the dining experience.

What does a chef grow in his garden? Rusty is a proponent of organic methods so I'm not surprised he also gravitates to the heirlooms.

Heirloom vegetables are open-pollinated. This means if you save the seeds, you can grow the same vegetables again next year. If you save the seeds from the best individual fruits and vegetables, you improve the variety the next year. Over time, you will have varieties ideally suited to Cheyenne.

Hybrid fruits and vegetables also produce seed, but plants grown from those seeds won't grow true to the parent plant.

"A regular hybrid is just a simple cross of two different varieties. They can create viable and productive seed. But now 'hybrid' means what is known as the F1 hybrid. These don't create good offspring, so hold off on saving this seed." — Shane

Rusty is experimenting with seed saving, but he also shops Johnny's Selected Seeds of Maine, High Mowing Seeds of Vermont (which offers only organic seed) and Territorial Seed Company. For a while, his chief source was Baker Creek Heirloom

Seeds. The catalogs are 350 pages of delicious photos of vegetables and fruit from all over the world with exotic names and long descriptions.

For a gardener, it's like being in a candy shop. But it is important to keep in mind our local climate and look for short-season veggies. Now that he is selling at the market, Rusty also looks for varieties not sold at the grocery store.

There is so much to choose from. Offerings include purple tomatoes, oddly-shaped squash, a multitude of greens, pointy cabbage, red carrots. But in the end, they need to produce in Cheyenne, and they have to pass the taste test — appealing to a gardener who cooks.

Rusty shared with me a nine-page, single-spaced printout of his garden records for the past three years, organized by vegetable type, variety, heirloom status, year trialed, seed company, how many days to maturity, description. There are 360 entries to date, but some vegetables did not make the cut and were not planted a second year.

This scientific analysis is similar to Rusty and Vally's training in the science of food preparation. Cooking is one part art and a large part science. You need to understand how ingredients interact with one another. If you invent a good dish, you need to be able to reproduce it, just like scientific studies need to be replicable.

Vegetable gardening is also science, trying to produce the best crop each year.

Rusty prepares new beds by smothering grass with cardboard or

Rusty grows a wide selection of vegetables for his booth at one of the Cheyenne farmers markets.

metal plates (he makes folk art from junk metal), then he rototills it. Once a bed is established, however, he only uses a garden fork to loosen things in the spring and add compost.

His compost system is nearly keeping up with the garden's needs and he fills in with more from the city compost facility.

But Rusty also uses Espoma Plant-tone to add microbes and nutrients organically, and in the fall, he adds old cow manure. And now that he has chickens, he'll be adding old chicken manure.

Rusty hand-pulls weeds and hand-picks potato bugs early in the season. This was the first year for the chickens and he's not sure how helpful they will be, but he said he also uses several other methods for pest control:

- Neem oil has worked very well for aphids.

- Releasing ladybugs and lacewings in the spring, also for aphid control, seems to be working.

- Using Bt (a friendly bacterium) for cabbage whites (butterflies) for the first time this year seems to help.

- Agribon, a light-weight, white polypropylene fabric (floating row cover) spread over the carrots seems to be controlling the carrot rust fly.

To get an early start on the season, in late March or early April, Rusty uses low tunnels, stretching plastic sheeting over hoops placed over his beds.

Much of the garden area is irrigated using drip tape (flattened plastic hose that has a series of small holes).

So, what was planted in the Brinkman / Gollogly garden this year? Lots of varieties with delicious-sounding names. Rusty will know soon which ones have performed well enough to make the cut next year. If customers aren't quite ready for 'Tronchuda,' a Portuguese variety of kale, no matter. Rusty can take it home and turn it into dinner or prep it for the freezer.

"Silvery Fir Tree" is a short-season heirloom tomato variety that does well in Cheyenne.

CHAPTER 20: **TOMATOES**

My first year growing tomatoes I searched out someone with more experience. That is how I found myself immersed in Laramie County Master Gardener Michelle Bohanan's tomato forest, though perhaps "jungle" would be a better term, because plants seemed to be climbing on each other to reach the best sunlight.

Heirloom queen of the plains

Michelle grew 40 varieties of heirloom tomatoes from seed the summer I visited, one plant of each, down from 70 varieties the previous year. Each plant gets its own 5-foot tall, 16-inch-diameter tomato cage formed from concrete reinforcing mesh — the kind with the wires welded about 6 inches apart — wide enough to reach through to pick fruit yet suitable for tucking in a straying branch.

The tomato plants are spaced about 3 feet apart in the main tomato patch in the side yard and tucked into other spaces as well. By the time I visited mid-August, some plants had shot up and spilled over their cages, summer squashes were climbing the outsides of others, winter squash filled the paths between and were hiding basketball-sized fruit, and tassels of corn waved overhead.

Beans and parsnips added to the solid mass of dark green leafy textures. Flowers punctuated the vegetables and overflowed the flower beds.

Six or seven years ago, this island of vegetative exuberance was a desert of pea gravel spread over native clay soil. Michelle has worked bag after bag of fall leaves into her beds, plus compost from her coworkers. She used to use a rototiller, but now that her beds are three bricks high, a multi-tined digging fork can do the job better. No additional fertilizer is necessary.

Heirloom growing

Michelle finds heirloom tomato diversity through both the Sand Hill Preservation Center and Seed Savers Exchange, both out of Iowa, as well as groups of online seed exchangers.

About the end of February, beginning of March, she starts 10 seedlings of each variety. When they are big enough, she moves them to her plastic-wrapped back porch that's warmed by the sun, the dryer vent and heat escaping from a basement window. She takes the excess plants to the annual Master Gardeners' plant sale in May.

Michelle shares some of her harvest with her coworkers and cans whatever isn't eaten fresh. She hasn't always been keen on eating tomatoes, but now that she has taste-tested so many varieties, she has found her favorites.

I was sent home with tomatoes of five varieties, including one called "Absinthe" which has a peppery taste and stays green even when it is ripe.

Psyllid stuff

Michelle has only one pest, psyllids, tiny little things that inject poison into a tomato leaf, leaving parts of plants looking like a collection of brown and green rags and fruit growing half its normal size. She learned by saving seed from afflicted plants that they do not grow more resistant in the next generation. Rather, the next generation is more likely to succumb to psyllids more quickly.

Less than 10% of her plants seem to be affected. Incredibly, the plants next to the afflicted ones can be completely untouched. Perhaps they attract more lacewings and ladybugs or whatever preys on psyllids.

Other tomato pests and diseases

Those of us who have read the standard tomato cultivation information worry about diseases in crowded conditions, such as powdery mildew on leaves, but using soaker hoses and Cheyenne's normally breezy weather helps keep leaves dry and those types of diseases at bay in Michelle's garden.

A few of my tomato branches became leafless, maybe denuded by the tomato hornworm, but as a percentage of overall growth we're talking a hundredth of a percent, certainly not something needing any kind of chemical warfare. Besides, I found out tomato hornworms are just one stage in the life of hawk moths, those hummingbird-sized hoverers that enjoy my tubular flowers.

Prevention seems to be the best cure for all the nefarious pests illustrated in *The Encyclopedia of Natural Insect and Disease Control* from

Rodale Press. Follow good cultivation practices: Grow well-watered and well-fed (not overfed or over-watered) plants with plenty of fresh air and sunshine. Provide trap crops that divert predators or companion plants that ward off attacks.

Diversity seems to work in Michelle's tomato patch the same way it does in wild nature. There are always varieties that resist problems more than others or are better suited to a particular garden's climate and microclimate or one growing season's weather.

Rather than rotating tomatoes on a three year-cycle with other crops, Michelle achieves a rotation of tomato varieties.

"The main reason you rotate tomatoes is to prevent disease. I found that with regular early season use of fish emulsion, which acts as a natural fungicide, I had no disease and thus no reason to rotate. Still got great yields." — Shane

Weeds?

Michelle doesn't have to weed. There aren't any because her crops shade out everything else, though self-seeding cosmos has to be uprooted from the middle of the path to the rose garden.

COMPANION PLANTING

There is much literature about companion planting. Some vegetable combinations are based on the complementary way the plants grow, such as the indigenous "Three Sisters:" corn provides a trellis for the beans and squash shades the ground around them. The beans fix nitrogen for all three.

Some combinations are based on plants that don't compete for the same nutrients. Other combinations are based on the idea that highly aromatic herb plants might ward off pests on vegetables while other plantings might divert pests and become sacrificial.

There is no satisfactory scientific proof for companion planting. However, growing flowers around vegetables will attract more pollinators and could improve yields.

The Cheyenne Botanic Gardens displayed Andy Corbin's 1100-pound pumpkin and 336-pound squash in 2020.

CHAPTER 21: **PUMPKINS**

TRY (GIANT) PUMPKIN GROWING TIPS FOR SQUASH, TOO

A man has to be serious about pumpkins to wear a shirt made with printed pumpkin fabric. And that's what Laramie County Master Gardener Richard Franz wore, courtesy of the sewing skills of his wife, Sylvia, the day (in 2012) I visited him at his Cheyenne pumpkin patch.

Richard has been growing pumpkins since 1984, growing them in Cheyenne for 12 years. And not just any pumpkins, but giant pumpkins, because he competes every year to grow the biggest pumpkin he can.

He's part of a group of local pumpkin growers that haul their harvest to certified scales and submit their records to the Atlantic Giant Genetics Cooperative.

Today's prizewinning giant pumpkins, including this year's record-breaking 2009-pounder grown by Ron Wallace of Rhode Island, trace their genetics back to the Atlantic Giant variety grown by Howard Dill in Nova Scotia, Canada.

Serious competitors must provide parentage records when certifying their pumpkins. The pedigrees look like any genealogy chart, the individual pumpkins listed with three-part names: their weight, their grower and the year.

For as big as these pumpkins are, the actual number of seeds per pumpkin is only a couple handfuls.

Seeds from a prize winner can go for $4 to $5 for a packet of two, Richard said. You better hope your germination technique is faultless.

Richard collects seed from his best pumpkins and saves it. Normally, pumpkin seeds are viable for several years, but he is attempting to duplicate the preservation conditions used by national seed saving vaults, including very low humidity that could keep them viable for many more.

Taking a scientific approach to cultivation (he has a degree in geology with a minor in chemistry), Richard's pumpkins have progressed in size from 350 pounds in 1987 to 756 pounds in 2007, his biggest.

How to grow a giant

While there is a lot of pumpkin growing advice on the internet, it's best to seek out a local mentor because every location is different, calling for different techniques.

Ron Hoffman of Riverton, who has the state record, starts his seeds outside in May, Richard said, compared to his own inside method described below.

When I visited Richard, it was the day after our first killing freeze of the season, Oct. 3, 13 days later than average. The pumpkin leaves were all furled and it was easy to see the layout of vines, now frozen, which Richard had arranged as they grew. But Richard's pumpkins were safe, swathed in those quilted pads used by moving companies.

This year, his pumpkins are in the 200-300-pound range. Due

to an unfortunate accident, these were six weeks behind the typical growing schedule (note: never water pumpkins with water you've acidified for your experiment in growing acid-loving blueberries). Still, it's hard to imagine these fruits as big as exercise balance balls coming from mere pumpkin seeds.

Germination

Atlantic Giant seeds are available from many seed catalogs and through swaps and auctions listed on the Big Pumpkins website, which also has general information for novice growers.

Mid-March, Richard grinds a little of the seed coat off the end of a seed opposite where the roots and stem emerge. Some people soak seeds in water for eight hours. Then he plants it in a 2.25-inch pot, in regular potting soil and puts it under fluorescent lights in his basement. A Master Gardener for 26 years, he grows many other fruits, vegetables and flowers.

Transplanting

Very soon after germination, when the leaf-like cotyledons open up, Richard moves the seedling to a 1-gallon pot. It is very important, he said, that the plant does not get root-bound, with roots circling inside the pot. Unlike other plants whose roots can be untangled and spread out during transplanting, pumpkins are very finicky. "Pumpkins just don't like their roots messed with, like a person with ticklish feet," said Richard. He transplanted one root-bound plant that never grew beyond a half-dozen leaves.

Setting out

By the time the pumpkin seedling's roots hit the boundaries of the pot, about four weeks after germination, it's time to plant it outside, even though it's only mid-April. Richard warms the soil in advance by laying black plastic over it, leaving a planting hole in the middle. He usually grows two vines, planting on opposite sides of his patch, which takes up a quarter of his suburban backyard. Some vine growth sneaks out onto the adjacent prairie.

To protect his plants, Richard erects little hoop houses about 2.5 feet high and 4 feet long, clear plastic stretched over plastic pipe bent in half circles, sometimes having to extend the length of the houses as the vines grow. Old-style incandescent Christmas lights inside provide extra heat and an eerie glow at night that at first caused the neighbors some consternation.

A superstructure of metal pipe over the whole pumpkin patch can support a temporary canopy for hail protection.

Watering

Richard uses a grid of plastic pipe laid on the ground with sprinkler heads sticking up about 2 feet high at intervals. The entire patch needs to be watered, not just where the plants were planted, but where the vines root as they travel over the ground. While even well-watered plants have leaves that wilt for a

bit during the noonday sun, if they don't recover when it gets cooler, look for cucumber beetles or try a calcium treatment.

Fertilizer

Richard is experimenting with micronutrients but recommends a balanced fertilizer like 10-10-10 (nitrogen-phosphorus-potassium). More nutrients come from fall prep work: digging in the spent vines and leaves and adding lots of other compost. October is the perfect time to prepare for growing giant pumpkins.

Competitive growers have tried everything from injecting milk into stems (for the calcium), to fertilizing with molasses and raw manure, but "I haven't seen anything to make a big difference," said Richard.

Hand pollination

By the beginning of June, it is time to pollinate. Pumpkins have male and female flowers. Leaving pollination to nature is chancy, so serious growers get up before the bees and do the pollinating themselves, bagging the flowers so they aren't infiltrated by unknown pollen. If you grow vines from different seed sources, you can cross-pollinate and grow the resulting seeds the next season.

The roundest pumpkins have five ovaries, rather than four, and all have been fertilized.

Culling

To get the biggest pumpkin possible, allow only one pumpkin to develop per vine. There is some debate, Richard said, on whether this should be from the second or third female flower to develop, but because it sometimes happens that a pumpkin can quit growing after two weeks, he pollinates several and waits before choosing one. Then he cleanly cuts the others away. And every day or so, he must go out and cut away any pumpkins developing from natural pollination.

Keep the chosen pumpkin off the ground, on a board or some other surface that won't get soggy.

Harvesting

You need seven friends to get your giant pumpkin onto a trailer for weighing — to roll the pumpkin onto a special tarp and to lift it with handles that accommodate two people per side.

Carving

Richard and his family have had a lot of fun making giant jack-o-lanterns, all recorded in a wonderful scrapbook made by one of his daughters. A portable electric jigsaw with a 10-inch blade is now the preferred carving tool.

Preserving

Pumpkins can last in a cool place, like the garage, for months, providing their skin has no holes or scrapes that might let bacteria in.

Sylvia, Richard's wife, is a good sport about this pumpkin mania. With a master's in home economics, she has perfected many pumpkin-based recipes, which is good — half of a giant pumpkin's weight is edible flesh. Sylvia cuts it into chunks to give away or to bake, puree and store in the freezer for recipes such as Frosted Pumpkin Walnut Cookies, a favorite with participants at pumpkin weigh-ins.

"The best pumpkin for beginners and for our short season is Autumn Gold. You don't have to wait for it to turn from green to orange as it starts out that color from the beginning." — Shane

No room for giants? Try tennis ball-sized mini pumpkins like 'Jack Be Little.'

SYLVIA'S FROSTED PUMPKIN WALNUT COOKIES

Recipe provided by Sylvia Franz

½ cup butter/margarine
1 ½ cups packed brown sugar
2 eggs
1 cup cooked or canned
   pumpkin
½ teaspoon lemon extract

½ teaspoon vanilla
2 ½ cups flour
1 tablespoon baking powder
1 teaspoon salt
2 teaspoons pumpkin pie spice
1 cup chopped walnuts

Cream butter and add brown sugar, beating well. Add eggs, beat after each. Stir in pumpkin and flavorings.

Add dry ingredients. Stir in chopped walnuts.

Drop by teaspoons onto greased cookie sheet 2 inches apart. Bake at 375 degrees for 12 minutes. Cool, then frost.

Yield: 7 ½ dozen.

Maple frosting:

¼ cup butter/margarine
2 ¼ cups powdered sugar
Cream butter.

2 tablespoons milk
¾ teaspoon maple extract

Add 1 cup powdered sugar, beating with electric mixer. Add milk and rest of sugar. Add maple extract and beat well.

One of our hardiest and most prolific fruits is the chokecherry. Process with adequate sugar!

CHAPTER 22:
FRUIT TREES AND SHRUBS

APPLES, PLUMS, CHERRIES, PEARS, PEACHES? OH, MY!

Large-scale commercial fruit growing is not viable in the Cheyenne area, primarily because of the limited water supply and the vagaries of our weather, but in the home garden, especially if your other plants have low water needs, a few fruit trees and shrubs could be justified.

Water

I spoke with Catherine Wissner, the University of Wyoming Extension horticulturist for Laramie County, and she said watering fruit trees and shrubs is crucial to a successful harvest — not enough water and you won't even get flowering, much less fruit.

She said the rule of thumb is 10 gallons per 1-inch diameter of the trunk every 7 to 10 days during the growing season, adjusting for hot, dry and windy weather. You can even water once a month during the winter on warm days with the same formula. Fruiting trees and shrubs need more watering than the lawn they're planted in the middle of. Drip irrigation is the most efficient way to water.

Fruit types

Tree fruit grown in our area

includes apples (Chapter 23), cherries, plums, pears and even experiments with peaches. Look for fire blight-resistant varieties.

Fruiting shrubs like chokecherry, a local native, can be very bountiful. Cheyennites also grow serviceberry, elderberry, gooseberry, raspberry and currant.

The other crucial factor is selecting the right variety. Look for a variety of tree or shrub that flowers late enough not to be caught by a May frost or snow — yet has fruit ready to harvest before frost in September. Catherine is currently researching the best varieties for Laramie County. One apple that stands out, 'Yellow Transparent,' matures by late August. For a statewide look, see *Wyoming Fruit Variety Survey Data: Recommended Varieties* publication at the University of Wyoming Extension website.

Find out if the variety needs cross pollination with a second tree. This could be a second tree you plant or another close by in the neighborhood.

Planting

Once you find the right species, the tree or shrub can be planted anytime the ground isn't frozen, but it must be planted right (Chapter 55). The two best tips are to gently spread the roots and make sure the soil level is right at the transition between roots and trunk and below the graft if it is a grafted tree. For shrubs, soil level should be between stem and root, right where the soil line was in the pot.

American Plum is a Wyoming native shrub or small tree found along creeks, wherever there is enough moisture.

Fertilizing

Catherine said fruit trees and shrubs need fertilizer annually, preferably before June 1. The fertilizer should have numbers like 5-10-5 or 5-20-5, nitrogen-phosphorus-potassium, also abbreviated NPK. Remember, most of the roots are in the top 12 inches of soil and will spread farther than the tree's canopy.

Pruning and mulching

Pruning is essential for fruit trees. Homeowners tend to "limb up" their trees so they can more easily mow the lawn underneath, creating a shade tree with fruit benefits. Protect all kinds of tree trunks from lawn mowers by mulching 2 to 3 inches deep in a circle one to two feet wide around the trunk — yet keep the mulch from touching the trunk.

For shrubs, a circle of mulch is also good and can keep competing weeds and grass away from them.

Instead of limbing up, you can do what Catherine said commercial orchardists do, prune from the top down to keep the tree small and easier to pick fruit from. The top of my experimental apple tree grown from seed died back this winter, so I guess it will be a "prune down" experiment now.

Use standard pruning advice for removing deadwood and crossed limbs (Chapters 56 and 57). Research or ask Catherine about pruning methods specific to types of fruit trees.

Fruiting shrubs, like the chokecherry hedge in our backyard, need pruning regularly. Over the last 30 years we have removed a few stems each year that are more than 3 or 4 inches in diameter. They can get too tall and become trees. We'd rather they stay brushy. It's easier to pick the fruit and it provides a better bird habitat and privacy screen. Because chokecherries regularly sucker, there is always a new generation coming up.

Pests and diseases

Adequate watering helps keep fruit trees and shrubs stress-free and healthy. Remove the occasional diseased branches 6 to 12 inches below the infection using tool blades sterilized between cuts with 10% bleach solution — but do not put any "wound dressing" on any cuts — that goes for all kinds of trees.

Your best bet for identifying and determining treatment of pests and diseases is to photograph the damage and email it to Catherine. She does yard calls if necessary.

I asked Catherine how she protects fruit from predators, like birds and other animals. She isn't a fan of netting unless the mesh openings are less than 1.5 inches. Otherwise, the birds get tangled and often die.

She said to keep an eye on the ripening progress each day and pick the fruit before the birds or racoons do. But sometimes it seems the birds prefer their fruit less ripe than we do.

Picking

How do you decide when fruit is ripe? Taste test. Fruit gets sweeter the riper it is, although chokecherries never get sweet. And if apples fall off the tree, pick them up and make applesauce!

Christine and Steve Johnson grow Jonathan apples, an heirloom variety.

CHAPTER 23:
HEIRLOOM APPLES

HUNDRED-YEAR-OLD APPLE TREES ARE WYOMING-TOUGH

Most people's image of Wyoming doesn't include apple orchards.

However, back in the homestead era, settlers brought young apple trees with them and planted them above stream banks. They provided important food in territory where there were no stores nearby. Not only do some apple varieties store well, but others were made into cider or vinegar that was used as medicine and a food preservative.

An 1873 follow-up to the Homestead Act, the Timber Culture Act, gave homesteaders an additional 160 acres if they planted trees on 40 acres. Why not plant trees that provided food as well?

By 1880, entrepreneurs were planting orchards outside of Wyoming's major towns. Ed Young planted 3,000 apple trees near Lander, along with other fruit trees.

The Cheyenne Horticultural Field Station developed hardy Wyoming varieties during its years of operation, 1928-1974.

But by about the 1930s, modern apple storage methods, long-distance trucking and grocery stores started to put an end to the golden age of Wyoming apple growing. Farmers turned to growing hay and grain.

Funny thing, those abandoned apple trees persisted, if they weren't bulldozed. Some even continued to be taken care of. Many are now over 100 years old. With the interest in tasty local and sustainable food sources, Wyoming's heirloom apples are being sought after.

Jonathan Magby, graduate student at the University of Wyoming, at the time I talked to him, had for several years been helping botany professor Steve Miller on his quest to find, identify and preserve those apples through the Wyoming Apple Project.

The way apple genetics work, an apple seed will never grow up to be the spitting image of its parent tree. Instead, orchardists propagate apples by taking small cuttings. Jonathan and Steve are thus able to preserve heirloom varieties by taking these scions and grafting them to other apple tree cultivars (cultivated varieties) grown for their sturdy, Wyoming-hardy rootstock. They are being grown at experimental orchards outside Sheridan and Lander.

So far Jonathan has used DNA testing to identify 47 cultivars from old apple trees sampled around the state, though not all matched named cultivars.

The cultivar names are often descriptive, and they are often traceable back to Europe. There is evidence the Chinese grafted apples in 5000 BCE.

Wild apples have their roots in Kazakhstan, in Central Asia, which has landscape much like Wyoming's, which has native crabapples.

If you are the typical home gardener, right about now you are wondering where you could squeeze in an apple tree or two — and really you need to have two so that apples will form — or at least make sure someone nearby has apple or crabapple trees.

Next, you are wondering, of the kinds of apples that survived 100-plus years here, which are the best?

Jonathan listed his top 10 apples for me when we talked:
1. * 'Wealthy'
2.   'Haralson'
3.   'Patten Greening'
4. * 'Yellow Transparent'
5.   'Northwest Greening'
6.   'McMahan'
7.   'McIntosh'
8.   'Wolf River'
9. * 'Whitney No. 20' Crabapple
10. * 'Duchess of Oldenburg'
11.   'Dolgo'

Wait! That's more than 10! The *starred cultivars will do particularly well in Cheyenne as well as Florence Crab.

Each apple cultivar has its strengths and weaknesses, uses and flavors. When we lived in Miles City, Montana, in the 1980s, Mark and I had an old 'Yellow Transparent,' a hardy Russian cultivar. Its fruit ripened to a pale yellow in August. It wouldn't keep over the winter like some apples. In fact, it was practically applesauce as soon as the apple departed the tree. We froze lots of delicious applesauce.

The next question you home gardeners will ask is the harder one, where to buy these apple trees?

Check the Fort Collins Wholesale Nursery website for the list of retailers it sells to. One staff member, Scott Skogerboe, is a legendary propagator of heirloom apples and other trees. Hopefully, area nurseries will carry apple trees with rootstock suitable for Wyoming. Check the Wyoming Apple Project website for advice. Consult your extension agent.

If you have an old apple tree that might be an heirloom, see if Steve, in the University of Wyoming Department of Botany, is still adding to the Wyoming Apple Project database.

Laramie County Master Gardener Maggie McKenzie remembered the ancient apple trees on the place west of Cheyenne where she grew up and her family still lives. Jonathan was able to identify three out of four: 'Jeffries,' 'Wealthy' and 'McIntosh.' Most importantly, Maggie was inspired to get them some pruning love, helping to prolong their productive life.

This heirloom apple tree at Maggie McKenzie's childhood home survives on a prairie hillside overlooking Crow Creek. The slight depression where it sits collects enough moisture for it to grow.

Chris Hilgert grew these Seascape strawberries in a high tunnel in Laramie.

CHAPTER 24:
STRAWBERRIES

FORT LARAMIE STRAWBERRIES DEVELOPED IN CHEYENNE

"Fort Laramie Strawberries are from the 'ice-box' section of our nation, Cheyenne, Wyoming. This is a super hardy, wonderfully producing everbearing strawberry. You'll harvest your first berries this very summer! And what berries – HUGE, bright, scarlet-red berries...."

— *Burgess Seed and Plant Company, Bloomington, Illinois, online catalog description*

January isn't too early to order your strawberry plants for spring delivery.

The strawberry variety, 'Fort Laramie,' touted in many catalogs, was developed here at the U.S. Department of Agriculture's Cheyenne Horticultural Field Station, which opened in 1928. In 1974, it changed its mission and became the High Plains Grasslands Research Station.

Test plantings of strawberries began about 1934. The two most famous varieties, 'Ogallala' first and 'Fort Laramie' second, are still popular today.

Retired Cheyenne Botanic Gardens Director Shane Smith remembers Gene Howard, the last director of the hort station before it switched, telling him these successful strawberries could trace their genetics back to native strawberries in the nearby mountains. The station's successful plant varieties were often named for nearby places.

Selecting strawberry varieties

I talked to Jane Dorn, a veteran home strawberry grower who remembers spending summers with her grandparents on their ranch near Encampment and her grandfather growing 'Ogallalas.' She's grown the 'Fort Laramie' variety in both Cheyenne and in Lingle, where she and her husband retired.

'Fort Laramie' strawberries are classified as everbearing, compared to day neutrals that bear continuously, and June bearers, which are less hardy here.

In Cheyenne, "everbearing" means if there isn't a late frost that kills the flower buds, they will bear in June or early July. You'll get a second flush in the fall if an early frost doesn't get the flowers or ripening fruit. Their hardiness promise, Zone 3-7, is that with a little protection, the plants will survive from year to year.

While strawberries can be grown from seed, seeds are not as available as one-year-old plants. 'Fort Laramie' plants are widely available online and in spring at local nurseries. Should you want to try other varieties, Jane suggested looking for those labeled as blooming "late mid-season" or "late."

Chris Hilgert, University of Wyoming Extension horticulturist, says other than the hardy 'Fort Laramie,' 'Ogallala' and 'Charlotte,' other varieties might require growing in a hoop house to be successful. Or be prepared to cover your plants when frost threatens during berry development.

Chris will have a new publication on growing strawberries in Wyoming available in 2021 at the University of Wyoming Extension publications website.

Winter protection

Jane recommends straw or other winter mulch 6 inches deep. It can be pulled back from on top of the plants to around them in the growing season to suffocate weeds and keep the berries clean.

Planting

The best planting method for everbearers is the hill style. Soil is mounded about 8 inches high in a berm the length you need. The plants are spaced 12-15 inches apart in a double row. Removing runners allows each plant to put its energy into making more and bigger berries. Jane also uses raised beds, even an old water trough.

Planting starts is a bit tricky, Jane said. There's barely an inch of stem between roots and leaves. Dig a hole deep enough that the roots can hang straight before you fill in the dirt. She said two-thirds of the crown (where the leaves have been attached) should be above the soil line.

Renovating your strawberries will be necessary every three or four years. Check there's no disease before planting in the same place.

Watering

Don't skimp on watering. Figure one inch of water a week. Put a container out in the garden and see how long it takes to fill to the one-inch mark when you irrigate. Drip irrigation works well. Morning watering is best. If leaves are damp at night, it increases the likelihood of powdery mildew.

Fertilizer

Chris said fertilizing each year, and enough water, is the only way to get berries.

Jane is a fan of compost. Once she's established the strawberry bed, a top dressing of compost will work itself in. You can also buy specially formulated strawberry fertilizer.

Weeds

Jane weeds by hand. You don't want herbicides killing your plants and hoeing could disturb the shallow roots. Pull weeds frequently, while they are small.

Predators

Every bird and other kind of critter loves strawberries! You'll have to experiment with fencing, floating row cover and netting. Remember, some animals can tunnel under fences.

These Fort Laramie strawberries were grown by Mike Heath.

Disease

Shane mentioned red stele disease which is caused by a soil fungus. It is most prevalent when strawberries are grown in wet conditions in clay soils. The roots rot — the stele, or core of the root turns red. You'll notice your plants are less productive. He suggests starting a strawberry bed in a new location with resistant varieties.

Danny and Pam Glick (left) consult Chris Hilgert about their vineyard on the outskirts of town.

CHAPTER 25: **GRAPES**

WYOMING HAS WHAT IT
TAKES TO MAKE WINE

A vineyard is a rare sight in Wyoming.

When the Laramie County Master Gardeners' advanced class was invited to learn about and practice pruning grapes at a local vineyard in 2015, it was hard to believe one existed.

The destination was Laramie County Master Gardener Pam Glick and her husband Danny's place outside Cheyenne. You might recognize Danny as our county sheriff.

Good thing Prohibition is long past.

It was late April, a little bleak on the High Plains, and the vineyard was dormant — just gnarly trunks and leafless canes.

While there are several methods of training grape growth, the Glicks are set up for a two-wire system known as the "Four-cane Kniffin." It's named for William Kniffin, a Hudson River Valley viticulturist who, around 1850, discovered much better production where a fallen tree branch had pruned a vine this way.

The job was to look at each plant, now several years old, and figure out the best shoots to be the leader, and backup if necessary, and prune the others. The 12 students made significant progress on the 500-plus vines in an afternoon, getting more confident as they went.

The pruning seemed so ruthless. But the instructor, Chris Hilgert, state Master Gardener coordinator for the University of Wyoming Extension, assured everyone this is what is needed to produce grapes.

Even if a shady arbor is the goal, ruthless pruning will benefit it.

Still, grapes are very forgiving of novice pruning attempts.

Choosing varieties

In mid-August, I met with Pam to see how the grapes were doing and find out more about how she and Danny got into this agricultural niche.

A few years ago, Pam said she and friends went on a Wyoming wine tour, including Chugwater, La-Grange and Torrington.

That got her excited. So, she and Danny thought it might be a good investment for their retirement to get a small vineyard going. They did their research, including consulting Patrick Zimmerer who, with his family, owns the Table Mountain Winery and vineyard by Huntley, just south of Torrington.

As small and new as their operation is compared to Patrick's 11,000 vines, the Glicks have sold as much as 500 pounds of grapes to the winery one year. Production is dependent on weather more than anything, but vine maturity — and good pruning — can increase the yield.

The Glicks chose to grow 'Frontenac,' a red wine grape introduced in 1996, and 'Frontenac Gris,' a white wine grape introduced in 2003.

The varieties, with origins in Rochester, New York, were developed specifically for cold climates and disease resistance by the University of Minnesota, which holds the patents. According to their website, "'Frontenac' has the potential to produce outstanding dry red, sweet red, rosé, and port wines."

More recognizable French varieties trace their roots to grapes that are not hardy in our climate. But 'Frontenac' comes from a wild American grape ancestor and does well here. Success is also dependent on lots of sunshine, and sandy soils because "grapes don't like to have wet feet" – clay soils can hold water for a long time.

As for the vines? Despite the severe pruning we gave them in April, they grew and leafed out.

Planting

To begin, the Glicks made a bulk order that amounted to about $3 per vine. Each was about 2 years old, 1 foot tall, but with 3 feet of roots. They used an auger to make planting holes.

Blue plastic tubes provided collars to protect the new plants from rabbits. Of the 535 vines friends and family helped plant, only a few were lost, Pam said.

Growing

There are several problems to solve in a vineyard: watering, weed control and pest control.

The Glicks have drip irrigation set up to water the entire vineyard once a week overnight, 5 gallons per plant, with adjustments for the weather.

Weed control isn't so simple.

Pam, a recent graduate of the Laramie County Master Gardener program, does not use herbicides. She has been experimenting with different kinds of mulch, grass clippings, straw, discarded feed sacks and cardboard.

Tilling around the vines would disturb their roots. However, hand weeding has the added benefit of giving the viticulturist a chance to inspect the vines.

Vines need tying up as they grow and suckers need pruning. Every evening, Danny walks the vineyard for an hour, and early on Saturday mornings too, Pam said. It has become his therapy when his job is stressful.

Harvest hazards

In June, the vines were hit by a hailstorm that totaled the roof of the Glicks' house, but at the time of my visit nearly two months later, the vines had pretty much recovered.

The other hazard to grapes is birds.

I called Pam Sept. 14 to schedule another visit to see the ripe grapes. But she had bad news: The grapes were gone.

She and Danny had set aside a day in early September to put up netting. This protects the grapes until they are ready for harvest.

Unfortunately, that was the day they needed to respond to a family emergency.

Without the netting, the birds got every last grape while they were away, including the table grapes growing on the arbor by the house.

The Glicks were going to have a good grape crop before the birds got it.

As with other soft fruit, the birds seem to prefer their grapes tart - less ripe than we like them.

Despite losing their harvest, the Glicks will still have to perform fall chores in preparation for next season.

Table Mountain Winery

On Sept. 20, I stopped by Table Mountain Winery to see what 'Frontenac' grapes look like when nearly ready for harvest.

Patrick grows several other varieties, but said 'Frontenac' seems to be the one favored by birds. He also had hail earlier in the season so there were a few little dried brown grapes in his bunches, but only on the side the storm had come from.

A cold, late spring was responsible for the thick canopy of leaves hiding the grapes. He said each year's weather affects the taste of the vintage — one year he could taste the excess rain, another year, the effect of drought. The soil adds to the flavor, the "terrior," as well, and apparently in a good way. Table Mountain wines, which include grapes they grow as well as those from small Wyoming vineyards like the Glicks,' have won prizes at prestigious competitions in well-known wine-growing locations.

Time to tunnel?

Before this year's raid by the birds, Pam was thinking about enclosing the vineyard in high tunnels, something that is being tried in New York State and Canada, adding a layer of protection from wind, hail, early snow and birds.

Then perhaps she and Danny won't have their utility lines filled with robins making their own harvest plans.

Resources

If you are interested in growing cold-hardy wine grapes, visit University of Minnesota's grape website and contact Chris Hilgert through the University of Wyoming Extension website.

Visit the Table Mountain Winery website to see about visiting, holding an event there or where else to purchase their wines locally.

Linnie Cough identifies one of her many kinds of herbs with a sign.

CHAPTER 26: **HERBS**

GROW FOR SCENT, FLAVOR, FLOWERS AND FUN

Are you going to Scarborough Fair?
Parsley, sage, rosemary and thyme
Remember me to one who lives there
She once was a true love of mine.

— *Traditional English ballad verse*

I admit, my interest in growing herbs was sparked by old lyrics made popular by Simon and Garfunkel. In the Middle Ages, these four herbs mentioned were considered "essentials." Now I grow them for their scents, flavors and flowers.

The definition of an "herb" is a useful plant, the leafy part, used in smaller quantities than vegetables.

Spices come from other plant parts — roots, bark, seeds. Some are grown as medicinals. However, without the oversight of a trained herbalist, I wouldn't recommend experimenting with herbal remedies.

Instead, let's look at culinary herbs in my garden — all easy to grow. My experience in Cheyenne is that some are annuals, self-seeding. Some are short-lived perennials, and some survive a number of winters.

I usually mulch my herb garden in late fall with a 3 to 4-inch layer of crispy, curled, dried leaves from our ash trees. Straw can also offer protection.

Remember to never treat herbs with pesticides of any kind — herbicides, insecticides or fungicides — if you plan to eat or cook with them. Otherwise, they need what flowers and vegetables require.

Fall is a good time to check local nurseries, which might still have a few herb plants you can set on the windowsill for the winter and plant outside next spring. Having fresh leaves to pluck means you don't have to bother with drying.

In spring you can tuck your plants into a mostly sunny corner in your garden the way Laramie County Master Gardener Linnie Cough has, next to vegetables or flowers. Or pop them into a strawberry planter like Laramie County Master Gardener Kathy Shreve does. She sets it on the deck within reach of her kitchen door.

Herbs are happy in any situation, from containers to the symmetrical beds of formal herb gardens.

The four "essential" herbs

Parsley, *Petroselinum* species – This is a biannual classified into two groups, curly-leaved and the Italian flat-leaved. Mine self-seed and now new plants come up every spring. Chop leaves and add to soups, salads, Italian dishes, just about anything. Or dry or freeze them.

Sage, *Salvia officinalis* – Don't mix this up with sagebrush, which has toxic oils, even though it also has a woody stem. Culinary sage is evergreen and has leaves of sage-green (and now other colors). I've been able to keep plants growing for several years at a time. We flavor roasts with sage.

Rosemary, *Rosmarinus officinalis* – Another woody herb, it is often seen as a little potted evergreen tree.

Laramie County Master Gardener Michele Bohanan brings hers in for the winter. I've been able to mulch and overwinter the prostrate variety a few winters. Rosemary is great in meat and vegetable dishes.

Thyme, *Thymus* species – A low growing woody perennial in the mint family, some kinds work well as ground cover between patio stones. There are dozens of kinds, with different scents and ornamental leaves. *Thymus vulgaris* is the culinary type. We've admired its tiny flowers more than we've cooked with it. Perhaps we should put sprigs under our pillows, as they did in the Middle Ages, to aid sleep and ward off nightmares.

More mints

Lemon balm, *Melissa officinalis* – This can be made into tea. I like it for the lemony scent. But it is a mint and has invaded most of my raised bed. I yank it out wherever I want to plant something else. Wise gardeners keep it in containers as they would with chocolate mint, *Mentha x piperita* 'Chocolate,' peppermint and spearmint. The containers can be either above ground or in the ground.

Oregano, *Origanum vulgare* – It's one of my favorites — for Italian cooking as well as for the tiny flowers that attract lots of bees. It is a mint, spreading each year just enough to dig up and share some with friends.

The other Italian

Sweet basil, *Ocimum basilicum* – There are many varieties with leaves of different colors and flavors. This annual is easy to start from seed indoors and transplant to the garden, but the first hint of frost will finish it off. Besides Italian dishes, the leaves are also sprinkled in salads and soups. Pinch off flowers for better foliage but leave some for the bees. This year Kathy grew "Purple Ruffle" and Thai basils. Laramie County Master Gardener Susan Carlson harvests the flower stems before they bloom because there is more oil concentrated in the sepals (the green "petals") than in the leaves.

Edible flowers — usually just the petals

Chives, *Allium schoenoprasum* – A clump of chives is self-perpetuating. Mine is 30 years old. The grass-like leaves are easy to snip into any dish where onion would be at home. The ball-shaped purple flowers are also edible as individual florets. This is one of the culinary herbs native to North America.

Nasturtium, *Tropaeolum* – The showy orange and yellow flowers are reward enough for taking time to grow this annual, but the flowers can add color and a peppery flavor to salads. Direct seed it in the garden in spring.

Lavender, *Lavandula* – I love the scent in soaps and sachets. Leaves can be used with roasts and the flowers on desserts. "Munstead" is supposed to be cold hardy. Mine has overwintered several years now.

Calendula, *Calendula* – This is another self-seeder after it's been in the garden a season. I've grown it for years, though I haven't tried strewing the petals over dishes, like a

poor man's saffron. Its other name is "Pot Marigold."

Bee balm, *Monarda* – A variety I have with over-sized red flowers has been popular with hummingbirds that migrate through Cheyenne mid-July through August. A slow-to-spread mint, the crushed leaves smell interesting and the flowers can be added to salads.

Strawberry jars or pots have openings on their sides where individual plants can be inserted. Kathy Shreve has hers by her backdoor, planted with cooking herbs.

Other herbs to try

Cheyenne gardeners have good luck with other herbs: borage, chamomile, cilantro (the seeds are coriander, a spice), dill, fennel, lovage, Greek oregano and summer savory.

Ways to preserve harvested herbs

In her book, *The Garden Primer*, author Barbara Damrosch explains that what we're after, flavor or scent, is the result of plant oils. Harvesting and storage should maximize them — if you aren't just snipping a few leaves to add immediately to the soup.

Hang dry – The oils are at their strongest just before plants bloom. On a nice day, cut stems and hang them upside down, inside a paper bag, to dry. Strip dry leaves and store in airtight containers.

Freeze in ice cube trays – Basil doesn't freeze well. Damrosch suggests pureeing it with butter or oil and then freezing it in ice-cube trays, then popping the cubes into a zipper lock bag so it's easy to pull out what you need later.

Freeze whole in a sealed bag – Other herbs with less tender leaves can simply be frozen in a plastic bag.

Preserve in oils and vinegars – Another way to preserve herb flavors is in oils and vinegars. Recipes abound in cookbooks and online.

Seeds

I'll need to look for more seed variety in the specialty catalogs, like Richters Herbs, in which I counted 38 kinds of mint.

It is fun having a collection of herbs, even just for rubbing a few leaves so I can enjoy their scent while working in the garden.

"The absolute best herb seed catalog is Richters. It is more fun to read than a good book. They have dozens upon dozens of flavored mints, bubblegum, strawberry, etc." — Shane

Many garden herbs (oregano, left) and wildflowers (Britton's skullcap, right) are mints.

CHAPTER 27: **MINTS**

One winter I decided to research the mint family, *Lamiaceae* of which there are 7,500 species. I found tales of the good, the bad and the ugly.

Some mints were invited over to the New World because they were thought to be good garden plants, capable of providing medicinal uses, if not culinary flavor.

But some of them escaped the picket fences, becoming weeds that hang out on the dusty edges of civilization. Some poisoned live-stock. Others just didn't fit in the preferred landscape and have been periodically eradicated, especially the ones that insist on infiltrating the monoculture of the lawn.

New World natives, while never originally confined to the cultivated garden, were valued for their medic-inal know-how, but over time some recipes have been lost. They have been admired for their beauty and ability to thrive, each in its favorite wild place, providing sustenance to the local wildlife population. Only recently have we invited them into our cities and towns. But often we expect them to be made over into a showier version of themselves.

No matter where mints are from, they almost always share square stems and opposite leaves (leaves opposite each other on the stem), and they smell nice when you brush against them or crush their leaves.

Mints, like this beebalm, like to spread. May is a good time to dig up and share your excess plants.

Well-established garden mints

Immigrating people often take along their favorite plants from home. A surprising number of our favorite cooking herbs we grow in Cheyenne are mints that have travelled:

- Basil, *Ocimum basilicum*, traces its roots to India but is important to many cultures from Mexico to southeast Asia;

- Spearmint, *Mentha spicata*, Europe and Asia;

- Peppermint, *Mentha x peperita*, Europe and Middle East;

- Oregano, *Origanum vulgare*, Eurasia;

- Sweet marjoram, *Origanum majorana*, Middle East;

- Rosemary, *Rosmarinus officinalis*, Mediterranean;

- Garden sage, *Salvia officinalis*, Mediterranean;

- Common thyme, *Thymus vulgaris*, Europe;

- Lavender, *Lavandula angustifolia*, Mediterranean;

- Lemon balm, *Melissa officinalis*, Europe, Iran, Central Asia.

Garden mint turned weed

Horehound, *Marrubium vulgare*, is considered a medicinal herb, but has escaped cultivation. Originally from Europe, North Africa and Asia, it is now listed in the handbook, *Weeds of the West*, because it has invaded our native grasslands, including southeast Wyoming. Wherever there is a disturbance in the natural landscape, look for it. It's considered a weed because it is unpalatable to livestock.

Robert Dorn, in his book, *Vascular Plants of Wyoming*, lists other weedy mints in our county:

- Creeping Charlie, *Glechoma*

hederacea, from Eurasia, common in lawns, attracts bees, has been used in beer and cheese making, but is toxic to cattle and horses;

- Dead nettle, *Laminum amplexicaule*, from Eurasia and North Africa, problem in croplands and newly seeded lawns though one variety is considered good landscape ground cover;

- Motherwort, *Leonurus cardiaca*, from Eurasia, an herbal remedy, introduced for bees, now invasive;

- Lanceleaf sage, *Salvia reflexa*, is a Eurasian ornamental, listed in *Weeds of the West* because it is poisonous to livestock when chopped into or mixed with other feed.

Exotic and native mints excel

But here's a good mint that has become naturalized in Laramie County and elsewhere in North America: catnip, *Nepeta cataria*. It is native to Eurasia and Africa. A hybrid, *Nepeta x fassennii*, known as garden catmint 'Walker's Low,' became the perennial plant of the year in 2007.

For every difficult mint, there are more mints that contribute positively to society. Here at the north end of the Front Range, and elsewhere in the drylands of the west, we are looking for plants for our gardens that don't need much water. Some of those are natives and others from similar landscapes on the other side of the world.

Look at Russian sage, *Perovskia atriplicifolia*, straight from the steppes of central Asia. It's become an extremely popular landscape plant around here, plant it and forget it. I don't think anyone has taken advantage of its Old World reputation as a medicinal or put the flowers in salad or crushed them for dye.

Water-frugal homeowners are replacing lawn with various creeping thymes, Thymus species, and all of them hail from Europe, North Africa or Asia.

Horticulturists are always working on improvements and a catalogue like High Country Gardens shows examples. You'll notice cultivars (cultivated varieties) with cute names. The improvements can be better cold tolerance, better drought tolerance, longer blooming and or bigger, brighter blooms. Some species are native to Turkey, like a type of lamb's ear, *Stachys lavandulifolius*, or another from Arizona, another lamb's ear, *Stachys coccineus*.

Wyoming natives

What I am more interested in meeting these days are the Wyoming natives, the plants that know how to get along with the native wildlife, including birds, bats, bees, butterflies, and other insects.

Looking again at Robert's book, among the mints found in southeast Wyoming I saw:

- Dragonhead, *Dracocephalum parviflorum*;

- Drummond's false pennyroyal, *Hedeoma drummondii*, used as a minty flavoring in Mexico);

- False dragonhead,

Physostegia parviflora, related to obedient plant;

- Selfheal, *Prunella vulgaris*, a common lawn "weed" and Holarctic native—native to northern areas around the globe;
- Canada germander, *Teucrium canadense.*

Cultivated natives

Several plants show up in Robert's book, *Growing Native Plants of the Rocky Mountain Area*, (which he coauthored with his wife, Jane Dorn) that are Rocky Mountain mint cousins for our gardens:

- Giant (or anise) hyssop, *Agastache foeniculum*, also called hummingbird mint;
- Horsemint or purple beebalm, *Monarda fistulosa*;
- Coyote mint or mountain beebalm, *Monardella odoratissima*;
- Skullcap, *Scutellaria brittonii.*

Problem family members

Some gardeners have banned all mints from their gardens because they have heard they spread uncontrollably. That is true in my experience with the mentha species.

My chocolate mint, *Mentha × piperita* 'Chocolate Mint,' was well-behaved for 10-15 years until the summer I pruned back the big rosebush nearby and gave it more sun. It went ballistic. By fall I was ripping it out with my bare hands. Standard advice has been to keep crazy mints in pots so they can't spread.

My lemon balm goes to seed before I notice and seedlings pop up the next year, but it never complains when I dig it up to share and make room for other plants.

Live and let live

The old-time culinary mints share my same raised bed and keep each other in check. Even the Russian sage hasn't gotten out of hand as it would in a more open spot.

Maybe it's time to try some of those new native cultivars and spice things up — and see what the bees think.

Cheyenne has ideal conditions for growing lavender. Cathy Rogers tends hers on the northside.

CHAPTER 28: **LAVENDER**

FAMOUS HERB PERFECTLY SUITED FOR CHEYENNE

Lavender is an herb held in high esteem across the ages, even back 2,500 years when it was used in mummifying pharaohs in Egypt.

Lavender, a member of the mint family, is edible. As a dried wreath or spray, its soft gray-green leaves and stems of lavender, pink, blue or white flowers are classic. As an essential oil or dried herb, it has medicinal uses. It is often used in perfumes and other products because its scent has a reputation for calming the mind. Even photos of great fields of it in Provence, France, or garden borders in England give one a sense of peace.

All those attributes might have been what Laramie County Master Gardener Cathy Rogers was looking for when she went to her first lavender festival several years ago.

"I became interested in lavender because it has always been my favorite fragrance," she said. It led her to want to fill her pasture on Cheyenne's north side with mounds of lavender shrubs. She brought home several varieties to try.

Growing conditions

Growing conditions here are perfect for many kinds of lavender: dry weather, lots of sunshine and well-drained, low fertility, alkaline soil. The alkalinity enhances the fragrance.

Deer don't like lavender, but bees do — two more reasons to

consider growing it.

Although many of the 450-plus named cultivars of lavender are rated Zone 5, Cheyenne's growing zone, mulching after the first freeze will protect them from being killed by our region's tendency for multiple freeze-thaw cycles each winter.

On a hot day in August, Cathy took me out to her garden to inspect the kinds of lavender she chose from festival vendors as most suited to Cheyenne:

- 'Impress Purple'
- 'Gros Blue'
- 'Folgate'
- 'Buena Vista'
- 'Edelweiss' (Grosso white)
- 'Grosso'

Propagation

Lavender will seed itself, though it won't grow true to its parent. It can be propagated from cuttings, which is what Cathy did to establish the long row in the pasture.

She prefers to make hers from the softwood — the flexible, non-woody branch ends. She cuts them about 5 inches long and strips the leaves off the lower half. Then she dips the ends of the stems in rooting hormone and inserts them in seed-starting medium, usually a light potting soil made up of ingredients like peat, vermiculite, perlite — not plain old garden soil. You can try rooting the stem in water too.

Cathy had 80% success with her seed-starting soil method. It takes about three years for the new plants to mature. She waited a year before planting her cuttings out in the field where she had suppressed the pasture vegetation with weed-barrier cloth. Proper spacing is important — lavender shrubs can be as large as 30 inches wide as well as 30 inches high.

Care

Lavender requires little care most years once it's established. Cathy had only irrigated the row once as of mid-August. But plants require annual pruning when mature. Removing one-third of the shrub, usually in spring right after last frost, will give you more flowers. Cathy has found a battery powered hedge trimmer is a great tool for pruning the lavender. Much easier than using clippers or the scythe that the professionals recommend.

Harvest

But sometimes branches are harvested during the growing season.

When and what is harvested depends on what product is the goal. For decorative craft purposes, snip branches when the flowers are barely open. Potpourri and sachets use only the flower buds, again, barely open.

For use in food, often paired with lemon flavors in desserts or roasted with chicken or vegetables, check the recipe. Some call for dried or fresh flowers, others for the leaves. A little goes a long way — maybe two teaspoons of dried buds for an 8 x 12-inch pan of lemon bars.

There's also lavender infusions, lavender sugar, lavender syrup,

Lavender is harvested and used in many ways: fresh, dried, distilled, infused. It can be edible, aromatic and decorative.

lavender jam, lavender vinegar and lavender lemonade.

Distilling essential oils requires a big copper distiller like a moonshine still. It can use whole branches, leaves and all. Essential oils get used in cleaning and beauty products.

Information

Cathy's best sources of information have been the workshops and vendors at the Lavender Association of Western Colorado festivals. The association's website has detailed information on growing lavender in a climate similar to ours.

"I use '*The Lavender Lover's Handbook: The 100 Most Beautiful and Fragrant Varieties for Growing, Crafting, and Cooking*,' by Sarah Berringer Baden, as my primary reference, at least until I can get to Provence, France, or Sequim, Washington," Cathy said. Both are centers of the lavender industry.

"[Mrs. V.'s] theory is that if she finds a place where the weeds grow well there is nourishment enough there to grow annuals which are not particular. If the weeds struggle, then no annual is expected to make returns. She isn't a horticulturist, but she is a gardener who has adapted herself to the position in which she finds herself."

Dorothy Biddle and Dorothea Blom,
Garden Gossip: Chronicles of Sycamore Valley, 1936

PART 4

FLOWERS

Crocus is one of the first spring bulbs to bloom. They can come back year after year.

CHAPTER 29: **SPRING BULBS**

Remember your first sighting of blooming flowers last March?

No matter how many more snowstorms we had, crocuses, daffodils and tulips were the colorful optimists.

Did you say to yourself, "I want some in my yard"?

If so, August is the time to make your plans for spring-blooming bulbs. The catalogs have been coming in the mail since July, though the bulbs will be mailed at the appropriate time for planting, usually mid-October, before the ground freezes.

I've been succumbing to those full-color catalogs for more than 30 years, but I decided to check in with Laramie County Master Gardener Kathy Shreve and learn more. Kathy has headed up the Laramie County Master Gardeners' bulb sale for several years.

After struggling with Cheyenne's gardening challenges, it's a relief to know that we are well-suited to growing spring bulbs. Many of them originate in Iran, Iraq and Mongolia, which have a similarly dry climate, Kathy said. Just about all the spring bloomers, except jonquils — more suited to warmer climates — do well here.

Planting location

Think about where you want bulbs. All bulbs do well in sunny locations, including those areas that won't be shaded until the trees leaf out late spring. Avoid places where snow drifts last a long time.

Shady areas might do best with daffodils, snowdrops and squill, Kathy said.

If space is limited, consider planting different sized bulbs on top of one another. Because the big tulips and daffodils need to be planted the deepest, place them at the bottom of an appropriate-sized hole.

I usually dig one hole wide enough for a group of a dozen or more bulbs properly spaced — I prefer clumps to lines. Fill in with dirt until you reach the right depth for the next-biggest bulb, perhaps a smaller tulip or hyacinth, and top off with a layer of the smallest bulbs: grape hyacinth, crocus, snow crocus, snow drops, squill, Scilla species.

You also want to plant long-lived bulbs that keep returning every season where they can be left for many years. The Siberian squill I planted more than 25 years ago continues to spread and come up thicker every spring. Kathy mentioned that small bulbs like these can be naturalized in your lawn, if you don't get the urge to mow before they are finished.

You also need to think about what you want to grow over the bulbs in the garden for the rest of the growing season. A shallow-rooted or self-seeding annual works well because you won't have to disturb the soil. It can cover the dying tulip and daffodil leaves before they can be removed, which is when they are completely yellow and have finished feeding the bulbs.

The bulbs are dormant the rest of the year, but they do need some water. Pair them with summer flowers that also like it somewhat dry because bulbs will rot if it is too wet.

Choosing bulbs

Bulbs can be expensive. Breck's was advertising the *Ice Cream Tulip — A Tulip They Haven't Seen!* at an undiscounted price of $22 for three bulbs. There are many fancy tulips: fringed, double petals, multi-colored etc. Kathy said, "They're pretty but they're like annuals. They don't have the hardiness of their wild parents."

The bulbs that keep coming back are the "species" tulips, the ones closest to wild, which bulb breeders have messed with the least. The Kaufmanniana and Greigii types and the Darwin Hybrids are also good. These are also less expensive because they are older varieties. Kathy said in Cheyenne they don't require extensive soil preparation before planting.

I planted a sack of a dozen plain red tulips a few years ago and this spring I had a mass of 40 blooms. Some of them were a little small and Kathy suggested I dig them all up and replant the smallest bulbs somewhere else while they mature.

Keep in mind: The bigger the bulb you buy, the bigger the flower. The same variety of tulip or daffodil can be sold in different sizes. The purveyors with the best reputations will tell you how big their bulbs are so you can compare.

Choosing color and bloom time

Getting a great blend of flower colors is not my forte. I tend to go for the polychromatic look — any color I can get to grow. Sometimes clashing shades of red bloom next to each other at the same time.

Kathy, on the other hand, works with color palettes. For the Master Gardeners bulb sale one year, she chose tulips in the yellow to apricot family, with purplish blue accents provided by an allium and a hyacinth.

All bulb descriptions include an expected bloom time. What actual week any bulb begins blooming varies from year to year based on how quickly the soil begins warming, so it is all relative, but there is a progression. A warm microclimate next to a south-facing brick wall will speed it up.

First the small bulbs bloom: crocus, squill, snowdrops; then the medium-sized, hyacinth, and the species tulips and Kaufmanniana and Greigii; finally, the big tulips, like the Darwin Hybrids. Daffodils, sometimes referred to as "Narcissus," also come in a range of bloom times. You can have bulbs blooming from March through early June in Cheyenne.

Check that all the bulbs are suitable for our USDA Plant Hardiness Zone 5. I aim for colder zones though, 3 or 4.

Additional considerations

"Don't pick them if you want them to come back," Kathy said.

This was the most surprising new information I learned. I like to bring a few tulips inside to enjoy.

Apply fertilizer designed specifically for bulbs once in the spring as their leaves emerge and once in the fall. Kathy uses half the recommended rate.

If you have problems with predators, critters digging up and eating your bulbs, try daffodils and allium, Kathy said. Animals don't find them as edible. Pine straw (pine needle) mulch also seems to be a deterrent, says Jessica Friis, Cheyenne Botanic Gardens horticulturist.

And finally, the bulb companies have lots of advice on their websites. One, John Scheeper's, even sent me a booklet with my order that I found helpful.

BEST BULBS

Here are my picks for spring-blooming bulbs for the Cheyenne Botanic Gardens' Habitat Hero demonstration garden, designed to provide flowers early for bees and to be self-propagating from year to year, or "naturalizing" or "perennializing" as they say in catalogs.

In each category I picked the cheapest bulbs which, as Laramie County Master Gardener Michelle Bohanan agrees, is a good indication of how hardy and easy they are to grow.

- **Species tulip**, *Tulipa turkestanica*, blooms March/April, 8 inches tall, ivory petals with orangish bases, naturalizes.
- **Species or snow crocus mix**, March/April, 4 inches, white, blue, yellow, violet, deer resistant, naturalizes.
- **Iris reticulata mix**, early April, 4 to 6 inches, blue, purple, yellow, naturalizes.
- **Siberian Squill**, *Scilla siberica*, April, 5 inches, blue, naturalizes, deer and rodent resistant.
- **Glory of the Snow**, *Chionodoxa forbesii*, April, 5-6 inches, blues, naturalizing, deer and rodent-resistant, multiple flowers per bulb.
- **Large cupped daffodils**, April, 18-20 inches, yellow, naturalizes, deer, rodent and rabbit resistant. These varieties are the most popular of the 13 divisions of daffodils and are available in garden centers all over town.
- **Grape Hyacinth**, *Muscari armeniacum*, April/May, 6 inches, blue, naturalizes, deer resistant. Other *Muscari* species are white and even pale pink.
- **Species tulip**, *Tulipa linifolia*, May, 6 inches, red, naturalizes.
- **Single late (Darwin) tulip**, May, 22-30 inches, all kinds of plain and blended colors available. These are the most popular tulips and most available in local stores.
- **Flowering onion**, *Allium oreophilum*, May/June, 6-8 inches, deep rose. All the alliums, including the giant purple globes I've had rebloom for several years, are rabbit, rodent and deer resistant, and popular with bees. But not all allium varieties return reliably.
- **Fosteriana, kaufmanniana and greigii tulips** are good naturalizers and survive our spring snowstorms.

"'Snowdrops' is a little white flower. Not a showstopper, except it regularly blooms in mid-February in Cheyenne. A great cure for spring fever." — Shane

Market gardeners can specialize in cut flower arrangements. This one features two kinds of gladioli.

CHAPTER 30:
MARKET GLADS

FARMERS MARKET BOUQUETS FEATURE CHEYENNE-GROWN GLADIOLI

My guilty pleasure at the Tuesday Farmers Market is not the baked goods. It's the flowers. This year I caved and started bringing home bouquets every week.

This is the fifth year Vally Gollogly of Cheyenne has been offering cut flowers at the booth she shares with partner Rusty Brinkman (Chapter 19). They are also the proprietors of Crow Creek Catering. Their vegetables look delicious, but the flowers look like candy. I

think the grocery stores figured this out long ago.

Many of Vally's arrangements are under $10 and fit in glass jars, a personal size. I try to remember to bring my own drink cup to transfer them, so I can put them in a car cupholder for the trip home.

This year, the gladioli in the arrangements stand out — so many vibrant blooms lined up on one stalk.

I don't think of this elegant, exotic relative of the iris, its name Latin for "sword" (think "gladiator") being something easy to grow in Cheyenne.

A tropical plant, most of the 250-plus gladiolus species are not expected to overwinter here. They require "lifting," as the horticulturists say. When the leaves wither and before the first freeze, the gladiolus corms or bulbs, fat roots, need to be dug up and dried in the sun for a couple days. Then the dirt is brushed off and they are stored loosely indoors someplace that stays cool and dark — a place where any excess moisture evaporates rather than forms mold. Vally winters her bulbs in an old darkroom.

I can't resist gladioli at the market and Vally can't resist buying gladioli bulbs to grow.

- *Acidanthera bicolor* (fragrant, white with maroon center)
- *Gladiolus* 'Windsong' (pink with yellow centers)
- G. 'Atom' (bright orangey red with white edges)
- G. 'Glamini Charlotte' (buttery white)
- G. 'Green Star' (lime-green)

Vally is experimenting with *Gladiolus nanus*. It is among the smaller glads, 12-18 inches tall. It is rated as hardy in Zone 4, or 5 — Cheyenne's winter-hardiness rating on the USDA Plant Hardiness Zone map. I noticed High Country Gardens, specializing in plants for Rocky Mountain-area gardening, suggests they be well-mulched.

Anyone in Cheyenne who is a serious market gardener grows the tender vegetables, tomatoes, peppers and eggplant, in a hoop house, or high tunnel. Vally and Rusty have two. Much of one is devoted to gladioli, dahlias, Persian and regular

Gladiolus 'Atom'

zinnias and other cutting flowers. In the diffuse light the flowers, especially the dahlias, grow longer stems, great for flower arranging.

Juicy blooms, like juicy fruits and vegetables, require a lot of water. The high tunnels are on drip irrigation, so no water is evaporated by the wind.

Juicy blooms are appealing to pests. In summer, the tunnel sides are rolled up to regulate the temperature inside. This year, big yellow grasshoppers have volunteered to trim the dahlia flowerheads perfectly. They take off only the petal tips, leaving a tight cone of color. It's so perfect, you think it is supposed to look like that, good enough for a flower arrangement.

Vally's preferred time to cut flowers for market is the evening before. If a few leaves are left on the plant when you cut the gladiolus stalk, she said it helps it regenerate. Cutting either evening or early morning when they are unstressed means flowers will last longer — nearly a week for Vally's arrangements. Her greenery and other flowers come from the volunteers along the edges of the vegetable patches — whatever catches her eye before market day.

Having a good eye is important in the presentation of fruits, vegetables and flowers at the market, or at the Laramie County Fair. Vally walked off with 42 blue ribbons plus two Grand Champions and one Reserve Champion one year, not only in floriculture and horticulture, but also in the culinary department, especially preserves and dried foods.

Vally's enterprise echoes the Slow Flowers movement, the idea that we should support local flower growers instead of buying flowers flown in from South America. The Front Range of Colorado was a hotbed of floriculture until the U.S. encouraged South Americans to get into the U.S. cut flower trade in the 1980s in lieu of growing opium poppies, so I've heard. Buying local flowers at the farmers market is a first step in reclaiming our regional heritage.

Vally remembers the lush greenness of a childhood in Ireland and how tough it was to adapt to desert gardening when the family moved to Santa Fe. In comparison, she finds Cheyenne to be a happy medium. Growing flowers makes her happy. Bringing her flowers home makes me happy.

CUTTING GARDEN BOUQUETS

If you have the urge to cut flowers and put them in jars and vases, then you want to consider the cutting garden.

The vegetable gardener may scoff at flowers, but the enormous flower industry is meeting an important need, even if it is merely human happiness.

"Cutting garden" is a searchable internet term. The University of Vermont advised me to plant long-stemmed flowers in mono-species patches, like vegetables, in some out-of-the-way place where I won't have to look at the destruction I wreak when I regularly cut what's in bloom.

Cottage-style cutting gardens

However, the few blooms I bring indoors for closer examination and appreciation of beauty are never missed in my messy, cottage-style garden.

The true cottage garden of British fame leaves no turf inside the picket fence except paths,because the historical British cottager was growing food and herbs as well. It appears as a profusion of blooms and greenery spilling over borders.

Planning

Early fall is the time to prepare new flower beds and plant spring bulbs, the first of the cutting flowers. Leave paths so you can reach everything with pruners or scissors. Peruse the seed catalogs in January. Don't forget to grow greenery for your future flower arrangements.

Suzanne McIntire, author of *An American Cutting Garden, A Primer for Growing Cut Flowers,* advises us to correlate the cutting garden to future flower arrangements, but my bouquets are as informal as my garden. Any blooms that are incompatible, such as the violets that are too short for an arrangement with penstemons, get their own appropriately sized vase or jar.

As a long-time quilter, I never worry anymore if my quilts — or my flowers — match my décor. The more colors I have, the less it matters.

Keeping records

You'll also want to discover which flowers can last more than a day in a vase. If you are contemplating becoming a part of the Slow Flowers movement, selling cut flowers locally, you'll want to track what blooms and when.

Even in winter, there will be a few things to cut. The yarrow, rudbeckias and coneflowers left standing make nice dry flower arrangements.

In December I look forward to pruning coniferous evergreens or cutting a whole spruce or fir tree as is customary, the ultimate in cutting plants to bring indoors.

Rhea Halstead grows a charming rose garden. Most of her choices are hardy, some are only "annuals."

CHAPTER 31: **ROSE GARDEN**

YOU CAN PROMISE A ROSE GARDEN HERE

Gary Halstead probably didn't promise his wife a rose garden.

With the Cheyenne weather as it is, most people would bet on that becoming a broken promise.

But in 2004, when Rhea Halstead and her husband were finished with their list of major home improvements, she looked out at the backyard and was inspired to recreate a scene from Country Home magazine: a small, vintage travel trailer smothered in roses, with a little bistro table and chairs for two out front. The serene vision appealed to Rhea, who has a career that often brings her face to face with the dark side of humanity (she's retired since this interview was written).

Ten years later, on my visit, I am charmed by the oasis the Halsteads have grown, protected by hedges and trees. The tiny vintage travel trailer is there, embedded in roses, and should be covered in blooms within a month. Rhea found another, slightly larger trailer at a garage sale for $50 and fixed it up — antiques are her other passion. She calls it the Honeymoon Cottage.

Over to one side is a tiny cottage that's really the potting shed. Another small building is the summer kitchen — the Halsteads love to entertain outdoors. And there's the gazebo and a greenhouse. Circuitous gravel paths are sparked by a scattering of colored glass pebbles.

Rhea's 150 rose bushes are tucked into protected corners or in small beds in which white picket and other kinds of fencing provide backdrops. And everywhere there are bits of vintage memorabilia to discover.

Rhea was not a gardener when she decided to plant her first rosebush. Instead, she researched and learned from members of the local rose club.

How does Rhea grow roses?

Right location

Roses need 6-8 hours of sun, preferably morning sun, because afternoon heat fades blooms.

Right variety

Most of Rhea's roses grow on their own roots — they are not fussy varieties that require grafting onto sturdier root stock — and they tend to be repeat bloomers. Many are hardy enough that they don't need winter protection.

Spring planting

March and April are when Rhea consults her wish list and researches where to find new varieties she wants to try.

If you do plant a grafted variety, "grown on a union," bury that union 2-3 inches deep, Rhea said. For the latest, best planting instructions, search online for "how to plant a rose bush" at Wikihow or other sites.

Watering

Rhea waters as needed, which can be as often as every other day when it's hot. She has considered drip irrigation but has chosen to walk her garden with the hose.

"That's the whole Zen thing," and it helps her de-stress she said. It only takes 30 minutes and it allows her to spend time with the roses and see how they are doing.

Summer maintenance

Rhea tried using all the natural fertilizers, but the dogs ate them. Now when she checks mid-summer for the need to fertilize, she uses conventional products.

Each year she replenishes her wood chip mulch, which feeds the roses as it decomposes as well as re-presses weeds. And for weeds that do show up, "We get on our hands and knees and pick," Rhea said.

She aims for rose varieties that aren't as susceptible to pests and diseases, and if she needs to, she uses Neem oil and sometimes Bayer products.

Chlorosis can be another problem. Our alkaline soil can tie up iron and leaves will grow gangly and yellow. Roses like slightly acidic soil and so applying iron sulfate as directed can help. Consult the Laramie County Extension office for a definite diagnosis.

Deadheading, removal of flowers that are finished blooming, encourages the repeat blooming varieties to keep flowering.

Fall preparation

In September, Rhea quits deadheading to make it easier for the roses to go into dormancy. She reduces watering to once a week.

Winter covering

In November, about 60% of Rhea's bushes get covered, and always the ones in their first year in her garden. Covering is about trying to keep the rosebush cold so it stays dormant, she said. If she has a variety that doesn't die back, like the floribundas, it doesn't need a cover.

But hybrid teas and some others, and new bushes, do need a cover. Rhea buries the base of the bush in about 6 inches of topsoil, from either her garden or a garden center. Using an old plastic pot from a nursery, with the bottom removed, she places the cylinder over the plant and fills it with a mix of dry, brown leaves and a little more dirt. The open top allows water to leach in, but the leaves allow enough air to prevent mildew.

Spring uncovering

Rhea removes the covers between April 15 and 30. At the time of my visit April 26, she had removed the covers, but not the mounds of soil, which were fine protection for the coming spring snowstorms. Rhea said she did re-cover the bushes before the 11 inches of snow we had May 11 and 12.

Eventually, she waters out the protective soil, cuts canes back to the last green growth, blows the leaves out, picks the weeds and puts in new wood chip mulch.

Choosing roses for Cheyenne

Canadian roses, which are varieties developed by Agriculture Canada for harsh prairie conditions, are a better bet here in this climate. Some varieties to consider: Explorer series roses, 'John Davis,' 'William Baffin' and 'Alexander Mackenzie.' Also, 'Morden Blush,' 'Hope for Humanity' and 'Winnipeg Park' are solid roses.

Knockout roses seem to do well here. These are varieties developed in Wisconsin and introduced in 2000.

The David Austin roses were developed in England beginning in the 1960s and cross old garden variety roses with modern. These are very winter hardy: 'Winchester Cathedral,' 'Mary,' 'Crown Princess Margareta' and 'Strawberry Hill.'

If you go with a modern rose, floribundas are hardier than the hybrid teas. A few that survive well here and are quite beautiful are 'Europeana' and 'Strike It Rich.' They will require winter cover.

High Country Roses in Denver carries many older varieties of roses that do well in this climate.

Roses rated for Zone 5 on the USDA Plant Hardiness Zone map will mostly do OK here. Though Cheyenne is rated Zone 5, roses rated for Zones 4 and below do better here.

The Harison yellow rose came west with pioneers. It can survive on its own at abandoned homesteads.

CHAPTER 32: **HARDY ROSES**

ROSES AT ABANDONED PRAIRIE HOMESTEADS BLOOM

Roses are perennials, but the joke is, in Cheyenne, they are often annuals. These prima donnas of the garden are often killed by one of our episodes of harsh winter weather.

Sometimes, only the grafted part of the rose, the upper, fancy variety, dies and the hardy, usually less beautiful, rootstock lives on.

There's no shame in losing roses to winter, and you can replace each bush for about the price of a dozen cut roses. Even the folks at the Cheyenne Botanic Gardens replace theirs occasionally.

One day, I ran into Steve Scott,

head of horticulture for the Gardens at the time, now retired. Having just been inundated by roses while on a trip to the Pacific Northwest, I asked him what the deal was with these "annual" roses around here.

Rose varieties that bloom all summer don't prepare adequately for our winters, he said.

On the other hand, the species roses, close cousins to wild roses, bloom once in June for several weeks and then go into winter preparation mode, protecting canes and roots from future winterkill.

I recognize those roses: the big shrubs full of yellow blooms like the one my mother had at her old house in Wisconsin, or the one at my front door in Casper, and even the Austrian Copper rose (orange and yellow) in my Cheyenne backyard that has probably been here since the house was built more than 50 years ago.

These roses come with fascinating stories.

Persian Yellow rose

Europeans had no yellow roses until they discovered one in Persia, now part of present-day Iran. However, some people didn't like the way it smelled and named it *Rosa foetida*, "Fetid rose," fetid meaning stinky. But it has become an ancestor of all kinds of yellow roses we see today.

The Austrian copper rose shares ancestry with the Harison's yellow rose. It blooms in early June.

Austrian Copper rose

The gardener at Emperor Rudolf II's imperial gardens in Vienna first described *Rosa foetida bicolor* in 1539, a variety of the Persian Yellow rose in which the upper surface of the petals is red-orange and the lower surface yellow.

Harison's Yellow rose

Later, George F. Harison, a rosarian (someone who cultivates roses) found an interesting, hardy hybrid growing in his estate's garden in the New York City suburbs in the 1820s. It was apparently a cross between the Scotch Briar rose and the Persian Yellow rose, with flowers having more than double the normal five petals of wild roses — and a nicer fragrance.

Harison was a lawyer but he recognized a valuable rose when he saw one, so he gave cuttings to William Prince, a nurseryman on Long Island, who propagated it and began marketing it as 'Harison's Yellow' rose in 1830.

Oregon Trail rose

In little time, this new rose became so popular, it frequently travelled with the pioneers going to Oregon. Something from one's garden was much more portable and made a better memento of home than that chest of drawers that was eventually dumped by the side of the trail to lighten the load.

So sometimes 'Harison's Yellow' is known as the Oregon Trail rose. It's also known as the Yellow Rose of Texas, though the song by the same name is about a woman.

If you've ever ordered plants by mail, you wonder how anyone on the Oregon Trail, circa 1836-1890s, managed to keep a rose alive on a several-months-long trip. It was summer when the wagon trains made it to the Wyoming part of the trail — they liked to get to Independence

Rock, 60 miles southwest of Casper, by the 4th of July.

The pioneers carried this rose with the ends of the cuttings stuck into potatoes, wrote Donna Mileti Benenson, in an article for Early American Homes magazine.

Abandoned homesteads in the West are often memorialized by a cascade of yellow roses in June. Last month I saw a shrub near Bozeman, Montana, standing by itself, that was more than 6 feet high, and from which point the canes bent and descended nearly to the ground, loaded with blooms and creating a mound twice the usual diameter of 5 to 6 feet.

How to find hardy roses

Though 'Harison's Yellow' rose is a hybrid, meaning it won't grow true from seed, it suckers easily, sending up new canes that can be cut and rooted. I wonder if Prince, the original propagator, ever made much money once gardeners figured out how easy it was to share.

If you don't have a friend or family member with a Harison's, it and other hardy shrub roses are available commercially. Check local garden centers and High Country Roses in Denver.

Caring for hardy roses

If roses like 'Harison's Yellow' can prosper at abandoned homesteads, you won't expect to perform a lot of maintenance.

Cutting out dead canes in the spring will make them look nicer. An inch of water a week will make them fuller.

They aren't often plagued by insects and diseases, so don't spray pesticides.

Don't fertilize them less than six weeks before the first average frost date of Sept. 20 — that would be no later than the first week in August — so they can truly winterize themselves.

Once a shrub rose is finished blooming, it provides rose hips for the birds and a nice green backdrop for other flowers in your garden, maybe even some of those "annual" roses.

But while you try out fancy new varieties every year, keeping the rose breeders and growers in business, your 'Harison's Yellow' rose could continue to prosper, and even outlive you.

C and T Iris Patch in Eaton, Colorado, offers an ocean of iris choices.

CHAPTER 33: **IRIS**

There is an annual flower phenomenon less than an hour south of Cheyenne, just east of Eaton, Colorado, from mid-May through early June. And after you find it, you might think you'd been to Eden instead of Eaton.

It's thanks to a tradition among iris farms to open to the public while the iris are blooming. Last year was my first visit to C and T Iris Patch's acre of beauty, and it won't be my last.

There is a gap between the spring bloom time and the best time to transplant iris — July into August — but Charlette Felte, co-owner of C

and T Iris Patch, takes pity on spring visitors and allows them to take home select plants. I bought several and as per her instructions, cut the blooms and put them in a vase, then trimmed the leaves and planted the rhizomes (fat root-like appendages) in a sunny spot.

With 800 visitors per spring, it's good everyone doesn't succumb to immediate gratification and can wait until orders are shipped in summer. If you can't visit, the color photos in the online catalog are nearly as inspiring.

When Charlette reached retirement age, she announced to her husband Tim that she wanted to move to the country to raise iris. "Fine," he said. "Find some land." Two days later, Charlette had picked out a place.

Charlette knew a lot about iris already. Growing up, her father would send her and her siblings down the street to help an elderly neighbor who had an iris garden.

"I thought they were the prettiest flowers," Charlette said.

Variations

C and T Iris Patch opened in 2000. It now carries 3,200 varieties of iris. The largest category is the bearded iris (the beard being the fuzzy patch on the falls — the petals that bend downwards). Within bearded iris there are classifications based on height.

Here are the classes of bearded iris beginning with the earliest to bloom:

- Miniature Dwarf Bearded
- Standard Dwarf Bearded
- Intermediate Bearded

and then three blooming at the same time:

- Tall Bearded (mid-late spring)
- Border Bearded
- Miniature Tall Bearded

If you are lucky, your iris may rebloom in the fall — when temperatures resemble those during the spring bloom. Some varieties are identified as rebloomers because they have a propensity for it, but it isn't something to count on.

Now if you think all irises are blue or yellow, you need to check out what's available, either online or during bloom time. There's also peach, orange, pink, brown, red and violet. Some are bi-colored, tri-colored, spotted, striped and edged with accent colors. And for some reason, flower breeders are always trying for "black."

The names people dream up for each new hybrid are sometimes beautiful, 'Come Away with Me,' 'Kiss the Dawn,' 'Mist on the Mountain.' Sometimes they make you laugh: 'All Reddy' (a red iris), 'Awesome Blossom,' 'Coming Up Roses,' 'Darnfino,' 'Get Over Yerself,' 'Got Milk' (all white and ruffled). And some might be a bit naughty: 'Sinister Desire,' 'Sunrise Seduction,' 'Hook Up.' Or named for someone, usually a woman, 'Sarah Marie,' 'Raspberry Rita,' 'Evelyn's Echo.'

As I was perusing the catalog, I noticed that each description mentioned the date the hybrid was introduced. The fun of breeding new hybrids goes back centuries to the origins of these iris in Europe, North Africa and Asia. North America has wild iris, but they usually prefer swampy conditions.

In Charlette's catalog there are varieties from the 1930s: 'Rhages,' 'Wabash,' and 'William Setchell,' and from 1912, 'Romero,' and the oldest, from 1904, 'Caprice.' Among other kinds of plants, the older varieties are not as disease resistant. However, Charlette said that the older iris hybrids, especially from the 1950s through 1980s, are hardier. The newer, rufflier, lacier, frillier, don't winter as well. Plus, they don't have as much fragrance.

Growing iris

Irises are not fussy plants. They prefer drier conditions. They will rot if they aren't dry enough, so they fit with today's water-smart or water-wise gardens.

Charlette also recommends her Wyoming customers not choose the tallest, the 40-inchers, because they take so long to bloom, and Cheyenne is already two weeks behind Eaton. The delay is probably due to a combination of Eaton being 1,200 feet lower, 45 miles south, and having sandier soils that warm up faster in spring.

Iris leaves grow in fan arrays. In July, when irises are normally dug up for transplanting, the fan is trimmed to a 6-inch tall diamond. Otherwise, leaves are not trimmed until the following spring.

The rhizomes are covered with an inch of soil, up to the point where the leaves turn from white to green. Charlette recommends giving the transplants an inch of water the first time, and then about half an inch per week until mid-September. Deep watering is better than frequent shallow watering.

Charlette recommends rabbit feed (pellet form) for fertilizer, which is high in phosphates and other nutrients iris need for good blooms. They need very little nitrogen. The best time to fertilize is mid-to-late March, and again in July for the reblooming varieties or plants newly divided. Charlette warns on her website to never use manure.

Trim the flower stalks after blooming to keep the color of the bloom true next year. Trim dead leaves away after winter, Charlette said.

In three or four years, your irises will have multiplied and need to be dug up and thinned to keep them blooming. You can either increase the size of your iris garden or give the excess fans to friends.

New hybrids

While bees will pollinate iris and cause seed pods to form, Charlette recommends removing them. Unless you have controlled conditions, the seeds will not grow true to the parent plant.

I asked Charlette if she has ever registered her own hybrids and she said no, it's about a 10-year-long process. First, you must provide enough seed true to the hybrid for 75 growers around the country and overseas to grow it out. They keep records for four years and submit them to the American Iris Society, which will decide if your hybrid is different enough from all the registered varieties.

Visiting in spring

C and T Iris Patch is open to the public a little past mid-May to almost mid-June each year at no charge — except the cost of not wanting to leave without your own iris. The website has extensive information about growing iris.

Wild geraniums (left) and zonal geraniums (right) are not related, but both are good garden choices.

CHAPTER 34: **GERANIUMS**

THEY ARE EASY TO GROW, PROPAGATE AND WINTER OVER

Geraniums are one of my favorite houseplants.

Serious gardeners look at me askance: "But they are so easy to grow!" Exactly. Besides, in the summer I can set them outside to dress up the porch. In addition, there are the wild geranium cultivars (cultivated varieties) that seem just as easy to grow and propagate.

Zonal geraniums

The epitome of geraniums is the zonal geranium, not actually in the *Geranium* genus, but in *Pelargonium*, native to South Africa. The Dutch brought them to Europe in the early 1700s.

I like the big red flowerheads, about 5 inches across, made of many florets. They also come in white, pink and various combinations. The leaves are roundish and fuzzy with scalloped edges and sometimes a dark crescent marked on them, the "zone." The cottage with the white picket fence always has them in the window boxes or inside in the windows. There's also the ivy-leafed type.

"Ivy leaf geraniums are nice in hanging baskets and can make a good houseplant in a sunny window."— Shane

I double-checked what I've learned in 27 years of growing

This zonal geranium has spent winters inside and summers outside for more than 15 years. It is the source of many cuttings.

with a neighbor, Charlie Culp. One fall day, he handed me two plastic grocery sacks, each with a hot pink geranium he had uprooted from pots on his front steps. Frost was predicted and he told me I should winter them.

I potted up both and shared one with one of the teachers. All winter I enjoyed mine. In spring I took it back outside. Some years I planted it in the garden, sometimes I left it in the pot. Sometimes I took cuttings to bring in instead of the whole plant, especially if the plant got too big. Sometimes I ended up with half a dozen plants. This went on for 17 years.

The last year I took cuttings and put them in water, I couldn't find time to plant them and when I finally looked closely at them a couple months later, they were covered in aphids and never recovered. But soon a friend shared a beautiful red geranium and I collected shades of pink at the nursery.

For the last 14 years, I've hauled in four big pots of geraniums for the winter and put them in the big, southwest-facing window in our attached garage. It's well-insulated, including the doors.

There are only a couple weeks when it gets below freezing at night out there and we must bring in the plants from the garage. And yes, we drive our vehicles in and out a couple times a day. But the door is never open more than a minute and the temperature barely changes.

geraniums with information from the Old Farmer's Almanac and we agree: geraniums appreciate bright light. Otherwise, they still bloom but they get leggy. When that happens, I cut off the thickest stems, use a pencil to poke a hole in the soil in the same pot or a new pot and insert the stem. It's that easy to root a cutting. If soil is not immediately available, the stems can be put in water.

Back when I walked my kids to and from school, I'd stop to chat

A couple of tips: when you bring in geraniums for the winter, try to make yourself cut back the blooming stems to 6-8 inches tall so the plant won't be so spindly by spring. You can pot up those cuttings in potting soil (not garden soil).

Don't over-water, especially if you have the plants in their preferred cool location (50-60 degrees). Let the top inch of soil dry out. Fertilize sparingly, waiting until the days lengthen after the winter solstice. And don't forget to keep turning the plants so they won't grow one-sided.

Be sure to remove the flower heads when they get down to the last few florets blooming or remove the florets as they finish.

Wild geraniums

Real geraniums are in the genus *Geranium*, wild geranium. There are several species native to North America. Many of these wild species are also known as "cranesbill" because the seed pod is a long, beak-like shape.

Area nurseries are selling several Geranium cultivars (cultivated varieties) that will do well here. They have a roundish but palmate (having "fingers") sort of hairy leaf and a pinkish flower that is equivalent in size to the Pelargonium's individual florets.

My wild geranium makes a great ground cover in shadier areas. The leaves turn red in the fall and persist all winter. When mine started crowding out other plants in the raised bed, I decided to snip a few leafy stems and see if they would root in water so I could then fill in bare spots elsewhere. And it worked!

Monarchs require milkweeds for egg-laying, but many other insects enjoy milkweed, too.

CHAPTER 35: **MONARCHS AND MILKWEEDS**

WHAT WORKS FOR MONARCHS WORKS FOR OTHER BENEFICIAL INSECTS

Monarch butterflies are hard to find in Wyoming. This is partly because we have few people looking for them and because of the terrible decline in monarch numbers overall. I found a dead one last year. I hope this will be the year I see my first live one in my garden.

Monarchs in Wyoming descend from those currently wintering in Mexico, not from the group west of the Rockies wintering in California. It's the only North American butterfly that must migrate because it can't survive cold winters like other butterflies.

In spring, the generation that wintered in Mexico produces the next generation while on its way north, and that one begets another, and so on. After a few months, it could be the fourth generation we finally see here. There are several more generations produced over the summer and the final one makes it all the way back to Mexico in the fall.

Monarchs have been clobbered on both ends of their route. Mexico has established the Monarch Butterfly Biosphere Reserve in the relatively small area they cluster. Here in North America, besides building on and paving over habitat, the problem has been planting herbicide-resistant crops and spraying them with herbicide to kill weeds — which also kills milkweed.

While monarchs feed on nectar from a variety of flowers, they only lay eggs, tiny white dots, on milkweed — it's the only plant their caterpillars will eat. The good news is that there are about 100 species of milkweed found all along their migration routes. There are 13 species in Wyoming — and four right here in Laramie County.

In September, check roadsides and the unkempt corners of town for ripe milkweed pods to collect your own seed.

Local native milkweeds

If you want to join the effort to garden for monarchs, you want to grow our local native flowers. Of course, monarchs are not the only nectar-lovers that will enjoy them.

Two species, *Asclepias viridiflora*, green milkweed, and *A. pumila*, plains milkweed, are not seen commercially as seeds or plants. But the other two are quite popular.

Asclepias speciosa, showy milkweed, a perennial, has large round balls of pink florets on stems 2 to 4 feet tall. Its vigorous rhizomes help it spread. I got a few plants from my neighbor who was digging them out of her lawn. But on the other hand, their taproots are sensitive and not all my transplants survived.

I've also collected seed from showy milkweed in the unmowed corner of the field where I walk the dog.

Growing milkweed

Seeds are easy to grow if you leave them in the refrigerator for two months to cold stratify or use the winter sowing technique no later than March 1 (Chapter 6).

Plant showy milkweed in full sun for maximum number of flowers. Water it regularly the first summer to get it started. Around the county I see it alongside roads where it gets extra water from runoff when it rains. It is not going to bloom much in a very dry location.

The other local milkweed, *Asclepias incarnata*, swamp milkweed, I haven't grown myself yet. Laramie County Master Gardener Michelle Bohanan assures me that despite its name, it doesn't need a swamp. Like showy milkweed, it does best with a little more water than just rain to maximize blooms and nectar production. It grows 2-3 feet high, usually with pink flowers, though Michelle has a white variety.

Considering milkweed has been treated as a weed and grows unaided in weedy places, I wouldn't worry much about fertilizers or compost.

Milkweed in winter

If your showy milkweed gets ugly late in the season, don't cut it back until there's nothing left for caterpillars to eat. And even then, the dried plants are useful for catching snow — free winter watering. I cut them back in spring.

Avoid pesticides

All the websites devoted to monarchs say avoid buying all kinds of plants treated with systemic pesticides. The long-lasting neonicotinoids get in the nectar and poison the butterfly — and other pollinators. Avoid these herbicide ingredients: Acetamiprid, Clothianidin, Dinotefuran, Imidacloprid, Nitenpyram, Thiacloprid and Thiamethoxam.

Butterfly habitat

Butterflies are also looking for shelter from wind, for sun-warmed rocks and pavement to bask on and for places to puddle on damp sand to get a drink.

The great thing about growing a garden for butterflies is that it also works for bees and birds. But let's not stop at the garden gate. How about encouraging native flowers along our roads, in corners of fields, in our parks? I'm excited to hear that Nettie Eakes, the head horticulturist at the Cheyenne Botanic Gardens, has plans for more perennials in city beds. Many natives, we hope. See Resources section for seed sources and monarch information.

The University of Wyoming school colors, brown and gold, were inspired by Black-eyed Susans.

CHAPTER 36:
FALL BLOOMERS

FALL-BLOOMING PERENNIAL FLOWER CHOICES ABOUND

In the fall I look around town, especially the Cheyenne Botanic Gardens, to see what blooms late in the growing season that I might add to my garden for the benefit of bees and our own enjoyment.

Annual flowers are colorful right up to the first frost, average date Sept. 20. In some years and some parts of town in some microclimates, killing frost might wait until mid-October. But unless they self-seed, I can't justify buying flats of annuals every spring to cover all my garden beds, nor have I the greenhouse to start my own. Instead, I turn to perennials. Here are suggestions for you to add to your garden in the spring. Or find them on sale in the fall and plant them then.

Black-eyed Susan, *Rudbeckia hirta* and other *Rudbeckia* species. Their golden yellow petals and brown centers inspired the University of Wyoming's selection of school colors. There are many varieties based on native species: short or tall, diminutive or gigantic flowers, mid-summer bloomers or later. Some bloom a long time — over a month. Some are better at coming back year after year.

Fall-blooming asters, *Symphyotrichum* species, New England asters.

One variety is a 2-foot-tall shrub of lavender-colored, 1-inch flowers. It's come back every year for over 20 years, waiting until mid-September to bloom. But another, brighter purple aster in a sunnier spot started blooming three weeks earlier and continued to bloom much later. Nurseries so often move onto the next best variety so you might as well go for what's available rather than mourn what you can't find.

Blanket flower, *Gaillardia* species. A hard-working perennial native to North America, it can start blooming in early summer. Horticulturists have had a field day designing varieties with different color patterns. A member of the aster family, it has petals that can be plain yellow, yellow with bands of red, or nearly all red-orange with a little yellow trim. Some are short, some tall. The seed heads are prickly little balls. If you deadhead them when they are finished blooming, they will put out more flowers. If you don't, they will drop seeds that will sprout next year, like many other easy-to-grow perennials.

'Hot Pink' Salvia, *Salvia gregii*. Perennials that bloom in early summer may start blooming again in early fall — perhaps they don't like hot mid-summer temperatures.

Microclimates

Microclimates make a big difference as to when perennials bloom. Nettie Eakes, head horticulturist at the Cheyenne Botanic Gardens, said visitors are always telling her how the same flower in their yard is either behind or ahead.

The CBG's Paul Smith Children's Village is lucky to be protected by high stone walls. On their north-facing sides, they provide shade and make a cool, slow-growing microclimate. On the south-facing sides, they absorb sunlight and make a warmer, faster-growing microclimate which can also extend the growing season.

Sneezeweed, *Helenium autumnale*. The most noticeable perennial I found blooming Sept. 18 at the Children's Village was a 6-foot-tall plant with multiple small sunflower-type flowers, each with yellow petals and ball-shaped yellow centers. Nettie said they increase by sending out underground stems but are not very invasive. Helenium comes in many other variations and bloom times.

Giant hummingbird mint, *Agastache pallida* 'Barberi.' Three feet tall, this does not have shout-out-loud color. But it is a nice contrast: silvery spikes of tiny purple flowers. It could attract a late hummingbird — or hummingbird moth.

'Karl Foerster' feather reed grass, *Calamagrostis acutiflora* 'Karl Foerster.' This is a go-to plant for landscape designers these days, but that's because it looks so neat. Growing around four feet tall, it starts out green in summer. Then the seed heads ripen to a golden wheat color. Finally, the whole plant turns gold. It is tough enough to stand and provide color all winter before getting cut back in spring.

Russian sage, *Perovskia atriplicifolia*. A wispy, shrubby perennial, it is also favored by landscape designers in our area. Each branch sprouts from ground level, with silvery leaves on the lower half and small blueish lavender flowers on the upper half of each stem. It likes sunny spots and will spread.

Chatting with my Laramie County Master Gardener friends, Steve Scott and Kathy Shreve, I also have this list of fall bloomers for you to think about planting next year:

- Autumn crocus, *Colchicum* species. Corms are planted in July or August. The blossoms are much larger than spring crocus.

- Blue sage, *Salvia azuria*. Native to central and eastern North America.

- Goldenrod, *Solidago* species. Blooms are branches of tiny yellow flowers. Many are native to North America.

- Joe Pye weed, *Eutrochium species*. Another North American native, sometimes varieties are 5 feet tall, with panicles of purple-pink flowers.

- Maxmilian sunflower, *Helianthus maximiliani*. Native to the Great Plains, 2 to 10 feet tall, branches with many yellow flowers.

- Purple coneflower, *Echinacea purpurea*. Daisy-like, native to North America, many varieties, 1 to 4 feet tall.

New England Aster is a fall bloomer native to eastern North America. Europeans first grew it in their gardens in 1710, long before it became popular here. There are many cultivars producing different sized plants and flowers in many shades from white to pink to lavender to purple that are in our gardens coast to coast.

- Snakeweed, *Gutierrezia* species. A shrub with yellow flowers native to western North America.

- Rabbitbrush, *Ericameria nauseousus*, or *Chrysothamnus viscidiflorus*. Both are yellow-flowered shrubs. The native varieties grow on our drier prairies.

- 'Autumn Joy' sedum, *Sedum telephium*. A stonecrop, it has fleshy stems, grows 1-2 feet tall, and is topped with bunches of tiny purple-pink blossoms.

- Obedient plant, *Physostegia virginiana*. Looks like a 2 to 4-foot-tall snapdragon with pale lavender-pink flowers.

"I really love the Willowleaf Sunflower, *Helianthus salicifolius*. It is more behaved than the Maximilian Sunflower. What I love most about it is the structure of the plant, which makes it attractive all summer long. The leaves combine on the stems to resemble a miniature skyscraper that reaches close to 5 feet tall. Then it puts out wonderful little sunflowers at the very end of the growing season. When the nights get cold the stem turns a wonderful purple." — Shane

For a chart of perennials for Cheyenne, see Cheyenne Botanic Gardens website, Resources tab, "Gardening Tips."

PART 5

GARDEN TYPES

Barb Sahl has tried several types of raised beds including stock tanks.

CHAPTER 37:
RAISED BED GARDEN

ADVANTAGES AND STYLES ARE MANY

Rabbits made her do it.

Barb Sahl, Laramie County Master Gardener, told me she was a ground-level vegetable gardener for the first nine years at her place on Cheyenne's south side, but she switched to raised beds to keep the rabbits out of her garden.

There were other considerations too. Raised beds would help keep her dogs from running through the radishes and it was a way to deal with a persistent weed problem.

Barb was also thinking about her aging knees, knowing her days of kneeling would end in the future.

With that in mind, she installed eight beds using a system of landscape pavers, then added five stock tanks.

Here is information about the history, types and benefits of raised beds in our area.

Genesis of the raised bed

The stereotypical vegetable garden has rows of vegetables. The bare ground between must be kept weeded.

An alternative is to grow vegetables like flowers, using wide beds, 2 to 4 feet wide (depending on how far you want to reach) and grow your plants more closely. This shades out the weeds and you never step into the wide beds, keeping the soil from getting compacted. The paths between beds can be mulched or grassed.

A wide bed can be planted at ground level, or with a bit of soil excavated from what will be the paths, made into a flat-topped mound. The soil in the mound will warm up earlier in spring, allowing earlier planting, though the plants themselves may still need protection from frost at night.

If the bed is amended with compost or with soil brought in, fertility and drainage can be improved.

In 2012, I tried the mound method. I had few weeds and great results. The path around the bed was deep in tree leaves collected the previous fall. However, the edges of the mound tended to erode after heavy rains.

Last summer my husband and I converted it to what gardeners normally envision a raised bed to be, a contained mound.

Types of raised beds

Gardeners have been inventive at using whatever is at hand to make the walls of a raised bed: bales of straw (hay has too many seeds that will sprout), wood, rock, brick, concrete block, old stock tanks. Raised beds work for flowers as well as vegetables. Barb even has her raspberries in one to keep them from spreading.

Wood: Raised beds can be built to workbench-level ("elevated" beds) or the sides can be as low as a single 6-inch wooden board — though that won't keep the rabbits out. However,

Barb soon realized plain wooden boards would decompose and she would have to replace them sooner than she'd like.

Thirty years ago, raised beds using old railroad ties were fashionable, but it was found that wood preservative chemicals from that era are toxic and can migrate into vegetable plants.

Currently, "ground contact pressure treated" wood has an environmentally friendlier preservative but there is still controversy.

If in doubt, use cedar or redwood. Either, though more expensive, should last a lifetime.

Raised bed kits often contain posts with brackets that hold wooden boards. Another version I'm trying this year is steel plates 18 inches tall and bent 90 degrees, which fit around the outside corners of the bed and screw into place.

In another bed we built 20 years ago, using plastic dimensional lumber, the corners are held together by galvanized steel brackets on the inside. The brackets have not rusted out.

Pavers: Barb used a system she found from Lee Valley Tools that starts with a frame of pressure treated two by fours outlining the shape of the bed. She made hers 2.5 feet wide by 8 feet long. Steel brackets attach to the frame and are designed to hold pre-cast concrete pavers upright. Barb's pavers are 16 inches square. More brackets along the top edge of the pavers attach to another frame of two by fours, making the structure strong enough to sit on. The brackets

Boards can be held together by a corner brace (left) or a galvanized bracket (right).

are ordered as a kit and the gardener buys the wood and pavers locally.

Concrete block: Mark and I tried a concrete block raised bed for our vegetables last year, but we didn't stack the blocks on boards like Barb did her pavers. After this past winter's freezing and thawing, the walls undulate. Also, for the nine months of the year nothing is growing in it, the bed looks just like a pile of ugly gray concrete — right in the middle of the view from our favorite window.

Unlike concrete blocks, cinder blocks contain heavy metals from the fly ash they are made with, and that toxicity can be absorbed by vegetables. "I don't recommend using cinder blocks because they are not only ugly, but also toxic."— Shane

Stock tanks: This style is simpler, but perhaps harder to find, prep and install.

Barb uses this method and got the idea from a relative who uses rusted-out tanks in her garden.

Barb found her own stock tanks on Craig's list. We're talking about the long, narrow ones made of galvanized steel. Barb's are 2 to 2.5 feet across by 6 or 8 feet long by about 2 feet deep. Because they weren't rusted out on the bottom, she drilled lots of holes for drainage. If she were to do it again, she suggests just cutting out portions of the bottoms.

How to install a raised bed

Find a flat, sunny location within range of your hose or drip irrigation system.

Plan the bed's width so you can reach the middle comfortably and maximize the dimension of materials to be used. The shape can be square, rectangular or even L or U-shaped. Barb left enough room between beds for her wheelbarrow.

Because Barb has a weedy

infestation of skeleton-leaf bursage, she chose to cover her site with weed barrier cloth and then covered that with bark mulch between the beds. You could use layers of cardboard at the bottom of the raised bed instead of weed barrier cloth.

Under normal conditions, you would remove pre-existing vegetation as you would for any other garden, especially if you aren't building your raised bed very high — you need to allow for root growth.

Unless your building materials are temporary like straw bales, be sure to use a level to keep everything square and neat looking. Get corner posts set straight and boards horizontal.

How to fill a raised bed

Barb wanted completely different soil for her beds than what was in her yard, so she ordered a load that was a little sandier, with less clay. It's important that it is good quality, she said, and not full of weed seeds. She has grown a wide variety of vegetables in the eight years since, and she's very happy with the results.

If you are growing vegetables, you might want to mix in a lot of compost like that available through Cheyenne's compost facility. In future seasons you won't have to till, just add a couple more inches of compost, perhaps in the form of the organic mulch you use on the surface — leaves and grass clippings, etc.

For flowers, be aware that hardy native perennials do fine with less fertile soil.

Accessories

Barb has made tomato cages from concrete mesh that fit her raised beds perfectly. She can wrap them in plastic to protect the plants from frost early in the season.

Raised beds also lend themselves to the addition of trellises, cold frame covers, mini-hoop houses, hail guards and drip irrigation systems.

Barb Sahl's Raised-bed Kit from Lee Valley contained steel connectors that attached her 2 x 4s to pre-cast pavers she bought locally.

Phillippa Lack enjoys a variety of containers full of flowers on her back steps.

CHAPTER 38:
CONTAINER GARDEN

USE THE FILLER, THRILLER AND SPILLER FORMULA

When it comes to container gardening, Marti Bressler has a bit of everything: window boxes, hanging baskets that adorn even tree limbs, and concrete urns filled with flowers.

Below a large window at her historic home's carriage house is a window box. She plans to install more.

"I don't see many people using window boxes," she said. "I don't know why not."

Hidden around back is her husband Larry's vegetable garden, also planted in containers. He likes making use of what's available, including an old enamel cooking pot, a damaged trash can and plastic tote.

Marti said her sister, Judy Day, is also a fan of unusual containers, including old-fashioned laundry sinks.

"I love containers, they are easier to take care of," she said.

Types

Anything that holds dirt will work — even an old cowboy boot or a wheelbarrow. But containers need drainage holes, so drill a few if necessary. Even if you have experience watering plants in containers without drainage, keep in mind Cheyenne is subject to sudden torrential summer rainstorms. You don't want your petunias to float away or drown.

This year, I am growing my tomatoes, peppers and eggplants in large black plastic pots that were used by a nursery for growing trees and shrubs.

I was looking for saucers to protect the patio from staining. But I decided to do without — I don't want the pots sitting in excess water and besides, the winter sun bleaches out those water stains on the concrete.

If you need to protect your deck, you can use an old turkey baster to suck up excess water from the saucer. But otherwise, it is easier to place containers where draining water can seep into the ground.

Whether you use porous pots (clay, concrete, unpainted wood), or non-porous pots (plastic, metal, glazed clay, painted wood), consider aesthetics and utility.

Soil in non-porous containers won't dry out as quickly. Plastic is lighter, easier to move when it starts hailing. But, as Laramie County Master Gardener Kathy Shreve discovered, you might need bricks in the bottom to weigh them down so they won't tip in the wind.

Size is important. Kathy reminded me larger pots don't dry out as quickly. For annual flowers, you can crowd quite a few in one pot, but for vegetables, adequate root space is more important. The more root space, the more production. Tomatoes need soil that is at least 18 inches deep, said Catherine Wissner, University of Wyoming Extension horticulturist for Laramie County.

Neither plastic nor clay winters well when left outdoors. Freezing and thawing cause cracking and disintegration. Larry said he paints clear sealer on the outside of Marti's concrete containers.

On the other hand, I've had the same old oak whiskey barrel halves for nearly 30 years now, and they have never needed maintenance, though I suspect the bottoms have rotted out, so I don't move them. And I can overwinter perennials in them.

You can mold your own hypertufa container from a mixture of Portland cement, peat moss and perlite. The internet has numerous instructional resources.

Filling

Everyone warns against completely filling containers with garden dirt. Contained soil doesn't provide plants what the open garden does.

On the other hand, garden plants, especially vegetables, need a little more than a soilless (peat and vermiculite or perlite) potting mix.

For my vegetable pots, I mixed in some leaf compost, about one-third to one-half of each pot, with standard potting soil. I did it like combining fancy cake ingredients: a little compost, a little potting soil, water, stir, repeat several times. I don't have a place to use a shovel to combine piles of materials.

Unless your plants develop diseases, you shouldn't have to replace the soil next year.

Many sources recommend putting rocks or stones at the bottom to improve drainage. That is only necessary if there is a chance that the bottom of your container will be sitting in excess water — or you need the weight like Kathy did.

Fertilizing

Because so many containers are thickly planted for instant color, be sure to feed your flowers. Liquid fertilizers like compost teas or fish emulsion mixed in your watering can to the specified dilutions work well, as do time-release products such as Osmocote. Marti told me she adds cow manure from the ranch to her containers every year.

If a white crust forms on the soil surface, you've been using too much fertilizer and need to flush the salts out by over-watering your container and letting the water drain out and away — several times over a few hours.

Watering

One of Marti's chief garden pleasures is the time she spends each day watering everything with the hose, giving her a chance to deadhead and groom her plants.

But for those who can't be in the garden as often, there is the method I saw demonstrated by Stephanie Selig, who had a container garden installation business the summer I interviewed Marti. Her Fort Collins, Colorado, business, Sundrops and Starflowers, now includes landscape design installation.

For her busy clients, she sets up a drip irrigation system. From the distribution tubing she leads the ¼-inch tubing up through a drainage hole in the container before filling it and placing an emitter on the end of the tubing. Of course, to accommodate the tubing and make the pot sit level, you need some little feet to raise it up. Put a timer on your system and you might be good to go — even on vacation.

You know you are done watering your container when water seeps out the bottom. Don't let your pot sit in a saucer of water unless the water will evaporate in less than an hour or two.

Plants

When it comes to flowers, keep in mind the principles of flower arranging.

- **Filler:** Something tall like a "spike," like a dracaena, is very popular

- **Thriller:** Try a focal point of flashy flowers

- **Spiller:** Trailing petunias, ivy or vinca, work, especially for hanging pots

In the vegetable realm, look for smaller varieties. The labels might point out which are especially suited for container gardening.

Placement

A container that is on wheels or not too big and heavy can be moved to find where the plants in it get the right amount of sun and protection from the wind, without having to wait until next year to try a better location. And best of all, you can take your moveable plants inside on frosty fall nights.

Susan Carlson was quite satisfied with her experiment with straw bale gardening.

CHAPTER 39:
STRAW BALE GARDEN

SET YOUR STRAW BALE ANYWHERE, THEN INOCULATE AND PLANT IT

Does the thought of the work involved keep you from starting a vegetable garden? Does time for all that rototilling or digging in of compost never materialize? Or maybe you tried a garden in our clay soils and results were poor?

Susan Carlson, Laramie County Master Gardener, can recommend a solution: straw bale gardening. Her stepson, who lives in Minnesota, brought her the book *Straw Bale Gardens* by Minnesota native Joel Karsten, which describes his

miraculous method.

This is the second season Susan has used rectangular straw bales for vegetables and her results look good. She also included flowers.

The idea is that a straw bale is compost waiting to happen. Before the growing season begins, over a couple weeks, you add water and a little fertilizer — organic or inorganic — and it will activate an army of bacteria. The bacteria break down the straw, turning it into just what plants need. Plants can be inserted into the bale or seeds can be started in a little potting soil placed on top.

The bale is like a container or raised bed held together with baling twine. You can set it anywhere, even on a driveway. You don't prepare the ground underneath.

And, depending on how clean the straw is, you will have few weeds, or wheat or oat sprouts, that can be easily removed by hand. You'll have more sprouts if you accidently bought hay — which includes the heads of grain — instead of straw, which is just the stems. Little white mushrooms might sprout, but they melt away when the sun hits them.

Straw bales might also be the solution to vegetable plant diseases that persist in soil. Gardeners are always advised not to grow the same family of vegetables (especially the tomato-pepper family) in the same spot more than once every three years. You can start a fresh bale each year, although Susan managed to keep her bales intact for a second year.

Susan studied Karsten's book and here's what she did:

First, obviously, she found straw bales.

I checked a local farm and ranch supply store and their regular bale, about 3 feet long and 60 pounds, runs about $7 (2016). Avoid the super-compressed bales.

A bale bought in the fall from a farmer should be cheaper than in the spring, after they've had to store them all winter. In fall, you can put your bale outside to weather.

If you've had problems with mice or voles, as Susan has, lay chicken wire or hardware cloth down first. Cut a piece big enough to fold up and protect several inches of the sides of the bale.

Lay out your bale prickliest side up, and so the sides wrapped with twine are not against the ground. Susan bought five bales and formed them into a u-shape to fit within an area fenced to keep out her dogs.

Because she planned to grow beans, Susan made a trellis as well. She wedged two bales, lying end to end, between two 5-foot steel "T-post" fence posts (about $5 each) and then strung wire at about 10 and 20 inches above the bales. She can add more wire if the plants get taller. Karsten recommends 14-gauge electric fence wire (but you won't be plugging it in).

On the ground inside the u-shape of bales (or between your rows), Susan laid landscape fabric (weed barrier cloth). You could use some other material to keep light from germinating weed seeds, like a layer of thick straw, cardboard, wood, wood mulch, etc.

Next, Susan "conditioned" the bales, starting about two weeks before our last frost date, which is around May 25, though you can start a week earlier because the bales form a warm environment.

The first step here is to find cheap lawn fertilizer with at least 20% nitrogen content as Susan did the first year. Do not use one that is slow-release or that contains herbicides.

You can also use organic fertilizers, like bone or feather meal, or very well-composted manure, but you need to use six times more than the amounts given for inorganic fertilizer. The second season, Susan said, she is having good results using Happy Frog packaged organic fertilizer, but she's using much less because the bales were conditioned once already last year.

The conditioning regimen begins the first day with a half cup of inorganic fertilizer (or six times more organic) per bale sprinkled evenly all over the top and then watered in with your hose sprayer until all of it has moved into the bale and the bale is waterlogged, writes Karsten.

The next day you skip the fertilizer and water the bale again. Karsten suggests using water that's been sitting out for a while so it isn't as cold as it is straight out of the tap.

Days three through six, you alternate between fertilizer-and-water days and water-only days.

Days seven through nine, you water in a quarter cup of fertilizer per bale each day. The bales should be cooking by now and feel a little warmer on the outside.

On day 10, add a cup of 10-10-10 garden fertilizer. The numbers mean 10% nitrogen (N), 10% phosphorus (P) and 10% potassium (K).

Next, lay out your soaker hoses on top of the bales if you are going to use drip irrigation as Susan has.

On day 12, Susan transplanted one cherry tomato plant directly into the bale, wedging it in. Smaller plants are easier to plant than large ones and will soon catch up.

"Bacteria are breaking down the inside of the bale and making this nice environment," said Susan.

Mostly, Susan wanted a salad garden, and so she started everything else from seed: edible pod peas, haricot vert beans (a type of tiny French green bean), lemon cucumbers, broccoli, spinach and various lettuces.

She packed a couple of inches of sterile potting soil (not garden soil) into the tops of the bales in which to plant the seeds. The warmth of the composting straw got them off to a good start.

She added shade cloth overhead to protect the lettuces from too much sun and started cutting romaine and butterhead lettuce by mid-June.

Susan also used shade cloth on the west side fence to keep the wind from drying out the bales too quickly.

And there you have it, a vegetable garden — or a flower garden if you prefer — ready to grow. All you need to do then is to garden as you normally would: enough water, fertilizer once a month, and pull the occasional weed that might sprout, or pick off any little slugs or insects.

Maybe because of our dry western climate, Susan was able to use her bales this second year. The bales shrank a little so she patched the gaps between bales with bits of chicken wire on the sides and filled them with potting soil.

One question is what to do with the old bales. They are great compost for conventional garden beds. Susan reached into the side of one bale and showed me lovely black soil. If you don't have any conventional garden beds to add it to, someone else would be happy to take the compost off your hands.

"This isn't the prettiest thing," Susan says of her straw bale garden, "but when it starts growing, you don't even look at the bales."

Ask to see the hoop house at the Children's Village at the Cheyenne Botanic Gardens.

CHAPTER 40:
HOOP HOUSE GARDEN

GREENHOUSE-LIKE STRUCTURES EXTEND THE GROWING SEASON

Farmers and gardeners in cold regions have always looked for ways to preserve their harvest, from root cellars to pickling crocks to canning jars.

But what if it were possible to grow cold-hardy vegetables over the winter?

There are many Cheyenne gardeners extending the growing season using cheap and easily available building materials to build hoop houses, also known as high tunnels.

If you've ever thrown an old

sheet over your tomato patch on a chilly night, you'll understand how Laramie County Master Gardener Maggie McKenzie took that idea several steps further.

If you've ever dreamed of becoming food self-sufficient, you'll appreciate how Clair Schwan uses the hoop house concept to produce hundreds of pounds of produce.

You can visit the hoop house in the backyard of the Paul Smith Children's Village at the Cheyenne Botanic Gardens when it is open.

Several other season-extending tools exist, such as cold frames which are bottomless boxes with clear glass or plastic lids, and low tunnels. But

Mark Gorges's cold frame is topped by a polycarbonate skylight dome.

a hoop house is high enough to walk in, giving it that greenhouse feel, and it is typically heated with nothing more than sunlight.

Hoop house location

Because hoop houses need to capture as many solar rays as possible, one long side faces south. Both Clair and the Children's Village have shielded their north-facing lengths by locating their structures against existing windbreaks of trees or fences.

Having level ground to build on is important to the integrity and longevity of the structure, although as Clair says, "The plants don't care in the least. They still grow like crazy and provide you a bounty the likes of which you won't see in an outdoor garden."

Hoop house structure

A hoop house is typically formed by bending plastic PVC pipe:

- Tap short lengths of rebar into the ground at measured

intervals on either side of the area you wish to cover.

- Slip the end of a length of PVC pipe over the rebar on one side and slip the other end over the rebar on the opposite side.

- Then do the next set and the next and, ta-dah! —now you have something that looks like the ribs of the top of a pioneer's Conestoga wagon.

That's the basic method, but everyone does it differently.

Maggie started out bending 4 x 16-foot cattle panels for her tomato plants to climb, and then in the fall, she added half-inch PVC ribs to extend the width when she decided to enclose the space. She figures she spent about $400 for her 10 x 13 structure, half of that for the glazing, or covering.

The much larger structure at the Children's Village, now under the management of Tyler Mason, assistant education director (who has since this interview, earned his

PhD in horticulture and taken a new job), was built last summer with 2-inch PVC pipes.

Clair used chain-link fence top rail pipe, which requires simple equipment to bend each length into the same arc.

Then there are purlins, boards that run the length of the hoop house — one on each side and one along the top, at a minimum — to keep the hoops stable.

Hoop house skin

Plastic sheeting from the hardware store isn't going to stand up to Wyoming wind, much less the ultraviolet rays we have at 6,000 feet.

All three structures mentioned here use a translucent woven poly material treated for UV exposure.

Beds and covers

Inside the Children's Village hoop house, 4-foot-wide raised beds on either side of a center aisle are outlined by stacked concrete blocks. Their upward-facing holes are also filled with dirt, where Tyler expects to grow herbs. The south facing sides of the blocks are painted black to absorb more heat, warming the soil in the beds.

Maggie's tomato patch was already located on a double-wide raised bed delineated squarely with boards and help from her husband Don, an engineer by training.

Clair too, has raised beds 2 feet high, made by stacking used power poles, although he needed to cover them so they didn't leach poisonous wood preservatives.

Maggie McKenzie's hoop house uses a bent hog panel for structure.

On cold nights and cloudy winter days, the plants inside appreciate being covered by a floating row cover, a light, white, polyester fabric frequently used by commercial growers, often to protect crops from insects, but which Tyler said can add 3 to 4 degrees of warmth.

Heating

On March 1, Maggie's "Little Hoop House on the Prairie," was a toasty 70-plus degrees, while the sun shone, the outdoor temperature was 45 degrees and winds were gusting to 45 mph.

Being scientifically inclined — a biologist by training — Maggie has installed four probes recording maximum and minimum temperatures of the air and soil, inside and outside.

The hoop house's plastic skin has no insulation value to speak of. But a few simple tools can collect enough solar heat to keep the plants warm through the night.

Maggie uses dark-colored, covered, 5-gallon buckets filled with water. Tyler also uses water, storing it in a 55-gallon black drum, along with a collection of water-filled pop bottles that release a little heat when they freeze at night. Clair is retrofitting his operation with solar-warmed water that will circulate in pipes underground.

Cooling

Hoop houses can get too hot and cook plants.

"If it is 65 degrees and sunny, it can equal 90 degrees when solar rays are trapped," Tyler said.

The Children's Village hoop house has plywood doors on either end. The top half of each can be opened for cross-ventilation. The bottom halves can be opened as well on very hot days, but Tyler warned that fencing needs to be set up to keep the rabbits out.

Instead of burying the bottom edges of the plastic skin, Maggie has wrapped the lengthwise edges around PVC pipe cut to length. This way she can roll up the sides in the summer. The advantage is that the plants are aerated from a variety of wind directions, decreasing occurrence of fungal diseases. And bees and other insects can easily fly in and pollinate the fruit and vegetable blossoms.

Growing

Eliot Coleman's book, *Four-Season Harvest* explains how he manages his hoop houses in Maine, which lies in Zone 5, just like Cheyenne.

In February, the Children's Village's unheated hoop house at the Cheyenne Botanic Gardens holds perennial herbs, the remains of greens and tomato baskets waiting for spring.

In late summer he sows cold-hardy greens such as spinach, kale, chard and broccoli. By the time they are nearly mature, the weather is so cool and the day is so short, the growing nearly stops. The plants are in suspended animation, waiting to be harvested as needed. By late winter, early spring, there is room to get an early start on summer crops.

Tyler plans a secondary use for the hoop house, hardening off plants before putting them outside. The primary purpose is raising vegetables to share with Children's Village program participants.

Both Tyler and Maggie experimented with growing spinach this winter.

It was nice to see something green growing three weeks before winter's end. I asked Maggie if she had the heart to pick her hard-won green leaves.

"How can I harvest those brave little spinach plants when they've weathered such hardship and survived?" she asked.

She might have been only half-joking.

COOLING HOOP HOUSES

There are several ways to keep a hoop house from overheating.

- Open doors or vents at both ends as far as needed, as the Children's Village does.

- Use temperature-controlled vents installed at the top of the hoop house which sense when to open and close.

- Run an exhaust fan. Solar-powered fans are available.

- Roll up the sides of the hoop house as Maggie does.

Jane Dorn offers another idea. "We have found that cooling our greenhouse in summer, even with all the doors and vents open can still be a problem. We have recently added two floor vents with a tunnel dug under the greenhouse wall on opposite sides to bring in cool air at soil level in the summer. These are covered and screened the rest of the year."

"You can mix up some clay-based mud in a wheelbarrow and fling the mud on the outside of the hoop house, covering about 25%. The shading will cool the inside quite well. It will last a while and simply reapply as needed. It is ugly but free." — Shane

A native bumblebee enjoys foraging on a native purple coneflower.

CHAPTER 41:
BEE GARDEN

ATTRACT BEES AND KEEP THEM HAPPY

Bees are wildlife, though we tend to not think of them in the same category as mice, raccoons and deer. They, however, are much more beneficial for our gardens and crops.

We depend on honeybees and native bees to pollinate the flowers of the crops that produce up to a third of the value of foods in our grocery carts including almonds, avocado, watermelon, squash, apples — most fruits and many vegetables.

Even crops that are considered self-pollinating, like soybeans, will increase production if pollinated

by bees, said Catherine Wissner, University of Wyoming Extension horticulturist in Laramie County.

Both the honeybee, from Europe, and our native bees are declining in numbers for several reasons, especially habitat loss. Like other wildlife, native bees lose out every time their diverse native habitat is converted to a weed-less, flower-less lawn, or paved over, or sprayed with pesticides. What can we do to help them help us?

Catherine believes that if everyone offered blooming plants on their property, native bees could make a comeback, especially if native plants are used. They'd also improve our vegetable garden yields at the same time.

Native bees are more efficient pollinators because they will fly when it is cooler or cloudy. Honeybees want perfect weather.

Native bees are solitary and almost always friendly according to Catherine. Unlike honeybees, they don't have big colonies to defend. Bumble bees especially are slow and inoffensive. But it doesn't hurt to have an antihistamine like Benadryl in your gardening first aid kit, or a syringe of epinephrine if you already know you are allergic to stinging insects.

Getting bees to your garden

Helping bees (and butterflies and other pollinating insects) can be done by planting flowers — natives especially. For years I thought flowers were merely pretty faces to brighten my mood and the view, but now I see them as essential to the ecosystem.

In many ways, what I want in a flower garden is what the bees want as well: flowers that will bloom as early as possible and others that bloom right until first frost.

I also want as many different kinds of flowers as I can get to grow in my yard and bees appreciate the variety. I focus on perennials because they are less expensive and less time-consuming than having to start from seed or buy annuals each year. Perennials just get bigger and bigger or spread seedlings each year, offering more and more flowers.

I love the simple, old-fashioned garden plants and the native wildflowers. Turns out bees like simple flowers too. The latest, greatest double or triple-petalled kind are too difficult for bees to navigate through and they often don't produce pollen. Bees need to collect pollen and nectar to eat, inadvertently pollinating flowers as they move about.

As a lazy gardener, I grow plants close together to shade out the weeds and I don't prune back the dead stuff until late spring. The old stems help hold leaf mulch in place and interrupt the wind enough to drop a protective blanket of snow for parts of the winter.

This strategy works well, as Catherine said, because there are native bees, and other beneficial insects that nest in the overwintering stems.

Find a place to plant with an eye for shelter, water and safety for bees

Reevaluate your current garden with an eye for enticing bees. Instead of another flat of exotic annuals this spring, could you plant native perennials?

Can you remove that half-dead juniper and replace it with a flowering shrub like red-twig dogwood?

Could you expand or add a new garden bed? Is it close to your outdoor water faucet? Is it where you can enjoy looking at it? Will it be out of the way of unofficial paths and yard activities? Is it a sunny spot? Many of the most popular plants for pollinators prefer sun.

Protecting bees from insecticides at all times is absolutely necessary — even those labelled "organic" can negatively affect bees or kill them.

Certain native bees like nesting in tubular spaces. You can drill holes ranging from ¼ to 3/4-inch diameter close together in a block of wood.

Bees need water. If you use a bird bath or dish, be sure to refresh it every few days to keep mosquitoes from breeding. Catherine uses a soaker hose on a timer and has seen the bees line up along its length, drinking.

"You can partially submerge some sticks or small branches in the water. That gives bees a way to crawl down to the water's edge to get a drink without drowning." — Shane

Decide what to plant

Catherine has a rule of thumb when she visits a nursery — look for the plants buzzing with bees already.

Visiting nurseries is the easiest way to find perennials and there is a plethora of nurseries along the Front Range from here south. However, you may have a hard time finding the native plants recommended as nurseries are still learning about this gardening for pollinators movement.

The Audubon Rockies website has a Habitat Hero program section.

There, you can find a list of resources and local sources for plants. The closer to home the source of the plant, the better chance the plant will thrive in your garden.

Growing from seed is a possibility, but transplanting from the wild should be avoided unless you have the permission of the landowner and the site is about to be bulldozed anyway.

Be sure your selections are rated by the USDA Plant Hardiness Zone chart for our Zone 5 or colder, Zones 3 and 4. Get at least three of a kind to plant together to make them more noticeable to passing bees.

Look at your overall plan to see if you have a variety of bloom times, flower colors and shapes, plant heights and leaf textures. Different kinds of flowers provide the bees different kinds of nutrients in their pollen.

A pollinator garden doesn't need to be installed all at once. Half the fun is keeping a lookout for additions — who doesn't enjoy an excuse to visit a flower-filled nursery?

For a list of bee-favorite flowers, scan the Plant List in Part 9 for plants that reference Chapter 41.

Rainwater and snowmelt from the Laramie County Library parking lot waters this new garden.

CHAPTER 42: **RAIN GARDEN**

PLANT WHERE RAINFALL RUNS

Rain garden. It brings to mind splashy flowers seen from under the protection of an umbrella.

It doesn't sound like something that would be close to relevant in Cheyenne unless we have regular repeats of our soggy September 2013 weather. Those 6.95 inches (second wettest month on record) wouldn't be considered much in Ketchikan, Alaska, (153 inches annually) or even New York City (49 inches). But it is here, where the annual average is 15.90 inches.

Wouldn't it be nice if we could sock away moisture, even from brief cloudbursts? Wouldn't it be nice if it

didn't just run down the street and back up the storm sewer? Or run into your basement?

The problem

Nancy Loomis, Laramie County Master Gardener, who co-owns Antiques Central with her sister, Pam Loomis, was having problems with storm water getting into the basement of the store at 2311 Reed Ave. Nancy's problem is that rainstorms and snowmelt cause her street to flood and water backs up into a loading ramp sloping below grade level, leading into the basement. Some of that water was coming from the roof of her building.

A few years ago, she read a magazine article describing rain gardens. She learned they are a way to capture snowmelt and rainstorm runoff from impermeable surfaces, like roofs and pavement. These gardens hold the water temporarily so it can percolate into the ground. This recharges the groundwater, even more effectively than your basic lawn.

The city of Cheyenne has done something similar, creating basins for runoff, sometimes known as bioswales if they are designed to filter silt and pollutants. The one between Warren and Central avenues at Pershing Boulevard, informally called Pando's Pond, is the most noticeable. But no one is calling it a rain garden.

Rain garden definition

A rain garden is small, less than 300 square feet. It takes advantage of the additional moisture it receives to grow a variety of blooming plants, usually without the aid of additional irrigation — even here.

Have you ever noticed, while driving two-lane highways in Wyoming, how much greener the grass is near the shoulders of the road compared to as little as 10 or 15 feet farther out? Runoff from the pavement provides that much more moisture.

Digging

So, Nancy dug her first rain garden about 10 feet out from the building. Its size is based on a calculation of the size of the section of roof at one downspout, the infiltration rate of the soil and the amount of water in an average Cheyenne rainstorm. To it, she later connected a second garden.

Not only did she need to dig a 10-inch deep basin, but she had a mound of dirt to remove also. She admits it was a little crazy to be doing it by hand, hauling 5-gallon buckets away to the city compost facility, but she found some interesting historical objects and a nice block of granite. She learned much about her dirt she wouldn't have if someone else had done it with heavy equipment.

Plants

Plants for the rain garden need to be chosen from three categories, beginning with those that would be planted on the flat bottom that could have their "feet" wet for up to three days (longer would breed mosquitoes), though ideally it would only be for 24 hours. Even during the worst of the September storms, Nancy's rain gardens drained in three to four hours.

For the lowest level, Nancy chose Saskatoon serviceberry, "Blue Creek" and "Dappled" willows, currant, Joe-Pye weed, Siberian iris, hardy pampas grass, spiderwort and Japanese iris.

On the lower sides of the basins are plants that enjoy extra moisture but not a soaking: roses, butterfly bush, daylilies, tall garden phlox, daisy, columbine, cranesbill, summer onion, Jupiter's beard, bee balm, Maltese cross, candy tuft, hardy hibiscus and asters.

On the uppermost sides, and the top of the berm, are the plants that prefer more xeric conditions: Russian sage, Oriental poppy, agastache, salvia, cat mint, and aster. She chose cultivars (cultivated varieties) that suit our USDA Plant Hardiness Zone 5 cold hardiness, often selecting for colder Zones 3 or 4.

Watering

Nancy did irrigate her new plantings, but by the second season, they were on their own. Some plants are self-seeding or self-generating, growing into areas where the moisture level suits them.

Across the front of the building another garden gets watered by shovel — snow shovel, that is. The extra moisture from clearing the sidewalk by dumping the snow onto the garden means it doesn't need irrigation, even as late as mid-August, when I visited.

Help

Nancy was able to get a grant through the Wyoming Department of Environmental Quality to make this a demonstration rain garden. She named it the Historic Sunrise Rain Gardens Project because the building originally housed the Sunrise Creamery.

While DEQ grants are available for non-point source pollution projects (roofs and roads are dirty and rain gardens can provide filtering to clean up the water before it hits the aquifer), those grants are designed primarily for bigger projects than what the typical homeowner needs.

The Laramie County Conservation District can help you plan your rain garden: figuring best location, ratio of roof to depth and size of the depression, cost of excavation, need for gravel filter layer, location of overflow outlet, etc.

In the early 1990s, I discovered county officials were interested in what it took to move flood waters out of the county as fast as possible, even if it meant channelizing our two local creeks within the city. The idea of capturing the moisture has slowly taken over. Vegetation added to our municipal basins could add an additional layer of filtration. Wouldn't it be fun if what currently looks like giant soccer fields on East Lincolnway turned into gardens, even bird habitat?

Nancy said planning was the most time-consuming aspect of the project. The actual digging and planting only took a couple of weekends.

Flooding from the street is still a problem at her corner. A neighboring business recently paved its gravel parking lot, creating more runoff. Perhaps when the day comes when flooding also affects neighboring businesses, the owners can come over to find out what Nancy's rain gardens are all about: the beauty of utility.

NANCY'S LATEST RAIN GARDEN

Nancy Loomis, Laramie County Master Gardener, is also the project leader for Community Wildlife Habitat Project, West Edge District. Turning Laramie County Library's detention pond adjacent to the parking lot into the Laramie County Library Water-wise and Pollinator Bio-retention System is her latest effort. Planting started in 2019.

This large rain garden, or bioswale, collects runoff from a place like a parking lot and filters it through a planted depression. In partnership with the Laramie County Conservation District, Nancy and volunteers planted the swale with Laramie County and Great Plains native plants that will benefit pollinators and other species and that will survive on natural precipitation once established.

Nancy's Wish List of Native Plants for the Library's Bio Swale

Note to readers: This list is not correlated with the Part 9 Plant List. Many are difficult to find in the local nursery trade.

Shrubs, Semi-woody Shrubs, Trees

Antelope Bitterbrush
Apache Plume
Bluestem Willow
Fernbush
Fourwing Saltbush
Fringed Sagewort
Golden Currant
Green Rabbitbrush
Leadplant
Littleleaf Mockorange

Mormon Tea
Mountain Big Sagebrush
Mountainspray
Oregon Grape
Pussy Willow
Red-osier Dogwood
Rocky Mountain Maple
Rubber Rabbitbrush
Saskatoon Serviceberry
Skunkbush Sumac

True Mountain Mahogany
Wax Currant
Western Sandcherry
Western Sandcherry,
   var. Pawnee Buttes
Western Snowberry
Winterfat
Woods Rose

Grasses

Big Bluestem Grass

Blue Grama Grass

Shining Muttongrass

Forbs

Blue Vervain
Bridge's Penstemon
Butterfly Weed
Cardinal Flower
Firecracker Penstemon
Fireweed
Fragrant Evening
   Primrose
Garret's Firechalice
Harebell
Horsemint
James Buckwheat

Kinnikinnik
Lanceleaf Sedum
Lavender Hyssop
Mat Penstemon
Marsh Milkweed
Maximilian Sunflower
Meadow Blazing Star
New England Aster
Palmer Penstemon
Pasque Flower
Pineleaf Penstemon
Plains Pussytoes
Prairie Winecups

Rocky Mountain
   Penstemon
Scarlet Bugler Penstemon
Scarlet Globe Mallow
Shell-leaf Penstemon
Spotted Joe-pye Weed
Stiff Goldenrod
Suphur Flower
Wasatch Penstemon
Western Iris
Western Spiderwort
Western Yarrow

Lila and Garry Howell built this water garden and have enjoyed it for a number of years.

CHAPTER 43:
WATER GARDEN

WATER GARDENS PAINT PRETTY PICTURES

A water garden sounds too exotic to be true for Cheyenne. But I saw one last summer full of water lilies and swimming koi.

Laramie County Master Gardener Lila Howell and her husband, Garry, had had one for 15 years at the time of this interview. It's the centerpiece of a little, tree-filled glade next to their house, which is just a few miles beyond the eastern edge of Cheyenne.

Lila likes a challenge. But a water garden is only as challenging as you make it.

Location

Like any garden, you'll want to have it where you can enjoy it, close to the house, even visible through a window. The farther any garden is from your door, the more likely it is to be neglected.

A water garden is essentially a pool. It requires access to a water source as well as electricity for a pumping and filtration system.

A semi-shady place like Lila's is nice — it cuts down on evaporation, meaning she only tops off the pond every 10 days or so during summer heat. But with shade comes tree leaves falling in the water and they must be removed, Lila said.

Also, Lila pointed out, don't put the pond in the path of natural drainage, where rain and snow melt flow, because unwanted stuff will wash in.

Preparation

The pool for the Howell water garden is an irregular shape, about 13 by 18 feet, and a depth of 4 feet. If you don't plan to have fish, it could be much shallower.

Because of the contours of their property, the Howells brought in dirt, and arranged it to leave the depression for the pond.

Whether you arrange dirt by shovel or backhoe, Garry recommends using a plate compactor to compact the dirt. And be sure there are no sharp objects sticking up anywhere.

To be sure nothing sharp punctures your pond liner, use carpet pad under it. Old padding is fine. Some people use sand.

Alternatives

Any container that can hold water can become a water garden, perhaps an old whiskey barrel that's been waterproofed. With just the addition of an aerator and a water lily, you can dress up your deck.

Pond liner

It's essential to seal the bottom and sides of the pond. Replacing water that seeps out would be expensive, especially if the pond is near your house and the seepage finds your basement. Concrete is not desirable because it cracks as it ages.

Lila said sometimes roofing material is used because it is waterproof, but she said it kills fish. She likes her koi. They are fun to watch and they eat any mosquito larvae.

She said she and Garry were able to order a custom-sized pond liner online from Pondliner.com, and 15 years later, it's still working. The company also carries standard sizes. One that is 15 x 15 feet square runs about $150 today. The website, and others like it, carries just about everything you'll need for a water garden or fishpond, including the fish.

Lila and Garry have edged their pond with flagstones, which protect the edge of the liner. Also, by having the flat stones jut out a bit over the water, animals that might want to eat the koi are kept out.

The ledge doesn't perturb the Howell's dog, however, as it likes to soak in the pond on hot days. So, they have built an underwater ledge to help it climb back out.

Dirt

There's no access to dirt in the bottom of Howell's lined pond. Instead, water plants grow in special perforated baskets full of our regular old heavy clay garden soil. Regular potting soil has a lot of light-weight materials that will float away.

Lila adds a layer of pea gravel to the top of each basket to keep the dirt in and the fish from nosing the dirt out.

Plants

The first couple years, Lila brought the water lilies in each winter. But it was too much work.

Since she had chosen to grow hardy, rather than tropical, water lilies, she finally tried letting them over-winter in the pond and they have been fine. Just as the fish can stay low enough to avoid ice forming on the surface, the water lilies' main growing points are protected too.

Lila also has frog bit, with tiny leaves and flowers, and Louisiana iris. But she didn't want cattails because their roots would puncture the liner.

Water hyacinth is invasive in lakes and streams in other parts of the country and it is illegal to grow it in those places, but not Wyoming. However, Lila found her water garden was too cold for it to thrive, so she quit buying annual replacements.

Maintenance

In some ways, a water garden with fish is a cross between a swimming pool and an aquarium, except chlorine is bad for plants and fish.

Housed in the quaint miniature cottage Garry built at the side of their water garden is the filtration system. Water from the pond is pumped with a 1.5 horsepower pump past a filter and a UV light to kill microorganisms. In the winter, only the pump is running, bubbling the water to keep the koi supplied with oxygen.

Every winter, there are a couple weeks when Lila plugs in the tank heater, the same thing ranchers use to keep livestock water tanks open. It helps the pump keep an opening in the ice for the fish.

Lila recommends vacuuming up the muck in the pond in the spring and keeping up with it during the growing season, maybe twice a month during the summer.

Skimming fallen leaves needs to be done, otherwise when they decompose, they steal oxygen from the fish.

Algae blooms seem to run in cycles, starting with one in the spring. Garry can put on his waders and get in and clean things up, including dead plant parts that sink to the bottom.

"Once you put fish in a pond, you will get gigantic algae blooms. We found out about these copper anodes (see Resources, The Pond Guy) that are placed in the water line. You fine-tune it so the copper doesn't kill the fish, but does prevent algae. With our many ponds at the Cheyenne Botanic Gardens, this was a major labor saver!" — Shane

Lila has found the more plants she has growing in the water garden, and the more of the water surface they cover, the less of an algae problem she has because the plants take up the excess nitrogen the algae needs.

You must also be careful about yard maintenance adjacent to your water garden, Lila said. Fertilizer and weed killer will kill your plants and fish.

How the garden grows

Depending on the weather, the water lilies begin to sprout in April and begin blooming mid-May and on into October. The blooms come in dark pink, light pink, white and yellow. Each flower blooms for three to four days, closing at night.

At the time of my visit last August, the day after a hailstorm, the big water lily leaves looked a bit tattered, as well as the flowers that had been blooming. But Lila said not to worry, the leaves quickly regenerate and the tattered ones sink away, leaving her and Garry once again with their very own Monet water lily painting.

Several varieties of water lilies are hardy enough for Lila Howell's water garden.

Wendy Douglass has experimented with several types of gardens made with rocks.

CHAPTER 44: **ROCK GARDEN**

TAKE INSPIRATION FROM
MOUNTAINS AND PLAINS

Rock gardens became popular in the 1800s when tourists started visiting the Alps.

Travelers were enthralled by the tough but colorful plants growing on the rocky slopes and brought home alpine plant souvenirs.

It took a few decades to figure out alpine plants need gritty soil, rocks and a cool climate to grow successfully. True alpine plants don't need compost or fertilizer.

Today's rock gardens aren't limited to cushions of small plants like the ones we see in our nearby mountains. There are plenty of kinds of naturally rocky places to emulate.

Laramie County Master Gardener Wendy Douglass takes her cues from the nearby mountains and the prairie surrounding her rural Laramie County home.

The following is a tour of different rock garden styles and options seen through the lens of Wendy's garden.

Mountain

In her backyard, Wendy has a conventional rock garden, emulating a group of rocks on a mountain side. On one side of it is a small waterfall that flows via recirculating water pump. On the other side, rocks have been arranged informally, leaving pockets to fill with soil and plants.

But because her yard doesn't get as much water as the mountains,

Wendy has arranged drip irrigation soaker hose throughout.

Another secret is that the base of the natural-looking pile of rocks started out as a pile of concrete blocks. No sense wasting purchased landscape rocks where they can't be seen.

Patio

Normally, when laying a flagstone patio, one tries to get the stones to fit as closely as possible. But not if you are planning to plant it. Tough little plants were blooming in Wendy's patio when I visited in June. They enjoy the sandy soil in the cracks. When it rains, the water pours off the flagstones and into the cracks, giving the plants more moisture than they would get in an ordinary garden setting.

Prairie-style

At the front of Wendy's house is a dooryard, or more pretentiously, a courtyard, protected on the west side by the garage and on the north side by a low wall. Much of it is planted as a prairie rock garden.

The topsoil Wendy brought in has been eroded by the wind over the last dozen years, leaving a gravelly surface like the real prairie. In fact, among serious rock gardeners, this might begin to qualify as a "scree garden" — emulating those mounds of gravel below the rock faces in the mountains.

Wendy has placed a few rocks among the plants, just as they might show up on the prairie — in fact, many come from elsewhere on the property.

However, this is a garden and so it is a souped-up version of the prairie — more flowers and the grasses tend to be ornamental. Plus, many prairie plants are much taller than the diminutive alpine plants of the traditional rock garden.

And it harbors another secret — an artificial boulder. Wendy and her husband experimented with a technique taught by Artificial Rocks, an Australian company that teaches how to start with a pile of rubble covered with a concrete mix and then artfully finished with colored mortar dabbed on by brush.

Trough

Similar to fake boulder-building, you can make hypertufa (lighter than concrete) troughs to display a particular collection of small rock garden plants. Multiple internet sites have directions.

Zen

Rock gardening took off in Europe and America in the 1920s and, based on the number of rocks installed by landscapers in local front yards, it continues to inspire people today. However, the Chinese and Japanese beat us to it by a thousand years at least.

Those gardens are more about emphasizing unusual rocks, not so much about plants. Wendy has what she calls her Zen garden, a tiny area protected by the house. The plants there can be pruned and shaped by Wendy, rather than the wind and the deer. Small rocks form a swirl on the ground. Sand can be raked in patterns as an act of meditation.

A word about collecting rocks and plants

Do not take home rocks you find out in the country without permission from the private landowners or permits from the public land managers.

It is illegal to remove anything from a national park — rock, plant or animal, dead or alive. Period. Wyoming's state parks also do not allow the removal of rock.

Our closest forest, Medicine Bow – Routt National Forest, no longer makes permits available for removing landscape rock for home use.

The Bureau of Land Management's Rawlins Field Office, which manages BLM lands in southeast Wyoming, was allowing rock collecting for personal use with stipulations. Contact them for the latest information.

Check local landscapers and rock companies to find out where they obtained their rocks, especially moss rock — the kind that has moss and lichens growing on it. It should have been bought from private landowners or bought via permit from public land offices. Quarried stone is less likely to have a shady past.

As for collecting plants, cross public lands off your list. Consider private lands only with landowner permission. But usually, the domesticated relatives found at local nurseries transplant better than wild plants. Check the North American Rock Garden Society website for specialty catalogs for rock garden plants.

My favorite rock gardens are tended by Mother Nature, up on the Snowy Range, especially along the trail that begins at Lewis Lake. The plants aren't labelled, but at the Forest Service visitor center above Centennial you might find a copy of a book published by the University of Wyoming Extension, *Plants with Altitude*. It identifies high-elevation plants that adapt well to gardens and that can often be found at local nurseries.

The Snowy Range in southeastern Wyoming has many examples of natural rock gardens.

The Cheyenne Botanic Garden's Crevice Garden features hardy plants from around the world.

PUBLIC ROCK GARDENS

There are several public rock gardens nearby from which to draw inspiration.

One is the Rock Alpine Garden at the Denver Botanic Gardens. Designed by Colorado landscape architect Herb Schaal (who also designed the Children's Village at the Cheyenne Botanic Gardens) and established in 1980, it is anchored by real boulders and every pocket is stuffed with plants from rocky habitats around the world.

The newest form of rock gardening is here too, crevice gardening, installed by Mike Kintgen. You know how freezing and thawing will cause rock to crack along parallel faults? These cracks, or crevices, can be simulated by laying flattish rocks on edge, stacked against each other. Gritty soil placed in the cracks is perfect for rock plants. Their roots are protected while they spread mats of colorful flowers.

Closer to home is the Gardens on Spring Creek in Fort Collins, Colorado. Arrangements of locally quarried rock display a colorful assortment of heat-tolerant perennials.

Here at home, at the entrance to the Cheyenne Botanic Gardens conservatory, is a crevice garden installed by Kenton Seth, owner of Paintbrush Gardens in Fruita, Colorado, with the help of Jacob Mares, former CBG horticulturist. Jacob said after three years with irrigation to get plants established, it was ready to exist on snow and rain only.

"Kenton Seth is probably the top crevice garden designer in the U.S. He is also famous in Europe and Australia. He is coming out with a book on the subject in 2022." — Shane

The Habitat Hero Demonstration Garden at the Cheyenne Botanic Gardens has mostly native plants.

CHAPTER 45:
NATIVE PLANT GARDEN

SUPPORT NATIVE WILDLIFE, SAVE WATER, PROVIDE BEAUTY

What we learned at the February 2020 Cheyenne Habitat Hero workshop is that there are three alternatives to the standard turf and foundation junipers for home and business landscaping.

Water-wise plantings

Western cities like Cheyenne and Fort Collins, Colorado, are encouraging businesses and homeowners to install landscaping that takes less water than bluegrass lawns so that there will be enough water for their growing populations.

Many Wyoming native plants — grasses, shrubs, trees and flowers — fit this definition, as well as many plants from desert lands in the U.S. and other parts of the world. Plant Select features these kinds of plants for xeric gardens, said Panayoti Kelaidis. He is one of the founders of Plant Select, senior curator at the Denver Botanic Gardens and was the workshop's keynote speaker. The plants can be found at independent Colorado nurseries and by mail order from High Country Gardens.

Pollinator-friendly/wild-life-friendly gardens

The drastic decline in native bees and butterflies has been in the news for years now. Choosing to grow flowering plants is a happy way to do something for the environment.

Native plants

However, not all flowering plants appeal to our native bees and butterflies. Douglas Tallamy, author of the bestseller, *Bringing Nature Home*, points out that native bees and butterflies are adapted to the plants native to their own area. Native insects need native plants so that they can become food for native birds.

There are different levels of native. If you are raising honeybees (natives of Europe), anything producing pollen will do, if it hasn't been improved by horticulturists too much — double and triple-petal cultivars are often sterile and have no pollen.

Plants native to distant parts of North America will not do much for most Wyoming native bees and butterflies and might require too much water for water-wise gardens.

Plants native to the western Great Plains — if they haven't been domesticated too much, will provide what our native critters crave. Skip the ones that naturally grow in wet areas unless you have a natural wet area.

Finding the right species (see Part 9's Plant List for plants from Chapter 45) is still difficult. Fort Collins Nursery has the closest large selection.

Maintaining native prairie

If you've got it, flaunt it. Laramie County Master Gardener Wanda Manley wants you to appreciate our native prairie — and treat it right if you are lucky enough to own a piece of it.

Don't treat the prairie like a lawn. Frequent mowing creates more of a fire danger. Mowing any time March through July kills ground-nesting birds. When you do mow, keep it high. Mowing too low deprives grass roots of shade and eventually thins the number of plants.

Keep an eye out for invasive plants and consider renovating your prairie. Consult with the Laramie County Conservation District.

Don't graze animals when the grass is actively growing. It's cheaper to feed hay than to repair the damage.

Locate and design your native garden

Laramie County Extension horticulturist Catherine Wissner can give you a three-hour lecture on how to select a site for a new garden. If you are proposing a new vegetable or ornamental flower garden, you look at sun, slope, wind, soil, proximity to water source and kitchen.

However, if you are replacing water-hogging turf with natives, you have more options. There are native plants that like sun (like vegetables), others that prefer part sun and a few that need shade. There are some that like sandy soil and others that are fine with clay. Some like rocky soil.

And for pollinators, you want to

strive to have something in bloom from late March to early October.

Figuring out which plants go where takes a little research. The Cheyenne Board of Public Utilities hopes to eventually have a plant finder database to help you match plants with your conditions.

Irrigation

You must water new plants the first year — even xeric species — to get them established. It's possible to pick plants that need little supplemental water after that — and maybe none.

But any irrigation that uses 50% less than what bluegrass turf requires is applauded by BOPU. Note: If you have trees you value, make sure they get enough water (Chapter 59).

You might still have one bed of traditional flowers requiring frequent watering and other areas that are more xeric. If you don't want to drag hoses around all summer, you can set up sprinkler systems and/or drip irrigation for differentiated zones.

Katie Collins, Fort Collins Water-Wise Landscape program manager, who spoke about and demonstrated the technicalities, has information at the City of Fort Collins website.

Prepare for planting

In spring, your best option for removing turf is with a shovel as soon as the most recent snow melts and the soil dries out a bit.

If you have really nice turf, you might be able to get someone to use a machine to strip it off and use it to repair damaged turf

elsewhere — which is what we did for the BOPU Habitat Hero demonstration garden.

Rototilling is not an option — it leaves a lot of grass that will re-sprout. But a shovelful of turf can be broken up, the roots shaken out and composted elsewhere and the soil replaced.

If you have time, you can suffocate turf with 12 layers of newspaper or some cardboard over a few months (usually winter), explained Laramie County Master Gardener Maggie McKenzie. Herbicides are a terrible last resort.

If you are building a vegetable garden, you'll want to amend the soil with lots of composted organic material, but that isn't necessary for native plants if you match them to your soil type.

Perennials from seed

Laramie County Master Gardener Michelle Bohanan supervised the winter sowing hands-on activity for all 105 workshop participants (Chapter 6). If it's too late for that technique for you this year, you can try direct sowing. Some catalogs specialize in prairie flowers, like Prairie Moon Nursery.

Picking and planting

Laramie County Master Gardener Kathy Shreve gave advice on finding healthy plants at a nursery. Be sure they are healthy and not rootbound or misshapen — especially trees and shrubs.

Plant so that the transition between stem and root is at surface level — not below it or above it. Loosen the roots — gently knock off some of the potting soil. For tree planting information, see Chapter 55.

Kathy reminded us that all plants, no matter how well-adapted, need to be watered for months when first planted. Not so much that they drown, but don't let them wilt.

Enjoy your garden often — it's also an easy way to see if problems are developing.

Become a Habitat Hero

The goal is to be recognized as a Habitat Hero. Take pictures of your yard transformation during the growing season. Visit the Audubon Rockies website for information on applying as well as more on water-wise planting for birds and other wildlife.

Popular Southeast Wyoming Native Plants

It is nearly impossible to find "straight species" at nurseries — you'll find horticulturally improved varieties instead. If the petals haven't been doubled or the leaf color changed from solid green, they will probably work.

Look in the shrubs and the plants native to North America categories of the Plant List in Part 9. Plants marked with a "w" are native to Wyoming.

HABITAT HERO GARDEN

My eyes were bigger than my garden in the spring of 2018. I blame all those luscious Botanical Interests seed packet illustrations.

March 1, a little later than usual for winter sowing (Chapter 6), I planted 25 cut-open milk jugs with perennial seeds and set them outside.

The seeds included species from these genera.

Columbine, *Aquilegia*

Milkweed, *Asclepias*

Tickseed, *Coreopsis*

Purple Coneflower, *Echinacea*

Blanket Flower, *Gaillardia*

Bee Balm, *Monarda*

Beardtongue, *Penstemon*

Black-eyed Susan, *Rudbeckia*

There were sprouts in every gallon jug by the end of April. The *Rudbeckia* seedlings formed a carpet.

I planned to have the front yard ready to plant, but between wet weather and various commitments, that didn't happen.

Then the Cheyenne Habitat Hero Committee got a query from the Cheyenne Botanic Gardens. Would we be interested in having a Habitat Hero demonstration garden site between the rose garden and the parking lot? I soon realized my winter sowing overflow would be perfect there.

On the other hand, the Cheyenne Habitat Hero Committee spent months over the winter planning a Habitat Hero demonstration garden with the Cheyenne Board of Public Utilities at their office, 2416 Snyder Ave. It shows how to save city residents and business owners money and water by planting a flower garden in place of a lawn. I wrote two successful grant proposals to National Audubon that funded nearly half of the $1,200 to buy plants, plus another for $3,500 for an interpretive sign.

The BOPU garden area was measured and plans were drawn digitally by Kathy Shreve, proprietor of Star Cake Plants. She chose an assortment of drought-tolerant species that over time will grow into a solid mass of colorful mounds of flowers attracting birds, bees and butterflies. An order was placed for plants in 4.5 and 2.5-inch containers, plus a few shrubs.

The turf was removed mechanically. Volunteers broke up the hard clay with shovels and mixed in compost. A flagstone garden path was installed as well as an irrigation system that snapped into existing lawn sprinkler heads. About 50 people showed up June 2 and planted 428 plants in two and a half hours — and watered them all in by hand and mulched them with wood chips.

At the CBG site however, rather than decide how many plants were needed to fill the space, Kathy helped me figure out how to use the 900 seedlings I started and any donations of other native-type plants. At least there was no lawn to remove and the soil is reasonable.

At home, my winter-sown seedlings go directly into the garden, but water wasn't immediately available at the CBG site, so the seedlings waited in the CBG greenhouse under the care of horticulturist Isaiah Smith and volunteers.

Seedlings can live indefinitely crowded together. The above-ground parts don't grow much bigger, but the roots get longer and longer and are harder and harder to tease apart so I started "up-potting." I claimed all the empty plastic containers from the BOPU planting and more from the CBG and bought six bags of potting soil, enough to fill 33 flats.

After 10 days the first 200 Rudbeckia Sandra Cox and I transplanted had grown 50 times larger than the ones that were still fighting it out in the four remaining milk jugs. I'd forgotten how my winter-sowing instructor, Laramie County Master Gardener Michelle Bohanan, had carefully counted out 16 or 25 seeds for each jug rather than spill an unknown number. Later, in the Botanical Interest seed catalog, where it states how many seeds are in each packet, it said the Rudbeckia packet has over 2,000 for only $1.69. Maybe it was a typo. Maybe not.

If all goes well with the CBG Habitat Hero project, by late summer we could see 450 Rudbeckia plants flowering brown and gold in time for the University of Wyoming football season.

Note: The rabbits ate the CBG seedlings the first summer, 2018 (Chapter 14). In spring of 2019 we fenced the garden, and many plants made a comeback, and more were added. Plants continue to fill in at both gardens by spreading and by self-seeding.

For the BOPU Habitat Hero Demonstration Garden plant list, see the Plant List in Part 9. Look for plants for Chapter 45B.

The BOPU Habitat Hero Demonstration Garden (late summer detail) is colorful all season long.

In August, the 'Blue Chip Jr.' butterfly bushes star in the Board of Public Utilities Habitat Hero demonstration garden.

By September, the Missouri evening primrose is fading, the blue avena grass has matured, and other plants are going to seed.

PART 6

LANDSCAPE

Bryan Gorges (right, 1990) was ready to start the improvements in his backyard (2015).

Jan. 3. 1990

CHAPTER 46:
LANDSCAPING

December is not a month for digging a new garden bed — even if there is no snow — Cheyenne's clay soils are frozen solid.

However, if you pay someone $3,000 to dig a 7-foot-deep trench to fix an ailing sewer pipe, you could end up with a 4-by-10-foot mound of freshly tilled earth. The neighbors stopping by with Christmas treats all wanted to know who we buried in our front yard.

The juxtaposition of the new sewer cleanouts and our rain gutter downspouts now presented obstacles for me as well as our mail and newspaper carriers, which got me to thinking about getting professional advice.

When a landscape architect is needed

When is it time to call a landscape architect? I asked David Ohde, of Ohde & Associates, who is licensed to practice in Wyoming and has been in business in Cheyenne since 1984.

David said when you should call a landscape architect is for serious issues like drainage, steep slopes, erosion, stabilization and meeting regulations like Cheyenne's Unified Development Code.

"We design outside spaces, not just plant trees and shrubs," David said.

Landscape architects deal with irrigation, grading, retaining walls, patios, outdoor kitchens and plant materials, however most of David's own business is commercial and institutional, rather than residential.

There is a limit to what licensed landscape architects in Wyoming can do. For instance, they can only design retaining walls up to 3 feet high without consulting a structural engineer.

David knows when to call the experts for other situations as well. He said you can hire a landscape architect to do a verbal consultation at an hourly rate. You can also go further and contract for a design that specifies dimensions, plant species and other materials, complete with sketches and cost estimates.

You, the client, own the plans and can do the installation yourself or hire a contractor. You can hire the landscape architect to oversee the progress of the installation to make sure plans are being followed.

Creative planning

Perhaps the client wants to screen a view — or frame a view. David can lay out the options — plant, trellis or wall — that are appropriate for the spot, based on whether it is in shade, sun or wind. If it's a planting, does the client prefer something that grows slowly and needs little maintenance, or do they like yard work?

Besides the nuts and bolts, landscape architects are creative. They interview their clients to find out what ideas they have already, how they might like to use their property, what their budget is, how much maintenance they want to do. They consider the architecture of the house and solve problems. Then they roll that all together into something functional and aesthetically pleasing.

It is important to recognize whether a landscape architect has a trademark style, and if it matches your style. A minimalist designer fond of Asian aesthetics is going to be hard-pressed to make a would-be English-style cottage gardener happy.

Hire local

Be sure a landscape architect you hire is familiar with Cheyenne's climate. Wyoming licensure is required for out-of-state landscape architects, but it is not necessary for working on single family residences, however an exemption is required.

If this sounds pricey for the average homeowner, you are right. It is no wonder over half of the licensed landscape architects in Wyoming are in Jackson, in the county with the highest average income levels in the state. However, without professional advice, David points out that landscaping mistakes can be expensive, for instance, a patio installed without regard to drainage might cause flood damage.

The cost of hiring a landscape architect should be looked at, David said, as "deriving benefit from professional service that has long-lasting benefits for the spaces we live with for years."

Garden designers

If you don't have a tricky landscape situation and you can't afford Monet fine art-type prices and you'd still like some creative ideas, look for a garden designer.

Garden designers are not licensed in Wyoming. They range from the self-taught to the well-educated.

Sometimes they are independent and you can see a gallery of their work at their website. However, they often work for a nursery or a landscape contractor.

Years ago, a local nursery sent out an employee to our house who measured our yard and drew up a plan for us at no cost. We bought the recommended trees and shrubs at that nursery.

For my current dilemma, a friend recommended Tyler Moore of Capital City Landscaping. He and his dad, Dan Moore, started the business in 2004. Tyler and his wife, Alicia, are now in charge of "creating your new piece of paradise."

Tyler and his crew, like most landscape companies in town, can tackle just about anything, including the blank slate left by new construction. Tyler was in construction and carpentry earlier in his career and he likes building decks and pergolas (gazebos). He takes classes in the winter, learning about the latest trends in landscaping.

Tyler is also creative and pointed out that I could solve part of my obstacle problem if the downspout extensions were changed out for underground pipes that lead to a pop-up drain far from the house's foundation.

What do his clients want? Often, low maintenance yards. But not always.

One eccentric, long-time client had Tyler build multiple terraces with garden beds he filled with his plant collections. Later he added a faux mine shaft to feature an old ore car he found, and he had a windmill plumbed to provide water to wildlife, whether it was windy or not. I was lucky enough to visit that wonderful garden, and gardener, a few years ago.

Just as we don't have to consult an architect or interior designer before remodeling the bathroom, we don't have to consult a landscape architect or garden designer before planting a bush. However, if you want new ideas, a new perspective (and to stay out of trouble on drainage and other serious issues), ask an expert.

Then the success of a project requires an expert who can imagine what the client doesn't know about his profession and who makes the effort to explain things. And it takes a client who is open to ideas and bothers to check in frequently while the work is underway, avoiding expensive miscommunication. Over the years, I've learned the success of building and remodeling projects requires good communication.

Landscaping is the same.

Plan your garden for interesting views from your windows during the non-growing season.

CHAPTER 47:
WINTER INTEREST

PLAN FOR TEXTURE AND COLOR IN THE OFF SEASON

"Winter interest" is a term you can Google. You'll get sites wanting to sell you plants that flower in winter — in Zone 10, in Florida. Or maybe you'll find Boise, Idaho, garden writer Evelyn Hadden's viewpoint that winter interest is anything that pokes up through the snow.

Cheyenne isn't the tropics or the snow-covered north. Though we sometimes have seven months between the first hard frost of fall and the last in spring, we can be snow-free much of the time.

Winter interest is about the view from your window, rather than the summer experience of being in the garden. It's about enjoying more subtle textures, such as different kinds of bark; and shapes. It's about the sculptural qualities of branches. It's about color, of which there is more than you might think.

Although our house was already 25 years old when we moved in, the winter view of the backyard was bleak: a flat lawn, clothesline poles, two big tree trunks, and all walled in by pink concrete block. Sending the kids out to play reminded me of sending them into a prison yard. It's improved now with various plantings, but maybe it could be more interesting.

In early December 2014, on what he calls a 50-50 day, 50 degree temperature and 50 mph wind, Shane Smith, Cheyenne Botanic Gardens director then, now retired, and I discussed winter interest and took a tour of the gardens looking for it.

Conifers

The backbone of any Cheyenne garden is the evergreens, providing a backdrop and wind protection. At the entrance to the gardens' greenhouse, a thick blue spruce hedge about 8 feet high blocks the view of the parking lot. (Note: When the conservatory was built, the landscape was reoriented and part of the hedge and other plantings were lost or moved.)

It started as a row of young, normal spruce trees planted 3 to 4 feet apart, but it's pruned every year, forming an impenetrable wall. It's important, Shane pointed out, that the hedge taper, becoming narrower towards the top. Otherwise, the lower branches are shaded, don't get enough sun and die off.

Besides the typical Christmas-tree shapes, we saw a weeping variety of spruce, developed from trees that are naturally prostrate but can be trained to reach a certain height before cascading.

Junipers perform several functions. Low-growing varieties become ground covers, but Shane said to skip the low kinds, only 6 inches tall, because they allow weeds to grow up through them.

Another, the Woodward juniper,

developed at the old Cheyenne Horticultural Field Station, grows tall and narrow, providing a columnar shape that doesn't take up much ground, and it's a brighter green than some of the other, shrubbier junipers.

One of our native shrubs can provide dried flowers. Rabbitbrush blooms yellow in the fall and the feathery, pale-colored seed heads persist. The leaves are evergreen. Different varieties can range from a yellow green to a silvery color.

"There are many kinds of rabbit brush. There are bluish colors and those that are mostly green. There are dwarf (only reaching 10 inches), medium and tall (reaching up to 6 feet). If they get any supplemental water, you probably need to prune them back by July so that they still bloom in August and September." — Shane

You can also check out sagebrush, the epitome of Wyoming's open spaces, which has silvery leaves year round, plus that quintessential Western smell when you brush against it.

However, both these natives need to be planted where they won't be irrigated after establishment. Receiving more moisture than our natural precipitation can kill them.

Deciduous trees and shrubs

It's easy to think bare branches will be just black silhouettes. But with our abundant, sunny winter days, there is more to see, from gnarly cottonwood to smooth redtwig dogwood. Shane said to keep in mind that for dogwood and other shrubs with colorful bark, only the younger wood will show much color, so it is important to prune the older stems back, close to ground level, every few years to encourage new growth.

Maybe you can choose trees and shrubs with fruit, red rosehips on rose bushes, orange berries on mountain ash, crab apples that cling after the leaves fall away — though how long they last will depend on how hungry the squirrels and birds are.

Other plants Shane recommended, some of which are growing at the gardens, are ephedra, with its weird bunches of long, match-stick-like twigs; mahonia, which reminds one of holly; mountain mahogany and various hawthorn trees.

Grasses

Ornamental grasses have become part of the professionally designed landscape, including the entrance to the Laramie County Library and many local businesses.

They dry to a nice tawny gold. Unlike other, stronger vegetation, they require only the lightest of breezes to accent the view with motion.

One kind Shane pointed out at the gardens is a variety of Karl Foerster grass growing in a 2-foot tall clump with feathery seed heads.

Another, blue oat grass, resembles a fountain of thin, bluish-green and silver strands which looks good as a lone specimen or as a herd of small, shaggy beasts. Shane said if you have a protected, south-facing exposure, there are other grasses you might try.

Two native grasses turn a reddish hue in the fall, little bluestem, *Schizachyrium scoparium*, and big bluestem, *Andropogon gerardii*.

If, at some point, the grasses are smashed by snow or it's closing in on spring green-up, it's time to cut back

The Cheyenne Botanic Gardens' Children's Village took a formal approach to winter interest, planting 'Karl Foerster' feather reed grass to mimic the columnar shape of the 'Woodward' juniper.

the tall grasses. Rather than clipping them, Shane simply grabs a bunch and saws through near the base with a small, folding pruning saw.

Perennials and annuals

Vegetable gardens are rather hopeless looking in winter. A good gardener cleans out all that stuff that turns slimy with the first frost. But maybe you left the sunflowers for the birds. Maybe before the end of the growing season you planted a cover crop that can become mulch next spring.

Some perennial herbs have winter color: silvery-looking sage (the cooking kind) and purple-y oregano or wild marjoram. And some even stay green.

In the perennial flowerbed there are lots of plants that don't need to be cut back right away. Black-eyed Susans, yarrow, and asters have interesting dry flower heads. In my garden, hollyhocks and mullein have big stalks that attract downy woodpeckers.

At the gardens, Shane and I found a clump of golden stalks with dried purple flowers, a kind of ornamental onion. And there was a sedum that had dried nicely.

But there will come a time when some of these dried points of interest break down and you will want to remove them.

Bulbs

Next fall, before heavy frost, get some of those early spring bulbs planted, even if it is just a handful here and there. Finding a crocus in March makes two more months of snow potential much easier to bear.

Ground cover

We still have some bluegrass lawn at our house. Where the wind doesn't blow off the occasional snowfall right away, it gets moisture and looks quite presentable. Native grasses look nice too.

Vinca, a vining ground cover, stays green, but can be invasive. Leaves of some other low-growing perennials might also stay green.

Use organic materials as mulch to cover bare spots around trees or in gardens. It's good for the soil as it decomposes, and it can be interesting to look at, whether it is dried leaves or bark, natural or dyed color. Shane likes the look of pine needle mulch. He's found if it's ground up a bit, it doesn't blow away.

Garden embellishments

Nothing says calendar page photo like snow gathering on a garden bench, wagon wheel or split rail fence. My favorite embellishment is a bird feeder or two, attracting bird color and movement and, even through window glass, cheerful bird sounds.

Kathy Shreve packs a lot of garden into her tiny front yard in the Avenues.

CHAPTER 48: **WILDSCAPING**

HOW TO GO NATIVE AND HAVE MORE FUN

The idea of wildscaping, landscaping your yard for the benefit of wildlife, has been around for a long time.

But there is a new spin on it. Here, the emphasis is on using native plants to provide shelter and food for wildlife.

Why native?

Let's say you plant a shrub that is native to another continent — an alien. It might produce berries our birds will eat, but it did not evolve with our local insects, entomologist Douglas Tallamy explains in his book, *Bringing Nature Home, How You Can Sustain Wildlife*

with Native Plants.

Our native herbivorous insects usually find the alien leaves to be inedible. And that is exactly why alien plants are so popular with gardeners.

But, Tallamy writes, if you fill your yard with at least 80% insect-edible native plants, there will be plenty of insects for birds to feed their young, and your yard will be contributing to the health of the greater landscape — and indirectly, human health.

Don't worry, in a healthy habitat, your plants won't be leafless.

A stand of native trees and shrubs supporting native insects could produce more birds than say, a stand of Russian olive trees, an invasive exotic in Wyoming that has crowded out native species in many places. In fact, land managers are now working to eradicate it.

Gardeners can also choose native plants that will provide nectar and pollen for butterflies and bees. That's important, as both are suffering declining populations.

Our natives are better adapted to our location, plant biologist and author Susan Tweit told the 100 people who took part in the first Habitat Hero workshop in Cheyenne in March 2015, organized by Laramie County Master Gardeners and the Cheyenne-High Plains Audubon Society.

Plants native to our area are also more resistant to our weather extremes, often require less water than aliens, and little or no fertilizer, she added.

Designing wildscapes

Tweit also discussed landscape design, another of her specialties.

Landscape design is about pleasing combinations of color, form and texture at each season. Wildscaping considers appearance along with providing habitat functions.

The mingling of layers, from trees to shrubs to ground cover, besides aesthetic appeal, provides shelter, or cover, and foraging areas for a variety of species that might each prefer different heights and microhabitats.

Tweit cautioned that "going native" does not mean a weedy-looking patch. You can still choose formal, cottage style, meadow or minimalist. Simply fill the space with natives.

How to transition

The trick is to keep your high maintenance, water-loving conventional aliens, if you still want them, in one area of your yard. Don't mix these with native plants, as too much water on the natives can be deadly for them.

You can gradually replace your alien trees and shrubs with natives. Replace alien annuals (like petunias) with native perennials. Widen your flower borders. And one year at a time, replace sections of your Kentucky bluegrass turf, which is another alien species, with native buffalograss (Chapter 53)

How to become a Habitat Hero

Audubon Rockies has a program, Habitat Hero, to recognize everyone who strives to make their yard more wildlife friendly. Check their website to find out how to nominate your yard.

Demonstration gardens

There are two public Habitat Hero Demonstration Gardens that were planted in 2018: at the Cheyenne Botanic Gardens and in front of the Cheyenne Board of Public Utilities office. In 2020, Jeff Geyer from the Laramie County Conservation District and Nancy Loomis spearheaded the planting of the swale adjacent to the Laramie County Library parking lot and a planting at the Civic Center Commons across from the city offices.

CHEYENNE NATIVE PLANT SUGGESTIONS

This list is courtesy of Jane and Robert Dorn.
See this book's Plant List for the botanical names.

Trees
Bigtooth Maple
Boxelder
Colorado Blue Spruce
Common Hackberry
Lanceleaf Cottonwood
Pinyon Pine
Rocky Mountain Juniper

Shrubs
Redosier Dogwood
Rocky Mountain Maple
Silver Sagebrush
Western Serviceberry
Western Chokecherry

Perennial and Annual Flowers
Annual Sunflower
Black-eyed Susan
Common Blanketflower
Orange Butterflyweed
Penstemon (many kinds)
Prairie Blazingstar
Purple Beeplant (Cleome)
Purple Coneflower
Western Columbine
Wild Bergamot (Monarda)
Winecups

Grasses
Basin Wildrye
Big Bluestem
Bluebunch Wheatgrass
Buffalograss
Indian Ricegrass
Switchgrass

Bob Lick (left) added metal roof, plastic deck and gravel to make his home west of Cheyenne "firewise."

CHAPTER 49: **FIREWISE**

RIGHT LANDSCAPING HELPS KEEP PROPERTY SAFE

In the summer and fall, when we smell smoke from forest fires, we might think we are safe here in Laramie County.

But grass fires are a threat, whether we live within the city limits or "out in the county," as people say around here.

It only takes an ignition source (lightning, a burn pile, a cigarette ember), fuel (dry grass, resinous wood, anything flammable) and oxygen.

There are things you can do with your house and landscape, especially if you live in what the firefighting community calls the wildland/urban interface, to reduce fuel. This will improve your chances of firefighters being able to defend your home.

Firewise Communities

The Laramie County coordinator for Firewise, a national program that works through the Wyoming State Forestry Division, helps property owners, especially in forested areas, assess their fire risks and develop mitigation plans. Sometimes funding can be found to implement the plans.

The Firewise Communities program, in which a town or a group, like a homeowners' association, works together, is most effective.

Bob Lick of Granite Springs Retreat, a development in the ponderosa pine forest 25 miles west of Cheyenne, attended a Firewise talk and realized his homeowners' association needed to get onboard immediately.

This is the second year (this interview was in 2015) since it qualified as one of more than 1,000 Firewise communities nationwide. This Firewise committee educates neighbors and takes actions such as thinning pines along access roads and establishing one location where everyone can bring their tree prunings for safe burning.

On a rainy day in early May, as I visited Bob and his neighbors, it was hard to remember the approaching hot, dry and windy summer days ahead. Ironically, a wet spring means grasses will grow tall and lush. But when cured brown by mid-summer, they will provide perfect tinder.

The less flammable house

The Firewise website has recommendations for the least flammable roof, wall, window and vent materials.

Decks and fences attached to the house are considered part of the house. Bob and another Granite Springs Retreat resident, Marty Gill, have both used plastic lumber for their attached decks, which will melt in a fire, rather than burn.

Wooden fences need to be separated from the house with something that is not flammable, such as a metal gate or a brick pillar.

When there's threat of fire, homeowners should remove straw welcome mats, patio cushions and other flammables.

The first 5 feet

The good news is that landscaping with rock is in fashion these days. Bob is in the middle of arranging a 5-foot-wide border of rock along the edge of his deck. Around the rest of the house is gravel, including his driveway, and more underneath the deck, to make sure nothing can grow, dry out and provide a rogue ember with tinder.

Barb and Milt Werner have built a terraced stone patio against one side of their log house that does double duty as a firebreak.

The three homes have hardly any foundation plantings. But with a beautiful natural setting, why bother?

Here in the city or out on the prairie, foundation plantings seem more aesthetically necessary.

Even though I live only 200 feet away from a fire hydrant, Betsey Nickerson, Laramie County Firewise coordinator (at the time I interviewed her) thinks I should remove the junipers that grow against my house. More than any of the other evergreens, junipers are about as flammable as a can of gasoline, she keeps reminding me.

Also consider the pine trees that lean over people's homes, shedding needles on the roof and in the gutters. Talk about good tinder.

Deciduous plants are much less flammable than evergreens. The list of less flammable plants on Natrona County's Firewise website is a roll call of native plant species found in mountain meadows. They are becoming more available through local nurseries.

A Firewise demonstration garden planned by Betsey and Laramie County Master Gardeners was installed in 2015 at the Curt Gowdy State Park visitor center. The plants and signage show there are lots of aesthetically pleasing flowering plants that are fire resistant.

30 feet out

When firefighters refer to "defensible space" around a home, homeowners get a vision of moonscape. True, you wouldn't want your propane tank here, or the cute shed with the wood shake shingles, or your wood pile.

Trees are fine, in small, isolated islands, not in a continuous mass like a windbreak. Short shrubs, mowed grass, and gravel paths between flower beds can make a charming, fire-resistant landscape.

Even pine trees can be acceptable if they aren't too close together. One secret Bob learned is that you can remove one pine in a clump of three, for instance, to allow the other two to take up more water, making them more fire resistant.

Also, limbing a pine tree — removing the lower branches — keeps a ground fire from laddering. That is when, using branches, fire can easily make its way up the tree to reach the crown. Here, the flames catch more air and wind, then billow out and throw fire-brands at nearby roofs and trees.

The recommendation is to

Granite Springs Retreat homeowners reduced fire risks to qualify as a Firewise Community

remove evergreen limbs up to 6 to 8 feet above ground level. However, the pine trees near Barb and Milt's house are hardly 12 feet tall so they use the other rule: remove no more limbs than those in the first third of the tree's height.

One unexpected benefit is that more grass grew under the trees, Barb said.

While her gardening is limited to half a dozen containers well-fenced to keep deer out, Barb does put a lot of effort into raking up pinecones and excess pine needles that could be fuel for a stray ember.

30-100 feet out

Those in neighborhoods with less than 100 feet between their house and property boundary realize the need to work with their neighbors.

Out on the prairie, after the ground-nesting birds have fledged in late June to early July and the taller grasses begin to turn brown, you might get the urge to mow this zone. But it is important to mow high, to shade grass plants. Otherwise, without shade, short grass can be more flammable than taller grass.

Homeowners in the forest might have grass to mow there also, as well as trees and shrubs to manage as in the 5- to 30-foot zone.

Maintenance

Once you've had your property assessed for wildfire risk, and you spent the next few years completing all the recommended risk mitigation, you still must keep up with maintenance. Check for leaves and needles in gutters, debris under the deck, dead wood, vegetation growth and clutter.

Just chant the Firewise mantra: "clean, lean and green."

Insurance

Short of moving downtown, following Firewise principles is the best insurance against the increasing risk of wildfires during hotter and drier summers, and even dry winters.

Would using Firewise make a difference in home insurance policies? Betsey said she hasn't heard of anyone receiving a discount, though it might help prevent loss of insurance.

But it should make for more restful nights for the increasing numbers of homeowners who take fire preparedness into their own hands.

Martha Mullikin's clematis grows on a copper pipe trellis (left) and her grapes on a wrought-iron arbor.

CHAPTER 50:
TRELLIS AND VINE

CREATE TRELLISES FOR WYOMING-HARDY VINES

Once the leaves are gone for the winter, we have as many as seven months to admire the structure of what's left behind (Chapter 47).

So how about adding more vertical interest to your garden or the side of your house with a trellis?

Trellis purpose

The purpose of a trellis is to get vining plants off the ground, which is handy in the vegetable garden. The simplest methods involve stakes, string or wire cages. But these are temporary.

Instead, let's look at more permanent trellis ideas used with ornamental vines.

Some trellises are attached to walls, some are free-standing, and some are formed into arbors meant to be walked under. Some can even be sculptural parts of dead trees or scrap metal. Or perhaps one of the porch posts will do.

Sometimes, the desire for a trellis comes first, rather than the desire to grow a vining plant. Is there a plain wall or fence that needs something to dress it up? Is there a view you would like to block? Is there a view you would like to frame with an arbor? Are you looking for some shade?

Need a little height to give your garden some pizazz?

Kinds

Trellises with engineered straight lines and perfect curves can offer contrast to natural vine shapes. Trellises with a less formal structure can blend in with nature.

As you drive around town this winter, look for trellises. Some are obviously the kind you buy, the simple fan shapes, lattice panels or ladder shapes. But there is some original artwork out there.

Wood is the easiest for most of us to build with, but if you are thinking long-term, be sure to use wood that will endure, like cedar. You don't want to get trapped into having to paint your trellis, especially if you are contemplating a perennial vine that adds growth from year to year. But if the vine gets cut back annually, re-painting might be possible.

Metal is the best. Wrought iron looks good for a long time and it is sturdy enough for heavier vines.

Or how about pipe? Copper looks good and might not be so hard to work with, although you don't want it to be publicly visible or someone will steal it for its cash value.

But perhaps you aren't a welder. Then it is time to think creatively about repurposing. My friends Mary and Jeff Weinstein had an old box spring they needed to dispose of. After removing the cloth and wood, the springs were attached to their wood fence and covered by their grape vine.

An arbor or pergola is roof-like. It can include sides that are trellises

Carla and Bruce Keating enjoy the Victorian rose temple he built.

or just the support posts. The roof can be flat or arched. Short arbors form a doorway from one area of the garden to another. Martha Mullikin, Laramie County Master Gardener, makes sure her arbors frame views, even a focal point as simple as a container of bright annuals. Despite her several arbors being made of different materials, she chose them all to be flat-topped, echoing the same form.

More elaborate is the "Victorian Rose Temple" in Bruce and Carla Keating's garden that Bruce welded, offering support for climbing roses on all sides. Plus, it is a shady place to sit.

Recommended vines

As artful as a trellis may be, it

needs a vine. I asked Susan Carlson, also a Laramie County Master Gardener, for her list of recommendations for our area, and checked the Cheyenne Botanic Gardens.

Susan said perennial vines are not going to cover the new trellis at once.

"Annual sweet peas and morning glories can act as filler for a few years where slower growing vines are planted. It takes a few years for the roots to become established."

And she had some advice on where to plant vines.

"Some protection from wind would be beneficial," she said. "I have vines on all sides of the house, except the west."

As I researched each of the recommended vines, I noted they all prefer sunny to partly sunny locations. All vines flower, some more noticeably than others. Except for grapes and hops, any fruit produced is appropriate for birds, not people. All vines mentioned are perennial, except morning glory and annual sweet pea.

Trumpet Vine, *Campsis radicans* — Orange-red flowers attract hummingbirds. It can be an aggressive grower. Flowers on new wood, so it can be pruned in early spring without affecting blooming.

Clematis, *Clematis* species

Clematis is just starting to climb another Mullikin arbor made of wood.

— Needs to keep its roots cool, either shaded by low growing perennials, mulch or a rock. Many species and varieties are available with different growth habits. Recommended for Cheyenne:

- **'Jackmanii'**— purple flowers, spring & early summer blooming, can be pruned in early spring.

- **'Henryi'**— white flowers, blooms in June on last year's wood, later blooms again on new wood.

- **'Nelly Moser'**— pink flowers, late spring and summer. Prune no more than top third.

- **'Sweet Autumn'**— fragrant white flowers bloom on new wood so prune after blooming. Native and very hardy.

Hops, *Humulus lupus* — Odd, but interesting green flowers. It dies back after frost and grows new shoots from the roots in spring. Hops are an ingredient in many beers. Once established, it can become invasive.

Morning Glory (annual), *Ipomea purpurea* — Blue-flowered varieties are most popular. Blooms most prolifically beginning in late summer. Needs lots of sun and water. Can be seeded directly when soil temperature is 60 degrees, but speed things up by starting inside three weeks early. Prefers poor soil. Supposedly grows 8 feet long but mine went 18 feet this summer. Grow multiple vines in each location.

Perennial Sweet Pea, *Lathyrus latifolius* — Purplish-pink flowers fade to white and are not fragrant. Blooms mid-season. A low water and low maintenance plant. Seeds are poisonous.

Sweet Pea (annual), *Lathyrus odoratus* — Fragrant blue, pink, purple and white flowers. Prefers cool, but sunny locations and lots of water. Plant seeds up to 3 weeks before last spring frost.

'Kintzley's Ghost' Honeysuckle, *Lonicera reticulate* — Yellow flowers in late spring, but large, silvery leaves are its hallmark. First propagated and grown by the Kintzley family in Iowa in the 1880s and rediscovered in Fort Collins and propagated by Scott Skogerboe.

Trumpet Honeysuckle, *Lonicera sempervirens* — Red trumpet-shaped flowers bloom much of the summer. Blooms on previous year's wood, so prune after flowering. Japanese honeysuckle is less hardy here but is considered an invasive problem in 29 eastern states.

Virginia Creeper, *Parthenocissus quinquefolia* — Flowers are not noticeable, but the birds love the berries and drop seeds that sprout all over my yard. Leaves turn red in fall. Little disks allow vines to adhere to walls, a problem when removing them.

Silver Lace Vine, *Polygonum aubertii* — White flowers bloom in late summer, early fall, and sometimes well into October, Martha told me. It is considered a relatively fast and hardy grower and can be invasive in nicer climates.

Climbing Roses, *Rosa* species — Technically, climbing roses don't twine around or attach themselves to trellises, but they can use the support.

American Grape, *Vitus labrusca* — Table grape varieties that do well in our area include Concord, Valiant, Reliance, Himrod and Swenson Red (Chapter 25).

See Cheyenne Botanic Gardens website, Resources tab, "Gardening Tips" for more information on vines.

A pink-flowered, mini dianthus groundcover flows along the edges of a path at the Mullikins.'

CHAPTER 51:
GROUND COVERS

TRY COLORFUL OPTIONS TO TURF

Gardeners consider ground covers to be short plants that act as living mulch, suppressing weeds and preventing erosion.

The bluegrass lawn is a ground cover. Because it is so popular, its growing needs are well known (Chapter 52). You can easily find someone to grow and mow it for you. Even simpler is growing native grasses — less water and much less work (Chapter 53).

When I surveyed the Laramie County Master Gardeners for their favorite perennial ground covers, a variety of short, flowering plants were listed requiring various amounts of sun and water.

Advantages

All have big advantages over mulches like gravel or wood chips.

Established ground covers out-compete weeds. Rock and wood chip mulches, on the other hand, eventually fill with weeds.

Plants keep the ground around themselves cooler. Rock mulch makes an area hotter.

Plants recycle carbon dioxide and make oxygen. Rocks and wood chips don't.

A blooming ground cover offers

more for bees and butterflies than rock, wood chips or a plain lawn.

Planting

You can combine plant species in a mosaic, or in what's being called a tapestry lawn by researchers at the University of Reading in Britain.

Avoid planting ground covers adjacent to lawns without some kind of barrier in between to keep the grass from invading.

Plant in the spring. If you instead plant a month or two before winter weather sets in, you should see most of your investment sprout the following spring.

How close together you plant depends on how big a hurry you are in to get an area to fill in.

When comparing hardiness ratings, keep in mind Cheyenne is rated as USDA Plant Hardiness Zone 5, but many local gardeners look for hardier varieties rated for colder Zone 4 and even Zone 3.

Laramie County Master Gardener picks

Stonecrop, *Sedum hybridum*, is recommended by Catherine Wissner, University of Wyoming Extension horticulturist. There are many varieties of these succulents, but this one is only 4 inches high. It produces yellow flowers in late spring and early summer. It needs full sun, low amounts of water (after establishment) and is rated Zone 4.

Birdseye Speedwell, *Veronica filiformis*, is another of Catherine's choices. This Zone 3 speedwell is only 2 inches tall. Fast growing, in some climates it can invade turf. Small blue flowers with white centers bloom mid-spring.

Turkish Veronica (or Speedwell), *Veronica liwanensis*, is one of three kinds of ground covers Martha Mullikin grows between flagstones. They all do well because they get the extra moisture running off the stone. This Zone 4 perennial becomes a blue-flowered carpet 1 to 3 inches tall in spring. It prefers sun with afternoon shade and a drier situation. Linnie Cough said hers blooms for two months. It is a Plant Select variety developed by the Denver Botanic Gardens and Colorado State University for thriving in western gardens.

Woolly Speedwell, *Veronica pectinata*, is a favorite of Susan Carlson. It is like Turkish Veronica, but the leaves are silvery instead of glossy. Both stay green over the winter.

Woolly Thyme, *Thymus lanuginosus*, and **Lemon Thyme**, *Thymus citriodorus*, are the other two forming mats over the flagstones at Martha's. Both are good to Zone 4. Both like full sun and do well in xeric (dry) conditions. Lemon Thyme has the added benefit of being considered a culinary herb.

Red Creeping Thyme, *Thymus praecox* 'Coccineus,' listed by Tava Collins, is a red-flowering ground cover that doesn't mind being stepped on a little. A Zone 4, it is drought tolerant once it has been established.

Martha is enamored with **Dianthus** 'Tiny Rubies,' *Dianthus gratianopolitanus*, which forms a 2-inch tall mat of leaves covered in pink flowers mid-spring to mid-summer. It prefers full sun and doesn't mind the colder temperatures of Zone 3.

Barren Strawberries, *Waldsteinia ternata*, will remind you of strawberries, but the small yellow flowers (Martha has a variety with pink flowers) produce fruit considered inedible by people — no word on whether squirrels like them. A Zone 4, it likes full sun to part shade, and is somewhat drought tolerant.

Small-leaved Periwinkle, *Vinca minor*, Kathy Shreve said, "can take shade, and will grow under a limbed-up spruce tree if given enough water." A Zone 4 less than 4 inches high, its periwinkle-blue flowers show up in May and early June. Mine, despite being in deepest shade, still plots to take over the world so I prune it and even pull it when necessary.

Sweet Woodruff, *Galium odorata*, is another that does well in shade (it doesn't like full sun), but I think mine would do better if I watered it more — it might reach the listed height of 6 to 12 inches. A Zone 4, its tiny white, fragrant flowers show up in May. Tava said when it is stepped on or cut (or mowed), you may get the sweet smell of hay.

Hummingbird Trumpet, *Epilobium canum ssp garrettii* 'Orange Carpet' also goes by *Zauschneria garrettii*. Kathy reports it is a "great xeric ground cover, does not seed around indiscriminately, and hummingbirds really do love the orangey-red flowers. Also, it blooms in late July-August when most everything else has pooped out." This is precisely when migrating hummingbirds passing through Cheyenne would appreciate it. A Zone 3, it is also a Plant Select variety.

Mary Ann Kamla recommended several plants including **Creeping Jenny**, *Lysimachia nummularia*, a Zone 3 with yellow

Periwinkle is an evergreen ground cover that does well in deep shade. It is very tough and aggressive, so think carefully before planting it.

flowers mid-summer. Mildly invasive, she keeps it contained with the edge of the patio.

Another that is doing well for Mary Ann is **Soapwort**, *Saponaria officinalis*. A Zone 3 with pink to white flowers, it appreciates water. Its leaves have historically been boiled to make a bubbly liquid soap.

Tava is a fan of **Spotted Deadnettle**, *Lamium maculatum*. She grows two varieties: 'Purple Dragon' and 'Pink Chablis,' the names describing the flower colors. Hers bloom throughout the season, Tava said. The leaves are silvery with green edges. These varieties are Zone 4, but some others aren't as cold hardy. Cutting back will encourage new blooms. The bumblebees love Lamium, Tava said.

Also on Tava's list: **Black Scallop Bugleweed**, *Ajuga reptens* 'Black Scallop.' Ajugas are good ground covers in general. This one has leaves that look nearly black when grown in full sun. Early summer it has blue flower spikes. A Zone 3, it can be invasive in the garden.

Richard Steele simply grows **White Clover**, *Trifolium repens*, instead of grass. It's mowable, takes less water, he says, and it feeds his bees, which provide him with honey. Establishing clover is much like establishing a lawn. You can also seed clover in an existing lawn.

"There are two brands of clover bred for lawns that have smaller leaves … one is called micro clover. They look a lot more manicured and fit in between the grass leaves. My backyard is almost all micro clover. Also, they have smaller flowers which attract fewer bees — fewer stings for barefoot kids." — Shane

There are two ground covers I planted this year that Shane Smith, Cheyenne Botanic Gardens director, now retired, has mentioned. One is **Creeping Phlox**, *Phlox subulata*. A Zone 3, it should have no problem coming back next year, but because it prefers sunnier spots, I'm glad to see its pink and white flowers will develop in our partly shady spot.

The other is **Snow-in-Summer**, *Cerastium tomentosum*, another Zone 3, with silvery green leaves. The first year it gave me one white flower. Four years later though, it had many flowers and had to be corralled.

See Cheyenne Botanic Gardens website, Resources tab, "Gardening Tips" for more information on ground covers.

Martha Mullikin knows how to keep her turf looking wedding-ready.

CHAPTER 52: **TURF**

Let's talk about growing grass today — or what folks in the landscape business call turf — and what you need to do to prepare a conventional, Kentucky bluegrass lawn for winter.

I asked Martha Mullikin, a Laramie County Master Gardener, to describe her lawn maintenance schedule.

She has a large lawn, large for being in the older part of town. It is where famous local architect William Dubois (1879-1953) once had a tennis court. It's large enough to host large weddings and other parties — which Martha has done.

Fertilize

Martha's rule of thumb is to fertilize on or close to the holidays, depending on weather: Easter, Memorial Day and the 4th of July. She uses fertilizer rated 10-10-10, the ratio of nitrogen to phosphorus to potassium. This is not a lot of fertilizer because, as she says, "the more you fertilize, the more you have to mow. All you're doing is watering and mowing."

And now that he's retired, that work falls to her husband, David.

They use Ringer Lawn Restore more in the summer, she said, "because it puts (good) bacteria into the soil."

It's available locally. Without chemicals, it introduces microorganisms that break down organic materials in the soil to make nutrients available to plants.

"We don't use the weed killer-fertilizer combinations because I compost grass clippings," Martha said. Otherwise, if the clippings aren't set aside for a year, the residual herbicide will kill flowers and vegetables in gardens treated with the compost.

After the final lawn mowing, she uses a "winterizer" fertilizer, one that is designed to be slow-release — you wouldn't want a big hit of nitrogen to encourage the growth of tender little grass blades right before winter weather.

It is equally important to read the directions on the packaging and apply the right amount of fertilizer and make sure it doesn't get washed into the street. Wasting fertilizer wastes your money and pollutes streams and groundwater — where someone — if not you — gets their drinking water.

In some patches of Martha's lawn, she has white clover growing. Clover is a nitrogen fixer, acting like fertilizer, so if it were growing with your grass all over your lawn, you could reduce the amount of nitrogen you use. Lawns with clover were standard until the 1950s when herbicides became popular. I remember my grandfather's lawn having clover in the 1960s.

Weeds

Martha usually digs dandelions and other weeds, seldom resorting to weed killer for persistent spots.

Every time the above-ground parts of a weed are removed, the weed's ability to feed its roots through photosynthesis is lessened, eventually starving it, and hopefully killing it, just like cows do when they continually graze their favorite plants.

Dealing with weeds on an as-needed basis rather than broadcasting weed-killer over your whole lawn means you save money and might get a sweet surprise, such as little violets blooming in your turf.

Watering

Martha has a well for watering, but pumping it has a cost as does using our municipal water. So, it makes sense to be as efficient as possible.

Using a sprinkler system like Martha's means you can set it on a schedule. But that schedule needs adjusting based on how rainfall and summer heat affect how fast your lawn dries out. The length of time an individual zone runs depends on how hot and dry it is compared to the others.

What you want to do is soak the top 12 inches of your yard. This is where most of the tree and shrub roots are, and where the grass roots should be reaching. Lightly watering often will keep roots too close to the surface where they may dry out and die. Plus, wetting a lawn too often encourages diseases.

Catherine Wissner, University of Wyoming Extension horticulturist, suggests one last deep watering before the ground freezes to benefit turf as well as trees and shrubs.

Also plan to water your yard if we have any of those long, dry spells in winter when it is warm enough to set out a hose and sprinkler. But don't forget to drain or blow out your sprinkler system in the fall before water in the pipes can freeze.

Remove leaves

Martha suggests using the lawn mower to pick up leaves with the grass catcher. "You have to get rid of those leaves or you will have snow mold," she said.

Considering leaf mulch can be used to keep down weeds in the garden, you can see how detrimental it might be to a lawn. The snow mold, a fungus, breaks down the leaves — and your grass.

The nice part about using your lawn mower is that you will be mixing grass clippings with dead leaves — a desirable combination of green and brown materials for composting. Also, small bits of leaves decay, or compost, faster than whole leaves.

If you don't have compost bins, use plastic leaf bags, leaving the tops open so moisture will be added by rain and snow. Or dig the chopped leaves into your annual flower or vegetable garden.

For protecting perennial flowers, I've found it's better to use whole leaves that are curled and dried — not

PRAIRIE SELDOM NEEDS MOWING

People moving to acreage and unfamiliar with the prairie are smart to contact Catherine Wissner, University of Wyoming Extension horticulturist, for basic instruction.

The worst thing to do to the prairie is mow it. But do mow the patch of bluegrass lawn the kids play on and the firebreaks immediately around the house and along fence lines.

Unmown prairie benefits you and provides bird habitat — grassland birds nest on the ground. Grasses shade the ground and keep it cooler and moister. They also will trap snow, giving it a chance to melt and sink in. Cooler ground is less likely to burn.

Mowed prairies make the prairie hotter, encouraging the short warm-season grass species at the expense of cool-season species, which keep the prairie cooler.

Don't mow the thistles! It encourages rhizomes — underground stems — to spread and pop up more plants. Catherine said to spray the individual plants when they are blooming or after the first frost. These non-native thistles are a tough, invasive plant that requires tough measures.

Our native shortgrass prairie attracts ground-nesting birds and other wildlife.

cottonwood leaves that remain flat and form an impenetrable layer. After the killing frost, add a foot or so of the curly leaf mulch. In windy locations, keep it from blowing away by laying some wire fencing over or around it.

Mowing

With our long, snowless spells, the grass roots benefit from shading by the grass blades, just as in summer.

"David usually mows 3 inches high. The last mow is 3.5 – 4 inches (as high as the mower goes) — pretty high. You don't want to shock it by cutting it very short," Martha said.

Rather than a weekly affair throughout the growing season, mowing should be done as needed, so that no more than one-third of the height of the grass is removed at one time. Mowing is needed more frequently in spring to keep up with growth, less often by fall.

Aeration

Considering our lawns often get a lot of traffic, including walking back and forth to mow, the soil can get compacted, making it difficult for water and fertilizer to soak in. And all the healthy soil microorganisms need air too.

"I really do think aeration helps. We like to do it in the spring right before we fertilize. A lot of places recommend two times a year, but we never have," Martha said.

Try renting one of those core aeration contraptions. Don't worry about leaving the plugs on the soil surface if you do it in spring like Martha. They

will soon break down.

If you have a thatch problem, core aeration is better than power raking.

"I don't recommend power raking. It damages the crowns of the turf. Instead, simply aerate and that will take care of the thatch by providing more oxygen to the microbes that will digest the thatch. Power raking is helpful if you need to overseed damaged turf." — Shane

The benefits of turf

Some people replace their lawns with rock and gravel, thinking it will cut back on maintenance.

However, dirt blows in on top, allowing weeds to grow, which require pulling them or using toxic weed killers. Then you must sift out the dirt every few years to keep it looking nice.

The advantage of a lawn is that all those growing grass plants add coolness and humidity to our homes' hot, dry summer environments. And all vegetation, including the lawn, helps absorb sound.

Lawn maintenance can be a lot of work if you use too much fertilizer and water, making the lawn grow faster than necessary.

But there are types of turf based on native grass species, like buffalograss, which require far less maintenance and water.

See Cheyenne Botanic Gardens website, Resources tab, "Gardening Tips" for more information on turf and drought, and dogs and turf.

Brent Lathrop chose native buffalograss for his lawn. It needs little water or maintenance.

CHAPTER 53:
BUFFALOGRASS

PLANT THE ORIGINAL LOW-MAINTENANCE LAWN

By the end of our long winter, our thoughts might turn to excuses to get outside, even working in the yard. But it doesn't take long before we remember the actual drudgery of lawn chores.

If you'd rather be fishing or biking or hiking or camping in the summer instead of mowing, get a tip from Cheyenne resident Brent Lathrop: buffalograss, *Bouteloua dactyloides*.

Kentucky bluegrass is the default lawn in Cheyenne. However, I know half a dozen homeowners like Brent who have switched to a grass species native to our High Plains.

Last fall, I went to see Brent's backyard, a swath of buffalograss. It was heading into dormancy, turning from green to the pale straw color of the winter prairie.

Because of the covenants in his neighborhood, his front lawn must be the conventional Kentucky bluegrass.

This is the fourth native lawn Brent has established, and the most difficult because of three droughty years at the beginning.

Beginning

The backyard of his new house was raw dirt when Brent seeded it in 2006 with a mix of 90% buffalograss and 10% blue grama, another native grass. By 2011, the lawn was finally looking the way he wanted.

Choosing to go native is a natural choice for Brent. "It's in my DNA because of what I do," he said. He works for The Nature Conservancy as the program director for southeastern Wyoming (retired since this interview). A low maintenance lawn, requiring less water, fertilizer and work, is a step towards more sustainable landscapes.

Once buffalograss is established, technically speaking, it doesn't need irrigation, but Brent waters it a couple times in the spring to help it green up sooner, to cater to his neighbors' lawn expectations.

Last year (2014), Brent spent only $194 on lawn watering for the entire growing season, including back and front yards, while his neighbors reported spending more than that each month.

Only 3-4 inches tall, buffalograss could be left unmown, but once again, Brent considers his neighbors' sensibilities and mowed six times last year, to keep it a little less ragged.

What he would really like to do is burn the grass. It evolved with fire and can get "decadent" without it but figuring out how to do that in a residential neighborhood with yards bounded by plastic fences is problematic.

Maintenance

Buffalograss appreciates a little fertilizer. Brent fertilizes once a year, mid-June, at half the recommended amount. Not bagging his clippings when he mows also adds nutrients.

Weeds are not much of an issue. Brent digs any by hand. Besides that, in my research I discovered buffalograss is susceptible to some of the common weed killers.

He will need to deal with some Kentucky bluegrass invading from other yards. But he also encourages native wildflowers to grow, just as they would on the prairie.

One of Brent's fringe benefits during the first years of his new lawn was horned larks hanging out — and nesting.

Now that the neighbors have all fenced in their backyards, the horned larks have moved on to the still open spaces under construction in the development. But other birds still visit — and more of them are seen on his grass, his jealous neighbors complain, than on their conventional lawns.

Pros and cons of buffalograss

Buffalograss is not a perfect substitute for Kentucky bluegrass.

Buffalograss greens up later than bluegrass and goes dormant in the fall earlier.

Buffalograss does not thrive in shade lasting more than half a day. But bluegrass will.

Buffalograss does not stand up to heavy, constant traffic because it spreads by stolons, connections from plant to plant growing above ground. Bluegrass spreads by rhizomes underground.

In its favor, buffalograss has excellent heat, drought and cold tolerance and few insect and disease problems compared to bluegrass.

Though if given too much water and fertilizer, buffalograss will become prone to weeds.

Buffalograss, like some of the other native alternatives, can be a little more work to establish, compared to rolling out a carpet of bluegrass sod.

"Because buffalograss is a bluish grey color, deep green colored weeds show up especially well. I would instead recommend growing either turf-type fescue or Blue Gramma grass, both of which are water wise and darker green to hide the weeds." — Shane

Pick the right cultivar

Buffalograss comes in several varieties that have been developed for different areas of the country. The newer cultivars (cultivated varieties) grow more densely and greener. Brent is growing one of those new ones, "Cody," developed in Nebraska. Avoid Texoka, which is more suited to growing conditions in Texas.

Seed is available at local garden centers, but you may have to shop online somewhere like Stock Seed Farms in Murdock, Nebraska, to find exactly what you want, Brent said.

Buffalograss is also offered as plugs and sod. These options aren't easy to find locally. One place Catherine Wissner, University of Wyoming Extension horticulturist, mentioned is Turf Master Sod in Fort Collins, Colorado.

Buffalograss plugs or sod would be worth finding if you have allergies because they are all female plants,

propagated vegetatively, so they don't produce pollen. Look for these cultivars: Legacy and Prestige.

How to plant buffalograss

The 4,900-square foot buffalograss lawn cost Brent less than $500 (2015) to install by seeding, the cheapest alternative.

The best time of year to start a buffalograss lawn is mid-April to early May, according to one source, or mid-May to mid-June. But it will depend on when we are clear of snow. Another possibility is mid-August to mid-September.

Replacing a bluegrass lawn with buffalograss, though, means removing the old lawn. Killing it with an herbicide is not the preferred method. It can be smothered with plastic or just dug up, stacking chunks upside down in your compost area where they will decay. You could opt for replacing a section of lawn each year.

Everything you know about preparing a site for bluegrass works for buffalograss. Get a soil test to see what fertilizer and organic matter might need to be incorporated before seeding.

Remove debris, but don't go overboard on tilling the soil — it shouldn't be "fluffy."

Spraying for weeds before seeding is mentioned in the handbooks, but Brent doesn't recommend it. Instead, when the weeds emerged, he knocked them down with the mower before they went to seed. The weeds provided a kind of cover crop while the grass got established. And remember, buffalograss is susceptible to weed killers when it is green.

How much seed do you need? For a small area with seed being broadcast using a hand-operated seeder, figure 3-5 pounds per 1,000 square feet. For larger areas where a tractor can pull a drill, figure 20-30 pounds per acre.

If broadcasting rather than drilling, take half of your seed and distribute it while traveling back and forth, and then distribute the other half while traveling back and forth at a right angle. Lightly rake seed in.

To get your seeds to germinate, you'll need to water lightly and frequently. Once they are established, you can gradually reduce watering.

If you were lucky enough to find plugs or sod, you need to water often enough that they stay moist — not flooded — especially under the sod.

Advice

There is plenty of advice about growing buffalograss — it was first used for lawns in the 1930s. The University of Wyoming Extension website lists this publication: *Low-Maintenance Grasses for Revegetating Disturbed Areas and Lawns*, (B1070).

BUFFALOGRASS BUDDIES' RESULTS

By Brent Lathrop, experienced buffalograss grower, and Jeff Geyer, Laramie County Conservation District water specialist, in an email to me:

Brent:

I do know that Stock Seeds has out a new buffalo variety called Sundowner that seems to be doing real well here.

Jeff Geyer replanted his back yard last year (2019) and with irrigation available it looks wonderful this summer, much better take than what I dealt with beginning in 2006.

He did have a better soil situation to deal with — the yard had been in bluegrass for probably six years — and he used the turf as a fertilizer when he sprayed it out and turned it under before seeding.

Jeff:

Ha! Brent is just jealous because it took less than a year to fill in my backyard. I selected two varieties of buffalograss – Legacy, plugs, and then Sundancer, seed. Both came out of Nebraska.

Plugs were very expensive, I think 70 plugs was well over $225, while seed to cover 6000 square feet of lawn was around $300.

I would not use plugs again as they were too slow to spread. Seed is the way. You need to kill out the bluegrass lawns early in spring so that you're ready to seed by early July at latest. Buffalograss is a warm season grass so by that time you should have some good heat coming on.

My water bill was significantly less this year (2020). The lawn greens up late April and goes dormant around September.

Jeff's process:

- Roundup the area three separate times with two weeks between each treatment.
- Till the entire area as deep as you can go.
- Harrow the area so that it's fairly level, and then wheeler pack it with whatever you can rent. I had a packer barrel on the back of my ATV. You don't want to compact the lawn like concrete but get it firm.
- Harrow or rake the surface by hand to create a good soil-to-seed contact surface.
- Seed at least 3 pounds per 1000 square feet. I did more like 4-plus pounds.
- Rake loosely over the seed again.
- Run the barrel compactor over it again, pressing that seed into the soil.
- Water just to keep the soil moist-ish, NOT wet.
- Wait — it usually takes between seven and 14 days to germinate.

PART 7

TREES AND SHRUBS

Find this sign at Lions Park by the beach. A map there shows where trees are identified with posts.

CHAPTER 54:
CHEYENNE TREES

WHICH TREES ARE TOUGH ENOUGH FOR US?

Summer is a good time to appreciate Cheyenne's trees. Each one is a bit of a miracle because most trees are not native to the High Plains except along creeks, most notably the cottonwoods.

In addition to enjoying their shade, you might want to study our landscape trees if you are thinking about planting one yourself (Chapter 55).

One way to find trees that grow well here is to follow the Tree Walk in the southwest corner of Lions Park, set up by the Cheyenne Urban Forestry Division. You can pick up a map with the tree descriptions at their office located nearby at West 8th and Carey avenues.

The Tree Walk features 37 trees (2021) marked with signs on posts. I'll highlight 12 here, illustrated in Part 9 in the Plant Gallery. Most of the photos are of 50 or 60-year-old trees from my own neighborhood so you can see them in proportion to the houses.

As you travel around Cheyenne admiring our trees, see how many more species you can find. If you need identification help and the Urban Forestry office is closed, try the Arbor Day Foundation website.

Tree traits

For more information on tree species recommended for Cheyenne and Wyoming, check Urban Forestry's website and the University of Wyoming Extension's publication available online, *Landscaping: Recommended Trees for Wyoming.*

Here are my codes for describing my top 12 trees everyone in Cheyenne should be able to identify.

E: Evergreen tree providing winter protection for birds

F: Fall color, loses leaves

H: Hail hardy

N: Native to the West

W: Wildlife likes the fruits

WW: Water-wise

- Ponderosa Pine, *Pinus ponderosa*
  E, H, N, W, WW
  Surrounding the Forestry office is a grove of extremely tall, skinny examples. However, in my neighborhood, single specimens look nice and full. I.D.: Look for bundles of two or three needles 5 inches or longer.

- Pinyon Pine, *Pinus edulis*
  E, H, N, W, WW
  Iconic, drought-tolerant trees of the Southwest, they're short, even after 50 years. If you are lucky, they could produce the prized pinyon pine nut. I.D.: needles 1.5 – 2.5 inches in bundles of two.

- Rocky Mountain Bristlecone Pine, *Pinus aristata*
  E, H, N, W, WW
  This is the Rocky Mountain species. It's the Nevada/

California species that lives up to 5,000 years. I.D.: drooping branches full of needles look like bottle brushes.

- Colorado Blue Spruce, *Picea pungens*
  E, H, N, W
  Growing several stories high, spruces can grow too wide, forcing homeowners to prune away their skirts. There are new varieties that are narrower. I.D.: needles are single, short, stiff and very prickly.

- White Fir, *Abies concolor*
  E, H, N, W
  It looks like, and grows as tall as a spruce, but it's a soft version. Another soft-needled, spruce-like tree is the Douglas-fir. I.D.: flat, short, single, flexible, soft needles.

- Rocky Mountain Juniper, *Juniperus scopulorum*
  E, H, N, W, WW
  There are many varieties of upright junipers available through nurseries. They all produce little waxy bluish berries. Birds also appreciate their windproof foliage. I.D.: no needles — just green scales.

- Plains Cottonwood, *Populus deltoides*
  F, H, N
  Wyoming's state tree has tough, heart-shaped leaves. But cottonwoods require a lot of water, and after about 50-60 years, these huge trees start deteriorating, dropping limbs on windy or hot summer days.

- Burr Oak, *Quercus macrocarpa*
  F, W
  We aren't too far from this species' native range. Slow growing, it might take a while to produce significant shade, but meanwhile, wildlife will enjoy the acorns. It can be hard-hit by hail, but will recover.

- European Mountain-Ash,
  Sorbus aucuparia
  F, H, W
  Bunches of little white flowers in the spring will develop by midsummer into orange berries that are quickly devoured by birds. The small leaflets seem to avoid hail damage.

- American Linden, *Tilia americana*
  F, W
  Hail can be hard on it, but this is a great shade tree. Plus, it has fragrant flowers and produces bunches of little fruits. I.D.: leaves are heart-shaped, but not tough like cottonwood. Mature trees are pyramidal-shaped.

- Honey-locust, *Gleditsia triacanthos*
  F, H, W
  Look for the thornless type. Its small leaflets somewhat avoid being shredded by hail. It might have 7-inch-long brown pods unless it's a fruitless variety.

- Flowering Crabapple,
  Malus species
  F, W
  These are hard to miss in spring, blooming profusely pink or white for weeks along Cheyenne streets and in parks and yards. Modern varieties are dwarf. They are popular with wildlife, which might eat the flowers as well as the fruit. I.D.: Oval leaves and small apples popular with birds. Some varieties hang on to their apples, though there are always a few left on the ground.

The High Plains Arboretum has been a source for propagating trees that will grow successfully in our area.

HIGH PLAINS ARBORETUM HISTORY

To the west of the F.E. Warren Air Force Base is the High Plains Grasslands Research Station run by the U.S. Agricultural Research Service. Back in 1930, soon after it was established, it was named the Cheyenne Horticultural Field Station. Thousands of kinds of fruits and vegetables were trialed to figure out what would grow in this area. The best varieties were introduced into commercial trade (such as 'Fort Laramie' strawberries, Chapter 24).

Plant explorers brought back tree materials from China and Russia and other parts of the world with climates similar to Cheyenne's and the high plains. In 1974, the station changed its mission to studying grasslands, but some of the trees lingered on, on their own with no irrigation or care.

In 2000, the Friends of the High Plains Arboretum, a subcommittee of the Friends of the Cheyenne Botanic Gardens, began to plan to protect the old trees and add new trees. They had a master plan prepared by award-winning landscape architect Herb Schaal.

The arboretum is open to the public but as of early 2021, the only amenities were a portable potty and signs about the arboretum on the south side of the entrance road, but that's about to change. Other than the arboretum and the entrance road loop, the rest of the station is not open to the public.

Steve Scott uses a pole to check that the tree's transition from trunk to roots is at ground level.

CHAPTER 55:
TREE PLANTING

USE LATEST SCIENTIFIC METHODS FOR BEST RESULTS

Tree planting is, in theory, as simple as dropping one into any old hole in the yard. The tree might survive, but then again, it might not.

Just what, exactly, do you need to do to make sure the tree survives and thrives?

We turn to a local expert, Steve Scott, head of horticulture at the Cheyenne Botanic Gardens, now retired. He had been planting trees at the gardens for 16 years at the time of this interview in 2014, long enough to see the results

of his techniques.

When and how to purchase

Steve believes spring — late March and April — is the best time to plant, before trees leaf out. It's easier to get enough water to new trees in spring and summer. Plus, tree selection at the nursery is better than in the fall.

Trees are either grown in containers (container-grow) or grown in the field and dug up, leaving their roots bare (bare root) or are in a ball of dirt covered in burlap (balled and burlapped) . Whatever type, it's important that roots have not been allowed to dry out at any point.

Bare root trees

This is Steve's favorite type. These might be little whips, 12 inches to 3 feet tall. Buying a bundle of them could be the way to go if you are establishing a windbreak or other large planting.

Besides being economical, studies show the smaller the tree, the more quickly it gets established and begins to grow. Within a few years, it will overtake a larger tree planted at the same time, even though that other tree started with a trunk diameter three times the size.

Steve demonstrated his planting techniques the day I visited with a tree he planted in the gardens' nursery as a whip five years ago. Today it's about 8 feet tall, maybe even 10.

Balled and burlapped trees

This is Steve's second preference. Back in the old days, it was thought that buried burlap would disintegrate and roots would grow through the wire basket, but my husband, Mark, and I discovered when we had a tree removed that we planted 20 years before that the burlap survived and there were roots that were deformed by the wire basket, causing deformed branches.

Steve suggests snipping away the wire basket at the bottom only, before setting the tree in the hole and then removing the rest of it, as well as any twine or fabric, before backfilling.

Container trees

These are the most problematic because the roots often start circling inside the pot. Steve doesn't hesitate to lift a tree from its pot to have a look at the roots before deciding to buy it. Roots should be firm and whitish. A nasty-looking root mass can be "butterflied," sliced in an X from the bottom, so that the roots can be spread out in the planting hole. Or in extreme situations, all the dirt can be washed off so the roots can be arranged properly.

The right tree in the right place

The U.S. Department of Agriculture Plant Hardiness map says Cheyenne is in Zone 5, minimum temperature of -15 to -10 degrees. But most Cheyenne gardeners select trees and other perennials for Zone 3 or 4 to avoid winterkill in those record-low years.

Around your house, plant evergreens on the north and west sides to protect it from winter winds and cut heating bills. Plant deciduous trees on the south and southwest sides to shade the house in summer and lower air conditioning bills, and later, when the leaves fall away, winter sunlight will warm your house.

People forget to plan for mature sizes of trees. Plant too close to power lines and you and the utility company will have to keep hacking away branches every year. Also, Cheyenne's safety zones require clearing vegetation 14 feet above the street and 8 feet above the sidewalk.

Aggressive growers, like silver maples, can damage concrete house foundations and driveways. Keep them at least 15 feet away.

Avoid planting trees with messy fruit, like mountain ash, where it might fall on sidewalks and parked cars.

Preparing the site

At least two days before you dig, you are required to call 811 to have your underground water, gas, sewer and electricity lines marked, at no cost, so you can avoid them.

Measure the depth of your tree's root ball, from the top of the upper-most root, and dig your hole 6 inches deeper. Measure the width of the spread of the roots. Dig your hole twice as wide. You might want to also remove grass farther out because it will eventually steal moisture and nutrients from tree roots.

Next, add back a 6-inch mound of dirt in the center of the hole. This is where you will set your roots. Allow the roots to drape gracefully.

Do not add any fertilizer, organic matter or other amendments to the hole, Steve said, otherwise the roots won't be encouraged to grow beyond that space, which they will need to do to anchor the tree firmly.

Setting the tree

One of the biggest reasons for the failure of trees to thrive is that they have been planted too deep, Steve said.

So, after you set your tree in the hole, take a stick or a rake handle and lay it next to the trunk, across the hole, to see if the top of the roots is at ground level. If not, remove or add dirt to the mound as needed.

Stake trees for one year using straps to protect the bark.

Staking the tree

Most people do this after planting, but Steve, because he usually plants trees by himself, finds staking holds the tree in place while he backfills.

He uses two metal, T-style fence posts set out a few feet from the trunk, to the north and south, so that the fence posts and trunk form a line perpendicular to the pre-vailing west wind.

He uses two fabric webbing straps, gentle on tree bark, each looped once around the tree trunk at about one-third of the way up the tree's height. A length of wire makes up the dis-tance between the grommets in the ends of the straps and the posts.

The old-school folks staked trees much higher, but if a tree doesn't get a chance to bend with the wind a bit, it won't develop proper taper — the trunk should grow widest at ground level.

After a year, two at most, stakes are not needed anymore and need to be removed.

Backfill and water

Throwing dirt back in the hole seems simple enough, but when only half full, Steve used the hose to water the dirt down between the roots before adding the rest of the backfill. To avoid injuring roots, don't tamp down the dirt with your feet or shovel.

Wait to prune until next year

Old-school methods would have you prune the top of the tree to match the size of the roots. But when the tree was dug up from the field for bare root or balled and burlapped, it lost 70% of its roots, Steve said.

You need all the leaves you can get because they gather the energy the roots need to regrow. Other than broken branches, wait until next year to start pruning for form.

Mulch

Mulch keeps down the competition, which is important to your tree because most of its roots are in the top 12 inches of soil and will eventually extend several times farther out than the branches.

The great thing about organic mulch, like wood chips, is that unlike weed barrier cloth, it allows in the nutrients — and it provides nutrients as it breaks down. The city composting facility has a ready supply of wood chips to renew your mulch each year.

Three inches of mulch chokes weeds and doesn't suffocate tree roots. But be sure to keep it several inches away from the trunk.

A side benefit to mulching trees is that it keeps the lawn mowers and weed whackers far away, so they won't injure the bark.

Trunk protection

Steve said for two or three years while the tree is reestablishing roots, the trunk needs protection in winter. He uses corrugated plastic drain piping slit lengthwise, putting it on at Thanksgiving and taking it off by Easter.

Relax, enjoy — and water

Tom Heald, a former Casper Extension agent, recommends finding out how long you must water to wet the top 12 inches of your yard's soil — where most of the tree roots are. Water for an hour (somewhere close by, but not over your new tree's roots) and then dig to see how far the moisture went. You might have to repeat the experiment in half-hour intervals, but once you know, you'll know how long to water.

The Cheyenne Urban Forestry Division has more information on tree care on its website, including when to water in winter.

Trees recommended for Cheyenne

One of the best resources for researching kinds of trees is the Cheyenne Urban Forestry Division website, CheyenneTrees.com, under the Education tab.

The other is the Cheyenne Botanic Gardens. Staff members have identified trees around the gardens so you can see what grows here (Chapter 54).

Make a cut under the branch first so the bark won't tear, then cut from the top.

CHAPTER 56: **TREE PRUNING**

PRUNING KEEPS TREES HEALTHY

"Train up a tree in the way it should go; and when it is old, it will not depart from it." — adapted proverb

Pruning a young tree might not be for the faint of heart.

I was sure Michael Smith was sucking in his breath as Catherine Wissner lopped off a nearly 1-inch-diameter, 4-foot long, competing leader on one of his cherished young aspen trees.

While I arranged for Michael, photo editor for the Wyoming Tribune Eagle at the time of this story in 2013, to take pictures of pruning techniques, he volunteered the trees in his yard for a house call from Catherine, University of Wyoming Laramie County Extension horticulturist. And he did have perfect examples of several situations requiring pruning.

Surprisingly, winter is the best time for pruning most trees.

"You can see their bones," Catherine said.

You can see all their structural, health and safety problems.

Being a season for dormancy for trees as well as insects and diseases, those problems are less likely to spread through the fresh cuts. Also, if you need to hire an arborist, he or she might not be as busy.

Millions of wild trees are pruned by nature, but on your own property you don't want to wait for the wind to do it for you, dropping a weak limb onto your car or onto your roof.

Arborists are trained to recognize a variety of situations, but there are a few that you can easily recognize and take care of while trees are young, which will save you (or the next homeowner) money and heartache a decade or two in the future.

But first, let's talk about how to cut. There are three caveats.

How to cut

First, make sure your tools are sharp and sanitary.

If you are cutting away diseased wood, be sure to disinfect tool blades after each cut. Catherine uses ¼ cup bleach to a gallon of water. Follow that up with a clear water rinse to keep the bleach from corroding the metal.

Hand pruners work for twigs and branches under 1 inch in diameter. Catherine prefers the bypass type (scissors-like) rather than the anvil type. A pruning saw is best for anything more than an inch. Bow saws are fine too but can be hard to get into position without damaging nearby branches.

Keep in mind chainsaws are likely too big for the job when it comes to young trees. You could end up doing some serious damage.

Second, never remove more than 25% of the tree's canopy in one year. Err on the side of less, rather than more pruning.

Third, cut in the best place. Every twig and branch emerges from a collar-like protrusion. Your job when removing them is to make sure that the collar is not damaged while you

cut as close to it as you can. It is what will help the tree "cork over," or grow bark over the wound, said Catherine. No wound dressing is necessary on a fresh cut of any size — it's been shown it only attracts insects and disease.

On the other hand, she said, "You shouldn't leave anything (stub) you can hang your hat on."

When shortening a branch, cut at an angle just above the juncture with a bud, twig or side branch.

No touching

The first rule of pruning is no touching. Look for branches that are rubbing on each other or are within a fraction of an inch apart and will rub in the wind.

"It's like a school dance," said Catherine, "and you are the chaperone. They aren't allowed to touch."

Branches that touch will rub each other's bark away, leaving wounds that are easily infected by tree diseases and insects. You could eventually lose both branches.

Instead, you can determine which branch to keep: the one that is stronger and or contributes best to the shape you want the tree to grow in.

The no-touching rule also applies to human structures. You don't want branches rubbing on your house or fence — it's bad for the tree and the object. Branches should be trimmed 4 feet above roofs so that there is plenty of clearance when they are snow-laden.

As for public safety, city ordinances require removing vegetation 8 feet above sidewalks and 14 feet above alleys and streets.

Only one leader

Everyone recognizes the pointy top of a spruce tree is its central growing point, which arborists refer to as the leader, but even most deciduous trees should have only one.

However, when I look at the 50-plus-year-old trees at my house, it's easy to see that accidents caused the trees to produce multiple leaders.

One of Michael's young aspens had the same problem. You could see the original, now dead leader pointing perfectly vertically to the sky, but on either side were two lateral branches now also pointing up, competing for the job.

Left to their own devices, the leaders use the tree's valuable energy competing with each other. Only the healthiest, best looking one should stay. The tree will be happier, said Catherine, when it can devote its energy to just one leader.

Branches never grow up

The height of where a branch attaches to the trunk never changes as the tree ages, Catherine told us.

One of Michael's aspens had lateral branches at about two feet above ground level. As the tree grows, they will only get bigger and begin to become obstacles while mowing the lawn. He could mulch around the tree, so mowing close wouldn't be necessary. One thing for him to consider is that some branches might still be at the eye-level of his children playing in the yard.

On the other hand, spruce trees should be left to drape their branches to the ground (that much less lawn care to worry about!). These draping branches help shade and hold moisture for the tree. Removing these branches can create stress-related problems to the tree and attract unwanted insects, said Catherine. It helps if they are planted where their branches don't interfere with human

Loppers and a pruning saw are enough for pruning young trees. When your tree outgrows them, it could be time to bring in professionals.

activity when they are at their mature spread of as much as 30 feet across.

Get the suckers

A tree might send up a sprout, or sucker, from the roots, or water sprouts on a main branch. They can grow as much as three or four feet in one year, with leaves larger than normal for the tree. These are a drain on the tree and increase its chances of acquiring disease, so they should be removed when the tree goes dormant.

Dead wood

Even in winter, dead branches in a deciduous tree are pretty obvious. Compared to live young branches, the leaf buds aren't plump, the skin looks desiccated and the branch is no longer as flexible.

If you are removing diseased wood, cut in healthy wood beyond the infection.

Volunteer trees

It will surprise people to know that there are a fair number of trees that plant themselves in Cheyenne.

The volunteers usually pick a microclimate with a bit of extra moisture or shade, like right next to your house foundation. Roots are stronger than concrete, so you are best off removing those trees before you get attached to them. However, the trees damaging Michael's fence — some kind of flowering plum — were probably planted too close.

Volunteers are usually softwood trees that don't last long in Cheyenne anyway, such as silver maple, elm, boxelder, poplar and willow, and are the most likely to shed limbs during storms.

Seek expert advice

Trees add value to your home, but only if they are healthy and not threatening people or property. You can do a lot for them yourself with a hand pruner when they are young. Get more specific information if you have fruit trees. Please call certified arborists for the big issues and big trees, especially if utility lines are involved.

The best information about our local trees and taking care of them is at the Cheyenne Urban Forestry Division's website. They have a list of licensed arborists, too.

The Arbor Day Foundation website has numerous videos on aspects of tree care.

To keep chokecherries as shrubs instead of small trees, remove the largest stems regularly.

CHAPTER 57:
SHRUB PRUNING

IT'S DIFFERENT, AND EASIER, THAN FOR TREES

By Jessica Friis, Cheyenne Botanic Gardens horticulturist

Shrubs are much more forgiving than trees. Pruning shrubs is more for aesthetic purposes.

Because trees get big, and the trunk and main branches are supporting most of the tree's weight against environmental stresses like wind and snow, structural pruning is important. It prevents limbs from breaking and ensures that the trunk develops strength as the tree reaches mature size.

Shrubs, on the other hand, send multiple shoots out from ground level and aren't supporting as much weight, so structural pruning is not as necessary.

Some of the pruning rules for trees also apply to shrubs. Dead wood should be removed, unless your shrubs are being used as a windbreak. In that case, you can leave the dead wood to provide more wind resistance.

Remove crossing branches to prevent rubbing and fusing, but don't remove more than a third of the total canopy during the growing season. For safety reasons, remove branches that touch structures, block views for drivers, and obstruct public sidewalks and streets.

Winter is a great time to prune deciduous shrubs. You can see the branches better (but see notes below on blooming shrubs). Cuts should be made at ground level if removing the entire stem, or just above a bud or secondary branch if removing only part of it.

Pruning for aesthetic reasons

Some shrubs benefit from pruning to emphasize their distinguishing characteristics. For example, pruning out the older, browner stems of red-twigged dogwood encourages the growth of younger, brighter-colored shoots. Their bright-colored bark against a winter landscape is what this species is known for.

The most common reason people trim their shrubs is to control their size and shape. While shearing, the practice of cutting off the tips of branches with hedge clippers to produce a formal shape, is tolerated by some shrubs, I don't highly recommend it, especially in Cheyenne.

Shearing is not necessary in most landscapes and it only cuts off the new growth. The middle of the shrub accumulates dead branches, which stop producing leaves when they are no longer receiving enough light. Then, if an early or late frost kills a patch of tender new growth, or a broken branch due to a heavy snow removes a chunk of the shrub, you end up with a gaping hole that could take years to fill back in, or never fill in at all.

I recommend paying attention to the mature size of the shrub and selecting those that will fit into your landscape. For example, some lilacs can grow to be 10 feet tall, so don't plant them in a place where you want a 4-foot tall shrub. If you do need to control the size of a shrub, cut the taller stems back at ground level, leaving untouched the shorter, newer stems (and remembering the one-third rule).

Some shrubs can be cut completely back to the ground if they need to be rejuvenated, but research

Hand tools might make for slow pruning, but they give you more time to think through what's best for the shrub.

first to make sure your shrub will tolerate it, and make sure the plant is properly irrigated and fertilized so that it has the energy and nutrients needed to grow back.

Pruning for pest control and plant health

Sometimes there are pests that prefer older wood, like the lilac borer, so it is recommended to cut the older, thicker stems at ground level to prevent the pest from invading your lilacs.

For shrubs that are susceptible to powdery mildew and other fungal infections, thinning out some of the stems to promote air circulation around the leaves will help.

Older shrubs that are not irrigated should be pruned very sparingly. Removing the dead wood is all that should be done during the growing season.

In general, removing up to a third of the older stems at ground level to make room for newer, healthier shoots will improve the look and health of most shrubs, so this is the best practice to start with. Dead limbs don't count as part of the third, so feel free to remove those at any time.

Pruning to promote blooming

If you have shrubs that bloom, it's important to understand what type of wood produces the flowers.

In some shrubs, such as lilacs, mock orange and viburnum, the flowers are produced on wood that grew the previous year. So, if you prune the shrub before it blooms, you will reduce the number of flowers you get that year. With those shrubs, it's best to prune as soon as possible after the blooms have faded, to give time for new growth that will provide next year's flowers.

Usually, the shrubs that bloom early in the growing season are blooming on last year's wood. Shrubs that flower on new wood, like elder and potentilla, produce flowers on wood that has just grown and can be pruned any time, but might produce more flowers if they are pruned in the winter or early spring.

Some shrubs, such as roses, hydrangeas and spirea, have varieties that fall into both categories, so you'll need to know which type you have. If you are unsure, my advice is to prune right after the blooms are finished, just to be safe.

Find more information on pruning shrubs at Colorado State University Extension's PlantTalk website.

A pine under stress from drought or unusual weather is more susceptible to a tip-boring insect.

CHAPTER 58:
TREE PROBLEMS

DROUGHT AND FUNGUS THREATEN TREES

The phone calls Catherine Wissner gets are a good snapshot of what is going on in Cheyenne yards. She is the University of Wyoming Extension horticulturist for Laramie County.

When gardeners or property owners notice something amiss with their lawns, trees, vegetable gardens, crops, houseplants that they can't figure out, Catherine gets their calls and will often visit. I asked her what the most frequent topic was the summer of 2019.

Trees and fungus

"Trees," she said. Mistreat a tomato plant and you don't get tomatoes. Mistreat a tree and you lose a major financial investment when it either dies immediately, or lingers for years, looking stunted and unhealthy.

This year we could blame the weather for a lot of tree problems, Catherine said. April through June we had nearly as much precipitation as our annual average, 12-15 inches. All that moisture aided the growth of fungus.

A common problem was verticillium wilt. It's in the soil and gets into trees, shrubs or other plants through the root system. Damaged roots are most susceptible. Sprays and injections don't work on this fungus.

The fungus moves from the roots through the tree's vascular system (think sap instead of blood) and within a month of showing signs of stress, the tree is dead.

Some tree species or varieties are more resistant, Catherine said. You must do your homework when looking for a replacement tree. But don't plant the new tree in the same place.

Another fungus affects oak leaves, leaving brown splotches. Just clean up the leaves when they fall off. Next year the trees might not be affected.

Pines can be attacked by a tip-boring insect — it bores into the tips of branches causing them to look lumpy. Because she values pollinator insects and birds, Catherine recommends pesticides as a last resort. In this case, without using a systemic pesticide like Safari, absorbed through the trunk or as a soil drench around the trunk, the tree could be lost.

Get Catherine's advice before choosing a pesticide. Read the directions and avoid methods that could cause the toxins to drift onto other vegetation, beneficial insects and other animals.

Trees and drought

July through most of September we had no rain to speak of. Trees depend a lot on the fine hair-like feeder roots in the top 2 feet of soil — and out much further than the reach of their branches. Many of the trees planted in Cheyenne are not drought tolerant, including cottonwoods. In nature, they grow along streams. They like deep, uncompacted, moist soil.

This year, many people in my neighborhood seemed to be saving money by not watering their lawns during those droughty months. That's fine if the grass only goes dormant. If it dies though, the noxious weeds will move in and you will need to start a new lawn.

No lawn watering means trees that are not drought tolerant start losing leaves prematurely and become victims of stress and disease. Catherine pointed out that watering your mature spruce tree is cheaper than the $1,500 it costs to have it removed if it dies.

Once a month in the fall, and on warm winter days, is the time to make it up to your trees. Water your whole lawn if you have mature trees.

Catherine makes yard calls for free or you can bring in a diseased twig (in a sealed plastic bag) to her at the county extension office. You can also email photos to her. Cheyenne Urban Forestry Division and the Laramie County Conservation District can also offer free tree advice.

A very sudden, huge drop in temperature too early in the fall killed pine needles, but not the tree.

CHAPTER 59:
WINTER TREE DAMAGE

SOME RED OR BROWN EVERGREEN NEEDLES ARE OK

Don't touch those red needles on your evergreens just yet cautioned Lisa Olson, director of Cheyenne's Urban Forestry Department (now retired) in late spring 2015.

Wait until June to see if your pines and junipers get new growth before deciding what to do, she added.

Over the previous winter, property owners noticed that the needles on the tips of pine and juniper branches turned reddish brown. The color indicates the needles (juniper leaves are technically called scales), are dead.

Cheyenne had warm weather later in the fall than usual, preventing some evergreens from getting the cues that they usually get from cooler temperatures to go into winter dormancy. When the temperatures suddenly dropped in November, the fresh growth froze and died.

While pines and junipers were most likely to be damaged, exactly which ones had the most seems to have been hit or miss. Upright junipers seem to have no damage while the spreading Pfitzer juniper shrubs were most often hit.

But the amount of damage seems not to be so much a factor of how

TREE LEAF SCIENCE

By Dennis Knight, University of Wyoming Professor Emeritus, specializing in vegetation ecology, and co-author of Mountains and Plains: The Ecology of Wyoming Landscapes.

It's quite a feat for any outdoor plant to tolerate everything that's thrown at it, and often they don't survive if one day it's warm and the next day unusually cold. If the transition extends over a few days, the plants become "hardened," which means that the cells produce more sugar and that lowers the freezing point.

Over the years in Wyoming, our native and ornamental plants have been selected in one way or another to have pretty short hardening periods, but mortality will occur. The whole plant may not be killed, but if too many of the leaves and buds turn brown, the chances of survival are slim. The plant may look completely brown, but if the buds on the twigs or at the soil surface have not been frozen, there's a good chance the plant will survive. Learning from experience, horticulturalists tell us which plants are most likely to survive in our state and which ones are not.

An unseasonable cold snap affected only one of two kinds of junipers growing next to each other.

Keep in mind that most evergreen plants, like the conifers and junipers, will still have some brown leaves, usually most noticeable in the winter and spring. The plants as a whole normally live much longer than individual leaves. "Evergreenness" is bestowed on some plants because they always have leaves that normally last at least one year before they fall off, and not all of the leaves fall off at the same time.

Plants with mostly brown leaves after an abrupt freeze may appear a little thin during the following year, depending on how many of the buds were deactivated. I hesitate to call them "killed" because the plant could be still very much alive. Such plants produce new leaves using energy stored in the twigs and roots."

exposed the shrubs were to cold wind as perhaps variety.

In one Cheyenne neighborhood, there is a sheared hedge of Pfitzers made up of five individual shrubs. After the freeze, one was totally green, the next three totally red, and the one on the other end was green with red tips.

A property owner's first urge is to cut off the dead stuff. However, this would add insult to injury for pines.

The bud for new growth is at the tip of the branch. A bundle of new needles grows from it in what is referred to as "candling." That's because it makes the tree look like it has hundreds of pale green candles before the bundles open.

Pine trees keep their needles for three to five years before shedding them, Lisa said. If you are patient, the new needles will "overgrow" the dead ones, which will eventually fall off.

There is no need to prune unless you have branches that need pruning for other reasons.

If a pine does not candle all over, it might not have enough new green growth to photosynthesize, to make new buds next fall. A year from now is when those results will show up.

Junipers grow differently than pines. Buds aren't just at the tips of branches, and if their buds weren't killed by the cold, they also might be able to "overgrow" the dead needles with new growth.

The Pfitzers allowed to grow naturally have dead needles only on the tips of their branches — the newest growth from last year. Older needles are still green. What happens to Pfitzers that have been sheared into tidy shapes? Many seem to be completely red. We'll just have to wait and see if they survive. (Note: The ones in my neighborhood all recovered.)

But Lisa says this might be a good year to consider replacing overgrown Pfitzers.

They are often used as foundation plantings, but after many years, they can grow 10 or 15 feet high and into odd shapes as their branches become deformed by the weight of heavy snow.

If you have one of these, you might consider not waiting for it to die to remove it and plant something fresh.

But otherwise, wait until June to see what grows before deciding what to prune.

"It's amazing how trees can come back," Lisa said.

A lodgepole pine battles pine beetles boring holes in its trunk by producing a lot of sap to try to push the beetles out.

CHAPTER 60: EMERALD ASH BORER AND PINE BEETLE

WHAT'S IN YOUR FIREWOOD?

Randy Overstreet wishes there were a sign at the border outlawing firewood from out of state, or at least a check station like there is for inspecting boats for invasive zebra mussels.

With the news this fall (Wyoming Tribune Eagle, Oct. 19, 2013) that the emerald ash borer, referred to by scientists as EAB, has been discovered in ash trees in Boulder, Colorado, a mere 92 miles as the pickup drives, one log of infected wood is all it would take to bring the pest here.

Randy was assistant director of the Urban Forestry Division of the Cheyenne Parks and Recreation Department at the time of this interview in 2014. He'd seen these invasions before. About 10-15 years ago, it was the bronze birch borer, in the same genus as EAB, which wiped out Cheyenne's birch trees.

The local mountain pine beetle invasion is just about over, Catherine Wissner, Laramie County Extension horticulturist, told me. "I'm not recommending spraying for mountain pine beetle at this time," she said.

Not having to spray is good news, though you might want to continue if your neighbors are still bringing in infected firewood from the forest.

While we are in the lull between invasions, let's look at how these insects operate and the best practices for handling them.

Beetle biology

First, the mountain pine beetle flies (or blows) in, around July and August, finds a lodgepole or ponderosa pine, even making do with other pine species. It chews into the bark of the trunk. The tree fights back by producing gobs of pitch at the point of entry, encasing the beetle and forcing it out.

But if a tree is drought-stressed it doesn't have enough water to make enough pitch when attacked by many beetles at once. Or if previous beetles have attacked and have infected it with blue stain fungus, it will interfere with the tree's plumbing system located just under the bark, which brings water up from the roots. The plan to pitch beetles out doesn't work.

This beetle is native to our forests. Experts believe the epidemic proportions of the infestation — hundreds of thousands of acres of dead trees in Rocky Mountain forests — is due to drought conditions and winters not cold enough to kill beetles.

The beetle eggs hatch and the larvae start eating in the phloem layer, eventually cutting off not only water, but the usual flow of food from needles to roots during photosynthesis. The next summer the needles turn red. Around July and August, the larvae, turning into pupae and then adults, chew their way out and find a tree to start the cycle all over again.

The wood cutter who cuts the tree after the eggs are laid and before the adults fly, and transports the wood to another location, is helping spread death to the pines in the new area.

Removing the bark onsite before moving the wood is the only way to be sure pine beetles are not accidentally transported.

Borer biology

The emerald ash borer operates a bit differently. In its native habitats in China, Korea, Japan, Mongolian, Russian Far East and Taiwan, it is kept in control by several parasitic, stingless wasps. U.S. scientists are breeding them to see if they can make a difference in the hard-hit areas. Michigan was the location of the first North America discovery in 2002, followed by the other Great Lakes states and Canadian provinces and the states adjacent to those.

There are 17 species of ash trees in the U. S., mostly in the eastern forests, and their loss is going to change ecosystems, maybe even cause extirpation of two dozen species of butterflies.

Green ash and white ash have been popular as street, park and yard trees across the country, and green ash is popular here in Cheyenne. Millions of dollars have already been spent in affected cities removing dying trees. But those of you with mountain ashes will be delighted to know those trees aren't related.

The EAB life cycle begins between mid-May and mid-August when an adult lands on an ash tree and lays eggs. They aim for the upper parts of the tree, so you probably won't catch a glimpse of the elegant, emerald carapace of the adult.

After a couple weeks, the eggs hatch and the emerging larvae tunnel into the tree. They, like the pine beetle, find the area just under the bark, where the tree's water and food systems are coursing. If you peeled back the bark, you would see s-shaped galleries — tunnels chewed away by the larvae between August and October.

The larvae are dormant under the bark over the winter, but from May to June they emerge from the tree as adults, leaving small but easily visible D-shaped exit holes. Should you see any in an ash tree, call the Cheyenne Urban Forestry office.

Unlike the pine beetle, which seems to finish off its host in one year, the EAB might take longer to kill an ash. Trees that were healthy to begin with might respond to injected systemic insecticides.

Protect your ash trees

Until EAB is reported in Cheyenne, don't let any tree service waste your money convincing you to spray your ash trees. You'll be killing beneficial insects unnecessarily. Protect your trees by not moving wood.

Don't move wood to Cheyenne

An EAB can supposedly make a flight of up to half a mile to find a suitable tree. Because there is no line of ash trees at half mile intervals between here and Boulder, it is unlikely any will arrive in Cheyenne on their own.

However, if you look at the map of infestation at the Emerald Ash Borer Information Network website, the whole state of Kansas and half of Colorado was between Boulder and the closest outbreak. The EAB arrived with human help, probably unintentionally. The original immigrants are thought to have arrived in Michigan via wooden

Finding D-shaped, ¼-inch holes in the bark of this green ash tree will be a sign of an emerald ash borer attack. So far, none found.

packing materials in shipments from Asia. Imported packing crates must now be treated.

Here, the most likely scenario is someone moving firewood. The eastern states all have strict regulations about transporting firewood, especially outside quarantined areas. We don't.

The website, DontMoveFirewood.org, run by The Nature Conservancy, is most concerned with people bringing firewood from home to parks and forests, or firewood sold by grocery and big box stores brought in from distant states and even other countries. Here in the middle of the prairie, we should be concerned with what is brought into town.

The best advice from the website is to not move firewood more than 50 miles. Try to find a use for your deadwood in your own backyard — make a bench or garden border or burn it in your woodstove, or at least move it only within your local community, says the emerald ash borer website. Don't bother bringing in ash nursery stock. Catherine is not recommending planting ash anymore. Young trees could be infected already or will have short lives if EAB comes to town.

Where the wood goes locally

While the Cheyenne compost facility accepts wood up to 10 inches in diameter and 6 feet long that they can chip, larger logs too big for their equipment have to go to the landfill. However, as of 2021, there was a man looking for large logs for woodworking and companies accepting logs for firewood. It is not known where the firewood goes.

On a personal, philosophic note

I've lived with our two green ash trees for 30 years (2021), half their lives. They have grown way too big for our backyard. Every three years or so they need expensive pruning jobs to keep them away from utility lines and from hanging over the neighbor's roof. When it is time for them to go, there will be more sunlight for the vegetable garden and a chance to plant trees better suited to a small space.

The Tiger Tree crew celebrates the planting of another tree for "Rooted in Cheyenne."

CHAPTER 61:
ROOTED IN CHEYENNE

LOCAL NONPROFIT PLANTS STREET TREES

Street trees and their canopy of green are prized, especially here in Cheyenne, located on the naturally treeless prairie. Trees keep cities cooler, break the wind's ferocity, add to property value, remove pollutants and sequester carbon.

Cheyenne residents started systematically planting trees in 1882 and have continued planting in successive waves.

The latest wave of tree planting was instigated by Mark Ellison, city forester. He noticed many street trees have disappeared, victims of disease

and old age. A windfall of $25,000 helped set up a tree planting nonprofit, Rooted in Cheyenne. The name harks back to our city's tree history and forward to a tree-full future.

The funds came from mitigation for the historic residential block replaced by Cheyenne Regional Medical Center's Cancer Center, said Stephanie Lowe, involved with Historic Cheyenne, Inc., the group set up to disburse the funds.

Mark and the Rooted in Cheyenne board organized an incentive program to encourage property owners to have trees planted in the right of way, between curb and sidewalk, or if the sidewalk abuts the curb, on the other side of the sidewalk.

In the spring of 2017 they bought 100 trees, and for $50 each, offered to plant a tree for a property owner as well as stake it and care for it for one year, including weekly watering in summer and monthly watering in winter.

Rooted in Cheyenne has continued to offer 100 or more trees twice a year. Some trees are available at no cost to people who qualify. This year, the actual cost of $150 per tree, including planting supplies, was also supported by a state forestry grant and the Laramie County Conservation District. Additional sponsorships and donations are welcome.

The trees in 2019 came from nurseries in Colorado, Nebraska and Oregon in 15-gallon containers. They were 8 to 10 feet tall with a caliper (diameter) of 1.25 to 1.5 inches.

Mark has taken the precaution of offering a variety of trees suited to our area. You can see photos and descriptions at the Rooted in Cheyenne website. It's a list to work from if you are planting on your own.

Consider volunteering on a planting crew for half a day. City Council Ward I member Jeff White is enthusiastic about his experience on a crew and the importance of the effort: "So many of the trees in our city have reached their shelf life. We would become treeless. It's important to have Rooted in Cheyenne."

Each crew plants 10 trees in four hours. A crew is led by one or two people from the green industry (landscapers, arborists, yard care company employees, etc.) who know how to correctly plant a tree.

If you plant trees yourself, see the Cheyenne Urban Forestry department's website, CheyenneTrees.com. Look under the Education tab for the Wyoming Tree Owner's Manual. It describes safe planting locations and best planting practices.

Volunteers are also recruited to do weekly summer watering. A crew of two drives a pickup around with a tank of water and a hose in the back.

WATER TREES YEAR ROUND

As of December 2020, 40% of the 425 trees planted by Rooted in Cheyenne were in the fair, poor and dead categories, according to a report by Mark Ellison. The most common problem was tree owners' failure to give the young trees enough water, 20-30 gallons for a 2-inch diameter tree, and often enough, once a week during the growing season and once a month during the dormant season on days over 40 degrees.

Depending on the precipitation levels and a tree's drought tolerance, more mature trees need supplemental watering as well.

Your tree planting benefits future generations, as the previous generations' tree planting at Lions Park has benefitted us.

PART 8

INDOORS

Chill spring-blooming bulbs outside or in the fridge and warm them up for mid-winter indoor color.

CHAPTER 62: **BULB FORCING**

CREATE SPRING INDOORS WHEN IT'S WINTER OUTDOORS

Early fall is the season for ordering spring-blooming bulbs, and October for buying them locally. But not all of them need to go in the garden. Some of them can be kept back for forcing.

Bulb forcing allows you to enjoy crocus, the small iris, hyacinth, daffodils and even tulips indoors earlier than they bloom outside. Think of them as a deep winter gift to yourself, or for someone else.

Cheyenne Botanic Gardens director Shane Smith, now retired, gave me background on the practice and a few tips.

The science and history

Shane said the trick is to use bulbs from temperate climates that need winter — such as the bulbs we plant in our gardens for spring bloom. They can get by with a shorter winter, or artificial cooling period, to bloom. Bulb growers in Europe started taking advantage of this about 300 years ago, as relayed by Patricia Coccoris of Holland in her book, *The Curious History of the Bulb Vase.*

The timing

Buy spring-blooming bulbs in early fall. Bulbs ordered from catalogs begin shipping here around the beginning of October because bulbs normally need to be planted outdoors when the soil cools, but before it freezes in December.

For bulb forcing, figure 12 weeks minimum of "cool treatment," however tulips need 13 weeks or more. Once the minimum is met, you can stagger when you start warming up the bulbs. You can aim for specific bloom times during our cabin fever months, January through March, or maybe even later into spring when we get those depressingly late, tulip-breaking snowstorms.

The best bulbs

Shane said he used to tell people to buy the premium-sized bulbs for forcing, but now he thinks he gets more bloom for his buck with the smaller grades of bulbs. Premium hyacinth bulbs go for more than a dollar apiece in the John Scheepers catalog, but you might find smaller bargain bulbs have more, if only medium-sized blooms, for the same amount.

Shane said some varieties of bulbs are easier to force and bulb catalogs often will mention which ones. Varieties seem to go in and out of vogue, so don't be surprised if Shane's recommendations are hard to find.

Hyacinth is the classic forcing bulb, growing 10-12 inches tall. Each stalk is covered in tiny florets. Shane looks for Pink Pearl, Queen of the Pinks, White Pearl, L'Innocence (white), Blue Jacket, Delft Blue and Blue Giant.

All varieties of crocus force well. Shane's favorite varieties are Remembrance (purple), Blue Ribbon, Giant Yellow and Jeanne d'Arc (white). Only 4-5 inches tall, they are usually planted as a mass.

Iris reticulata, though related to the summer-blooming bearded iris, grows only 4-6 inches high. Recommended for rock gardens, mine bloomed outside at the end of last February, but it would be nice not to have to brave winter winds to enjoy it. Shane said all the varieties force well. Scheepers lists eight ranging in color from white to blue to deep purple, all marked with a bit of yellow.

Almost any daffodil (narcissus) will work well for forcing, said Shane. The popular Paperwhite narcissus, however, is a tropical bulb, so it doesn't need cooling.

Tulips, said Shane, are the hardest to force. They need the longest cooling time, minimum 13 weeks. They also might get floppy and need staking. Look for the earliest varieties, those that would otherwise bloom outdoors here (USDA Plant Hardiness Zone 5) in April.

There are a variety of other, more difficult spring-blooming bulbs to experiment with: snowdrops; grape hyacinth, *Muscari*; and squill, *Scilla*.

Bulb-forcing vases

Bulb-forcing vases, usually glass, are pinched near the top, providing a cup for the bulb to sit suspended so that only its base touches the water. You watch as the roots grow to fill the rest of the vase and the flower stem sprouts. For this forcing method, you can cool just the bulbs in your refrigerator for the recommended time. Be sure hyacinth bulbs don't touch produce.

If you are lucky enough to find a bulb-forcing vase, remember to change the water regularly.

Potted bulbs

Shane pots his bulbs. Without a cellar between 35 and 45 degrees, he instead buries the pots in a 2-foot-deep trench in his vegetable garden. He then backfills the trench with straw or pine needles (I use leaves). The mulch allows moisture to percolate down, whether the bulbs are watered by hand or by snow, and it allows air in.

Pots can be plastic or clay. However, if you have a fancy one, you might want to use it as a cache pot in which you insert the utilitarian pot that was buried.

Put only one type of bulb in a pot because different types sprout at different rates.

The depth of the pot should allow 2 inches or more of potting soil under the bulb with the bulb tip just a little below the rim of the pot.

Shane said regular packaged potting soil will do. Potting soil can be very dry, so mix it with water in an old dishpan or bucket before spooning it into the pot as the layer that will be under the bulbs. Then set the bulbs on top, right side up. The root end can have bits of root left and the shoot end is usually pointier.

You can pack the bulbs in, nearly shoulder to shoulder, leaving just a little space between them. Then fill in with more potting soil. Shane said the top third of the bulb can be left exposed, but crocus and iris bulbs need to be covered a half-inch deep.

Label the pot so you remember what's in it — especially if you do more than one kind. Mark where you bury the pot. And mark your calendar for when to bring the pot in.

Chill out

While the potted bulbs are chilling in the dark, make sure the soil doesn't dry out. You may need to lift the mulch and water once a month if it's a dry winter.

Coming in from the cold

When you bring a pot in, Shane recommends putting it in a dim room at 60 degrees or cooler until the shoots are a few inches tall. Then move it to a bright window and 65 degrees. "Buried to blooming" may take two weeks. Turn pots every day to keep plants growing straight.

Flowers can last a week or two. Once in bloom, you can prolong it by setting the pot farther from the window and keeping the room's temperature at 65 degrees.

Afterwards

The advantage to planting forced bulbs in potting soil is that you can give them a second life. Cut back the spent flowers and keep watering until the leaves turn yellow. Plant the bulbs out in the garden when the soil thaws, where they might bloom again in one or two years.

My results

In October 2017, I buried a pot of crocuses and a pot of hyacinth as Shane explained. I also cooled some crocus and a hyacinth in the refrigerator to try in bulb-forcing vases.

In early January I dug out the

buried bulbs and removed the other bulbs from the fridge. The potted bulbs did well. The bulbs in vases didn't. They couldn't seem to grow enough roots. That hyacinth stalk of flowers was about 15% the size of the ones in the pot.

I felt sorry for the crocus bulbs in the tiny vases and soon planted them in dirt where they were much happier. That proves you could cool your bulbs in the fridge for the required time and then plant them in pots indoors, without wintering them in the garden.

Those forced purplish hyacinth bulbs bloomed bright pink indoors in midwinter.

A vertical gardening system works well for growing salad greens and other small plants.

CHAPTER 63:
VERTICAL GARDEN

GROW LEAFY VEGETABLES AND HERBS INDOORS OR OUT

When we slip into the dark half of the year, we don't have to say goodbye to growing our own fresh herbs, lettuces and other greens. There is an option for those of us without a greenhouse, hoop house or cold frame, even if we have limited natural light or limited space.

Think vertical.

Think "Farm Wall."

No more stooping over short little plants. No more weeds. No more intensive watering schedule.

Bright Agrotech, a Laramie-based start-up, perfected a system that maximizes production for every square foot. It works for farmers as well as hobbyists — indoors or out. The company had its start in Laramie, employing many people straight from the University of Wyoming. In 2017 it joined up with Plenty and still maintains a presence in Laramie.

As magical as this system sounds, it really works. Growers on six continents are using it. In 2015, the U.S. pavilion at the world's fair in Milan, Italy, installed a demonstration ZipGrow Farm the size of a vertical football field, like a giant billboard full of leafy vegetables.

In 2016, the system was used at

Cheyenne Central High School. There, agriculture teacher Ty Berry, now retired, had his classroom system set up on a cart so he could take it places, including the state and county fairs.

Elsewhere, Altitude Chophouse in Laramie grew edibles on an outside wall during the summer using this system.

How it works

The Farm Wall starts with towers. They will remind you of rain gutters upended, but they are made of food-grade white plastic that wraps around part of the open side, leaving a slot the length (or the height) of the tower for plants to sprout from. Towers come in 3 or 5-foot heights.

Bright Agrotech refers to these components as ZipGrow Towers. That's because the growing medium can be "zipped" in and out of the towers.

The plants grow in a matrix made of curly fibers from recycled water bottles. They have a brown, protective silicone coating. Otherwise, light would cause algae infestations in the originally clear material.

So how do you get the plant into the matrix material? Simple. The matrix comes in two halves. You "zip" it out the end of the tower, spread the two halves just enough to place seedlings in between at regular intervals and "zip" it back into the tower. The plants spill out the lengthwise slot.

As you can imagine, the plastic matrix isn't going to hold water well, so strips of wicking material are added with the plants.

The next step is to place the towers between the upper and lower horizontal gutters. The lower gutter is on the floor. The upper gutter can be slid onto a bracket on a wall (indoors or out).

What makes the Farm Wall water-smart is that it is a hydroponic system. Water constantly circulates. About once a week the water reservoir needs to be topped off. It looks like and is lined up with the other towers but has no growing slot. Water is poured into the top. At the bottom is a spigot that allows only a certain amount of water to sit in the lower gutter. A small submersible pump sends the water up through a hose and across the top, inside the upper gutter. There's an emitter above each tower, keeping it watered.

Without soil to provide essential nutrients, you must add them to the water yourself. What you add depends on what you are growing, which is where Bright Agrotech can give you advice. There are several commercial fertilizer mixes available, or maybe you'd like to try aquaponics, in which the water circulates through a tank of fish and picks up nutrients from the fish poop.

While on my tour in Laramie in 2016, one unexpected thing I learned from my guide, marketing team member Amy Storey, is that the more growing cycles a unit of matrix material has been through, the better it gets. All the old roots and all the potting soil left behind by the seedlings enables good microorganisms to get established and start helping with their usual job, making it easier for plants to absorb nutrients.

One plus of the Farm Wall system: no pesticides are necessary, if good horticultural practices are maintained. And there are no weeds because you aren't tilling the garden and causing weed seeds to sprout.

Considerations

There are several considerations with this system. The 5-foot high, four-tower package is $599 (2016). The two-tower, 3-foot high version is $369 (2016). There is also an 8-tower option. Beyond that size, you need to look at the commercial farm version.

You also need an electrical outlet for the water pump. While the commercial farming version needs to be hooked up to plumbing, the Farm Wall doesn't. But you might want to install it where a few splashes of water won't be a problem.

An electrical conductivity meter will help you know how you are doing with fertilization, though you might make do with nutrient package directions and your own observations.

You'll need someplace warm to start seedlings under lights.

Speaking of lights, you'll need some fluorescent grow lights set up vertically in front of the Farm Wall if it isn't set up outside or in a greenhouse.

Obviously, root crops are not going to do well in such limited root space. So far, the most successful crops have been flowers, herbs,

lettuces and other smallish greens.

The possibilities

For growing small vegetables commercially, vertical farming is certainly more efficient than one layer of 6 to 12-inch high plants, especially in a greenhouse. Also, in an urban area, the cost of lighting and water pumping might be less than transporting produce from elsewhere.

In Jackson, where the town is isolated and the growing season very short, Vertical Harvest grows for local restaurants, grocery stores and its own store in a 3-story glassed-in area on the side of a parking garage. On a tenth of an acre, they grow the equivalent of 5 acres of conventionally farmed land through the winter.

Ty's students planted beans in their classroom Farm Wall. It was paid for by an educational grant he wrote. Bright Agrotech provided curriculum ideas to maximize the educational possibilities.

I remember 30 years ago when Cheyenne parent-teacher organizations raised the funds to pay for computer labs for their schools. Now, computers are part of the school district's budget and every student seems to have what amounts to one in their back pocket.

Perhaps someday it will be completely normal for a wall of every school building to produce healthy food for school lunches. Unless kids are already packing Farm Wall salads from home.

Succulents and other houseplants give gardeners an excuse to play in the dirt in winter.

CHAPTER 64: **HOUSEPLANTS**

GROW A GREEN THUMB WITH HOUSEPLANTS

With as many as seven months or more between average first frost and last frost, without a greenhouse, houseplants become important for Cheyenne gardeners.

Do you think you have a black thumb when growing houseplants? The cure is as simple as having the right plant in the right place with the right amount of water.

Ironically, the best way to check the water needs of plants is by feeling the soil — and probably getting a little black dirt on your fingers.

Plants indoors provide several benefits besides accenting your décor. They produce oxygen and add

humidity. Some plants, including the spider plant and pothos, remove toxins from the outgassing of building and furniture materials — but you'd have to fill the room with a jungle for it to work.

Also, scientists tell us gazing at plant natural forms does something good for our psyches, especially over a long winter.

The right plant

Often, people complaining about their black thumbs are having a bad experience with a potted plant that came from a florist. It was in full bloom and now it's dead.

The likelihood of a beginning indoor gardener finding success with a hothouse flower is about the same as someone trying Mount Everest for their first hike.

Houseplants are often descendants of tropical plants brought back by Victorian-era explorers in a time when the wealthy could afford glass-walled conservatories. When glass became more affordable, houseplants proliferated.

But these plants come from many micro-climates around the world with varying amounts of humidity, rainfall, light and heat.

Your best bet is to start with the standards, plants that can tolerate a wide range of conditions. These tend to remain foliage plants in the climates provided by our homes and offices.

My three favorites, spider plant, jade plant and pothos, which looks like variegated philodendron, are also easy to propagate so you might be able to find a friend who will share cuttings or a starter plant.

With jade and pothos, planting a cut stem is as easy as poking a hole in a small container of potting soil with a pencil and inserting the stem. With the spider plant, a "baby" growing on the end of a long stem can be cut off (or left attached), laid on top of the soil and held in place with a paper clip bent in a u-shape. And then keep the soil moist — not wet — until they start showing new growth.

The right place

In nature, plants grow where they get what they need. To be a successful indoor gardener, you need to match the plant with the conditions at your house.

Many houseplants prefer sunny, south-facing windows. Others are fine with shorter periods of sunlight on the east or west sides of the house. Some plants prefer dimmer light on the north side or being placed a distance from a window. And for some varieties, bright overhead fluorescent office lights will be enough. Only fake plants survive very dim light.

How do you tell how much light your plant will need? Read the label that came with it. Or find out what kind it is by asking a Laramie County Master Gardener or look it up at the library or online.

Experiment with your plants. If they grow long and leggy, or older leaves fall off too soon, they might need more light.

Humidity can be important. I had an avocado I grew from the pit that did very well in a bathroom in which two teenagers showered every day. But then we got a new furnace with a stronger blower that dissipated the humidity better and the plant died. Short of growing humidity-loving plants in a terrarium, it helps to group plants together so they humidify each other.

Garden soil — at least our garden soil around here — is a bad choice for indoor plants. General, all-purpose potting soil that can be found at any garden supply center will work for most houseplants. Cactuses and succulents might prefer grittier soil.

All pots need drainage holes and a saucer that allows you to see when water starts draining out. A pot too big will make your plant look scrawny, besides, many plants prefer cramped roots — it encourages

By following care directions, Phalaenopsis 'Maestro,' my first orchid, has bloomed prolifically for as many as five months a year for the last six years.

some to bloom. My azalea has been in the same pot for 30 years and blooms regularly.

Watering

Don't kill your houseplant with kindness. Most types will drown, literally, if you keep the soil soaking wet. Roots need air and as soil dries, microscopic air pockets develop.

On the other hand, if you let the soil get too dry, especially some of the potting soils with a lot of peat moss, they can become hydrophobic and it's hard to get them to absorb water again.

During the winter, my spider, jade and pothos plants easily go a week between waterings. But other plants will dry out faster if they have soil that doesn't hold water well. Same with plants in clay pots, small pots or pots located near the heating vents.

The general rule is that the top inch of soil should dry out before watering again. A few days after watering, stick your finger in the dirt to see how fast it's drying. You can also learn to evaluate the soil's dryness by the color of the surface, or if you have small plants in light plastic pots, check how heavy they feel.

My watering method is to pour enough in to fill the pot nearly to the rim, but no more than the saucer below can hold. Then I wait, water other plants and come back in a couple minutes to see if any water is draining out. I repeat this until I see water in the saucer. If more water is draining out than what would evaporate in an hour, be sure to dump it or suction it up with a turkey baster so the roots don't rot.

Maintenance

A plant in a livable temperature, receiving the right amount of light and water, is not stressed and is resistant to pests and diseases.

Plants look greener if you trim away dead parts. If you occasionally wipe or wash dust off their leaves, they absorb more light and will grow better. Don't block pores with leaf polishes.

Directions for houseplant fertilizer might recommend frequent feedings, but be cautious, especially in the fall as days get shorter and indoor plants grow more slowly.

Wait until early spring to start fertilizing when plants are really growing again. Even then, don't be too generous. My three recommendations, spider, jade and pothos, do well enough at my house with hardly any fertilization. Cheyenne tap water seems to be about all they need.

Housecats

The tiniest bit of true lilies is extremely toxic to cats — call a veterinarian immediately. Even though I've had cats doze next to semi-toxic plants for years, "It's whatever is new and different, like seasonal flower arrangements," that gets even adult cats in trouble, said Rebecca Marcy, vet and owner of Yellowstone Animal Health Center.

Normally, plants that might be toxic in large quantities usually don't taste good enough to make the cat sick. Instead, try offering a pot of "cat grass" for a tasty distraction. This is usually a combination of oats, wheat and barley. Look for it at pet stores and garden center seed racks.

Make sure any plants with trailing parts can't be pulled down by a playful cat.

Vally Gollogly, to protect the bare soil in her big pots, said she covers it with smaller pots. You can also try planting a "groundcover" plant. I tried filling in with ponderosa pinecones once, but our kittens just pulled them out and batted them around. Luckily, their fascination with dirt waned.

Branching out

Beyond the standard foliage plants, I urge you to try my favorites: amaryllis and orchids. I don't force my amaryllis into dormancy and phalaenopsis orchids are uncomplicated. Both bloom sometime between January and April, usually.

Other fun categories of houseplants to look into are bonsai, fairy gardens and terrariums. There seems to be a society for every plant genus you can think of, from African violets to maybe the ZZ plant.

PART 9

PLANT LIST AND GALLERY

PLANT LIST

This is a list of plants mentioned in the chapters.

For more plants recommended for our area, see websites for the Cheyenne Botanic Gardens, the Cheyenne Board of Public Utilities and the Cheyenne Urban Forestry Division.

sp. – Abbreviation for "species." It is used because the species name is not known or there are multiple species in that genus that are not listed.

'Name' – A name in single quotes is a name of a cultivar or cultivated variety.

Synonyms – Some botanical names have changed and both names are listed.

Botanical names are in scientific nomenclature. The first part of the name is the genus, usually a group of plants with similarities and similar DNA. The second name is the species, or the name for a specific plant in a genus.

See also "Nancy's Wishlist of Native Plants," page 167.

Plant is pictured in the Plant Gallery.

Plants named in **bold** type are native to Wyoming, according to Robert Dorn.

Common Name	Botanical Name	Chapters
BULBS		
Allium 'Gladiator'	*Allium* sp.	29
Allium, Pink Lily Leek	*Allium oreophilum*	29
Crocus	*Crocus* sp.	5, 29, 36, 47, 62
Crocus, Snow	*Crocus chrysanthus*	29
Crocus, Autumn	*Colchicum* sp.	36
Daffodil	*Narcissus* sp.	5, 29, 62
Glory of the Snow	*Chionodoxa forbesii*	29
Hyacinth	*Hyacinthus orientalis*	29, 62
Hyacinth, Grape	*Muscari armeniacum*	14, 29, 62
Iris, Dwarf	*Iris reticulata*	29, 62
Snowdrops	*Galanthus* sp.	29, 62
Squill	*Scilla siberica*	62
Tulip, Darwin hybrid	*Tulipa* sp.	5, 14, 29, 62
Tulip, Emperor	*Tulipa fosteriana*	29

Common Name	Botanical Name	Chapters
Tulip, Greig's	*Tulipa greigii*	29
Tulip, Species	*Tulipa turkestanica*	29
Tulip, Species	*Tulipa linifolia*	29
Tulip, Water Lily	*Tulipa kaufmanniana*	29

FLOWERS, ANNUAL

Bachelor's button	*Centaurea cyanus*	Intro, 4, 7, 17, 48
Bee Plant, Rocky Mountain	*Peritoma serrulata*	41, 48
Cosmos	*Cosmos bipinnatus*	3, 41
Dahlia	*Dahlia* sp.	30
Forget-me-not	*Myosotis* sp.	41
Geranium, Zonal	*Pelargonium hybrids*	34, 64
Marigold, French	*Tagetes patula*	41
Marigold, Pot	*Calendula officinalis*	26
Nasturtium	*Tropaeolum* sp.	41
Sunflower, Annual	*Helianthus annuus*	Intro, 4, 7, 17, 48
Vervain, Brazilian	*Verbena bonariensis*	41
Petunia	*Petunia* 'Wave'	4

FLOWERS, PERENNIALS
NATIVE TO NORTH AMERICA

Aster, Alpine	*Aster alpinus* 'Goliath'	45B
Autumn Sage	*Salvia gregii* 'Hot Pink'	36, 42, 47
Bee Balm, Wild Bergamot, Horsemint	*Monarda fistulosa*	27, 41, 42, 45, 47, 48
Black-eyed Susan	*Rudbeckia hirta*	36, 45, 47, 48
Blanketflower	*Gaillardia aristata*	36, 41, 45, 47, 48
Blazing Star	*Liatris spicata*	48
Blue Sage	*Salvia azuria*	36
Canada germander	*Teucrium canadense*	27
Columbine, Colorado Blue or Rocky Mountain	*Aquilegia caerulea*	45
Columbine, Golden	*Aquilegia chrysantha*	42
Columbine, sp. (6 Wyoming species)	*Aquilegia* sp.	42
Columbine, Western	*Aquilegia formosa*	48
Coneflower, Cutleaf	*Rudbeckia laciniata*	11B2
Coneflower, Prairie	*Ratibida columnifera*	41, 45
Coneflower, Purple	*Echinacea purpurea* 'Magnus Superior'	36, 41, 45, 45B, 48
Coneflower, Narrow-leaved Purple	*Echinacea angustifolia*	45

Pictured in the Plant Gallery   **Native to Wyoming**

Common Name	Botanical Name	Chapters
Coyote mint or mountain beebalm	*Monardella odoratissima*	27
Cranesbill sp. (8 Wyoming species)	*Geranium* sp.	42
Dotted Gayfeather, Dotted	*Liatris punctata*	41, 45
Dragonhead	*Dracocephalum parviflorum*	27
Drummond's false pennyroyal	*Hedeoma drummondii*	27
Evening Primrose, Missouri	*Oenothera macrocarpa*	45B
False dragonhead	*Physostegia parviflora*	27
Fleabane Daisy sp. (46 Wyoming species)	*Erigeron* sp.	45
Goldenrod sp. (16 Wyoming species)	*Solidago* sp.	36
Harebell	*Campanula rotundifolia*	45
Hummingbird Mint	*Agastache foeniculum*	27, 36, 42
Hummingbird Mint, Pale	*Agasatche pallida*	36
Hyssop 'Sonoran Sunset' Texas Hummingbird Mint	*Agastache cana* 'Sonoran Sunset'	45B
Hyssop 'Sunlight'	*Agastache aurantiaca* 'Sunlight'	45B
Hyssop, Giant (or anise)	*Agastache foeniculum*	27
Joe Pye Weed sp.	*Eutrochium* sp.	36
Joe-Pye weed	*Eutrochium purpureum*	42
Lamb's Ear, Texas Betony	*Stachys coccineus*	27
Lewis flax	*Linum lewisii*	41
Maximilian Sunflower	*Helianthus maximiliani*	36
Butterfly Milkweed	*Asclepias tuberosa*	48
Milkweed, Showy	*Asclepias speciosa*	45
Missouri Evening Primrose	*Oenothera macrocarpa*	45B
Monardella, Coyote Mint	*Monardella odoratissima*	48B
New England Aster	*Symphyotrichum novae-angliae* 'New England Pink'	36, 41, 42, 45B
Obedient Plant	*Physostegia virginiana*	36
Penstemon	*Penstemon x mexicali* 'Pike's Peak Purple'	45B
Penstemon sp. (41 Wyoming species)	*Penstemon* sp.	41, 48
Penstemon, Rocky Mountain	*Penstemon strictus*	Preface, 45, 48
Penstemon, Sidebells	*Penstemon secundiflorus*	Preface
Plains Pricklypear	*Opuntia polyacantha*	18
Prairie Blazing Star	*Liatris pycnostachya*	48
Selfheal, Common	*Prunella vulgaris*	27
Self-Heal, Lacy	*Prunella laciniata*	45B
Skullcap, Britton's	*Scutellaria brittonii*	27
Sneezeweed	*Helenium autumnale*	36

Common Name	Botanical Name	Chapters
Spiderwort sp.	*Tradescantia* sp.	42
Tickseed	*Coreopsis lanceolata*	45
Winecups or Poppy Mallow	*Callirhoe involucrata*	45, 48
Yarrow, Common	*Achillea millefolium*	41, 45

FLOWERS, PERENNIALS
NOT NATIVE TO NORTH AMERICA

Bearded Iris	*Iris germanica*	33
Bergenia, Pigsqueak	*Bergenia crassifolia* 'Winterglut'	45B
Butterfly Bush	*Buddleia davidii*	42
Butterfly Bush	*Buddleja* sp. 'Blue Chip'	45B
Butterfly Bush	*Buddleja davidii* 'Miss Ruby'	45B
Candy Tuft	*Iberis* sp.	42
Catnip	*Nepeta cataria*	27
Daylily	*Hemerocallis* sp.	42
Frog Bit	*Limnobium* sp.	43
Garden Catmint 'Walker's Low'	*Nepeta x fassennii*	27, 42
Gladiolus 'Atom'	*Gladiolus nanus* 'Atom'	30
Gladiolus 'Green Star'	*Gladiolus* 'Green Star'	30
Gladiolus 'Windsong'	*Gladiolus* 'Windsong'	30
Gladiolus, Abyssinian Sword-Lily	*Gladiolus murielae* (Acidanthera bicolor)	30
Gladiolus, Dwarf 'Glamini Charlotte'	*Gladiolus* 'Glamini Charlotte'	30
Hardy Water Lily	Nymphaeaceae sp.	43
Hibiscus, Hardy	*Hibiscus* sp.	42
Hollyhock	*Alcea rosea*	11B2, 15, 47
Japanese Iris	*Iris ensata*	42
Jupiter's beard	*Centranthus ruber*	42
Lamb's Ear	*Stachys byzantina*	27
Louisiana Iris	*Iris* 'Louisiana'	43
Maltese Cross	*Silene chalcedonica*	42
Mullein	*Verbascum*, ornamental species	47
Obedient Plant	*Physostegia virginiana*	36
Oriental Poppy	*Papaver orientale*	42
Pasqueflower	*Pulsatilla vulgaris, Anenome pulsatilla*	45, 45B
Poppy	*Papaver orientale* 'Salmon Oriental'	45B
Primrose	*Primula vulgaris*	Garden Gallery
Rose, Canadian Parkland series 'Hope for Humanity'	*Rosa* sp. 'Hope for Humanity'	31
Rose, Canadian Parkland series 'Morden Blush'	*Rosa* sp. 'Morden Blush'	31

Pictured in the Plant Gallery   **Native to Wyoming**

Common Name	Botanical Name	Chapters
Rose, Canadian Parkland series 'Winnipeg Park'	*Rosa* sp. 'Winnipeg Park'	31
Rose, David Austin 'Crown Princess Margareta'	*Rosa* sp. 'Crown Princess Margareta'	31
Rose, David Austin 'Mary'	*Rosa* sp. 'Mary'	31
Rose, David Austin 'Strawberry Hill'	*Rosa* sp. 'Strawberry Hill'	31
Rose, David Austin 'Winchester Cathedral'	*Rosa* sp. 'Winchester Cathedral'	31
Rose, Explorer series "Alexander Mackenzie'	*Rosa* sp. 'Alexander Mackenzie'	31
Rose, Explorer series 'John Davis'	*Rosa* sp. 'John Davis'	31
Rose, Explorer series 'William Baffin'	*Rosa* sp. 'William Baffin'	31
Rose, Knockout	*Rosa* sp.	31
Runnerless Strawberry	*Fragaria vesca* 'Alexandria'	45B
Scabiosa or Pincushion Flower	*Scabiosa sp.*	Garden Gallery
Sedum	*Sedum sieboldii* 'October Daphne'	45B
Sedum	*Sedum spectibile* 'Autumn Joy'	47
Shasta Daisy	*Leucanthemum × superbum*	42, 15
Siberian Iris	*Iris sibirica*	42
Sweet William	*Dianthus barbatus*	11B2, 51
Tall Garden Phlox	*Phlox paniculata*	42
Wooly Creeping Speedwell	*Veronica pectinata*	45B

FRUITS

Apple, Dolgo	*Malus* sp.	23
Apple, Duchess of Oldenburg	*Malus* sp.	23
Apple, Haralson	*Malus* sp.	23
Apple, Jonathon	*Malus* sp.	23
Apple, McIntosh	*Malus* sp.	23
Apple, McMahan	*Malus* sp.	23
Apple, Northwest Greening	*Malus* sp.	23
Apple, Patten Greening	*Malus* sp.	23
Apple, Wealthy	*Malus* sp.	23
Apple, Wolf River	*Malus* sp.	23
Apple, Yellow Transparent	*Malus* sp.	22
Cherry, Nanking	*Prunus tomentosa*	
Chokecherry	*Prunus virginiana*	22, 41, 48
Crabapple, Florence	*Malus* sp.	23
Currant, Golden	*Ribes aureum*	22, 41
Currant or Gooseberry (12 Wyoming species)	*Ribes* sp	22

Common Name	Botanical Name	Chapters
Elderberry (3 Wyoming species)	*Sambucus* sp	22
Grapes	Vitis sp.	25, 50
Grape, Wild	*Vitis riparia*	
Grapes, Frontenac	*Vitis* 'Frontenac'	25
Melon		19
Plum, American	*Prunus americana*	41, 44
Raspberry (6 Wyoming species)	*Rubus* sp	22
Serviceberry	*Amelanchier alnifolia*	22, 41
Strawberry, Berried Treasure	*Fragaria x ananassa*	24
Strawberry, Fort Laramie	*Fragaria x ananassa* 'Fort Laramie'	24
Strawberry, Ogallala	*Fragaria x ananassa* 'Ogallala'	24
Strawberry, Seascape	*Fragaria x ananassa* 'Seascape'	24

GRASSES

Basin Wildrye	*Leymus cinereus, Elymus cinereus*	48
Big Bluestem	*Andropogon gerardii*	47, 48
Blue Oat Grass, Blue Avena Grass	*Helictotrichon sempervirens*	47
Bluebunch Wheatgrass	*Pseudoroegneria spicata*	48
Kentucky Bluegrass	*Poa pratensis*	45, 47, 48, 51, 52, 53
Buffalograss	*Bouteloua dactyloides, Buchloe dactyloides*	48, 53
Feather Reed Grass	*Calamagrostis acutiflora* 'Avalanche'	
Feather Reed Grass	*Calamagrostis acutiflora* 'Karl Foerster'	36, 47
Indian Ricegrass	*Oryzopsis hymenoides, Achnatherum hymenoides*	48
Little Bluestem	*Schizachyrium scoparium*	47
Switchgrass	*Panicum virgatum* 'Heavy Metal'	45
Switchgrass	*Panicum virgatum*	48

GROUND COVERS

Bugleweed, Black Scallop	*Ajuga reptens* 'Black Scallop'	51
Clover, White	*Trifolium repens*	51
Creeping Jenny	*Lysimachia nummularia*	51
Deadnettle, Spotted	*Lamium maculatum*	51
Dianthus 'Tiny Rubies'	*Dianthus gratianopolitanus*	51
Geranium, Wild (7 Wyoming species)	*Geranium* sp.	34
Hummingbird Trumpet	*Epilobium canum var. garrettii*	51
Periwinkle	*Vinca minor*	47, 51
Phlox, Creeping	*Phlox subulata*	51

Pictured in the Plant Gallery   **Native to Wyoming**

Common Name	Botanical Name	Chapters
Snow-in-Summer	*Cerastium tomentosum*	51
Soapwort	*Saponaria officinalis*	51
Speedwell, Birdseye	*Veronica filiformis*	51
Speedwell, Woolly	*Veronica pectinata*	51
Stonecrop	*Sedum sp.*	51
Thyme, Lemon	*Thymus x citriodorus*	51
Thyme, Red Creeping	*Thymus praecox* 'Coccineus'	51
Veronica (or Speedwell), Turkish	*Veronica sp.*	51
Woodruff, Sweet	*Galium odoratum*	51

HERBS

Borage	*Borago officinalis*	26
Chamomile	*Chamaemelum nobile*	26
Chives	*Allium schoenoprasum*	16, 26
Cilantro/Coriander	*Coriandrum sativum*	26
Common Thyme	*Thymus vulgaris*	27
Dill	*Anethum graveolens*	26
Fennel	*Foeniculum vulgare*	26
Garden Sage	*Salvia officinalis*	26, 27, 47
Greek Oregano	*Origanum vulgare*	26
Lavender	*Lavandula angustifolia*	26, 27, 28
Lemon Balm	*Melissa officinalis*	26, 27
Lovage	*Levisticum officinale*	26
Nasturtium	*Tropaeolum majus*	26
Parsley	*Petroselinum crispum*	26
Peppermint	*Mentha x peperita*	27
Rosemary	*Rosmarinus officinales*	26
Spearmint	*Mentha spicata*	27
Summer Savory	*Satureja hortensis*	26
Sweet Basil	Ocimum basilicum	26
Sweet Marjoram, Oregano	Origanum majorana	27, 47
Chocolate Mint	*Mentha x peperita* 'Chocolate Mint'	27

HOUSE PLANTS

Jade Plant	*Crassula ovata*	64
Moth Orchid	*Phalaenopsis* 'Maestro'	64
Pothos	*Epipremnum pinnatum* 'Aureum'	64
Spider Plant	*Chlorophytum comosum*	64
Zonal Geranium	*Pelargonium hybrids*	34

SHRUBS

Buffaloberry	*Shepherdia argentea*	45
Cherry, Nanking	*Prunus tomentosa*	22
Chokecherry, Western	*Prunus virginiana*	22, 41B, 45, 48

Common Name	Botanical Name	Chapters
Cinquefoil, Shrubby	*Potentilla fruticosa, Pentaphylloides floribunda, Dasiphora fruticosa*	57
Cinquefoil sp. (30 Wyoming species)	*Potentilla* or *Pentaphylloides* or *Dasiphora* sp	
Currant sp. (11 Wyoming species)	*Ribes* sp	
Currant, Red	*Ribes rubrum* 'Red Lake' or *Ribes silvestre* 'Red Lake'	45B
Currant, Golden	*Ribes aureum*	41, 45
Dogwood, Redtwig or Redosier Dogwood	*Cornus sericea*	41, 45, 47, 48
Ephedra	*Ephedra viridis*	47
Juniper, Pfitzer	*Juniperus scopulorum* 'Pfitzer'	59
Mahogany, Mountain	*Cercocarpus ledifolius*	45, 47
Mahonia	*Mahonia repens*	47
Maple, Rocky Mountain	*Acer glabrum*	48
Plum, American, Wild Plum	*Prunus americana*	41, 45
Rabbitbrush	*Ericameria nauseosa*	36, 41, 45, 47
Rose sp.	*Rosa* sp.	31, 32, 41B, 57
Rose, Austrian Copper	*Rosa foetida bicolor*	32
Rose, David Austin 'Mary Rose'	*Rosa* sp.	31
Rose, Harison's Yellow	*Rosa* 'Harison's Yellow'	32
Rose, Woods	*Rosa woodsii*	41B
Sage, Russian	*Salvia yangii* or *Perovskia atriplicifolia*	27, 36, 42
Sagebrush, Silver	*Artemisia cana*	45, 48
Sandcherry, Western	*Prunus pumila*	45
Serviceberry or Shadbush	*Amelanchier canadensis*	45
Serviceberry, Saskatoon or Western	*Amelanchier alnifolia*	22, 41B, 42, 48B
Snakeweed	*Gutierrezia sarothrae*	36
Willow	*Salix arenaria* 'Blue Creek'	42
Willow	*Salix integra* 'Hakuro Nishiki' 'Dappled'	42
Yucca	*Yucca glauca*	45

TREES

Ash, Green	*Fraxinus pennsylvanica*	60
Aspen	*Populus tremuloides*	11B2, 56
Boxelder	*Acer negundo*	48
Cottonwood, Lanceleaf	*Populus acuminata*	48B
Cottonwood, Plains	*Populus deltoides*	52, 54, 58
Crabapple, Flowering	*Malus* sp.	23, 47, 53

Pictured in the Plant Gallery **Native to Wyoming**

Common Name	Botanical Name	Chapters
Fir, White	*Abies concolor*	54
Hackberry, Common	*Celtis occidentalis*	48
Hawthorn sp. (5 Wyoming species)	*Crataegus* sp	47
Juniper	*Juniperus scopulorum* 'Blue Arrow'	45B
Juniper	*Juniperus scopulorum* 'Woodward'	47
Juniper, Rocky Mountain	*Juniperus scopulorum*	48
Linden, American	*Tilia americana*	Intro
Locust, Honey	*Gledisia (Gleditsia) triacanthos*	53
Maple, Bigtooth	*Acer grandidentatum*	48
Mountain-ash, European	*Sorbus aucuparia*	11B, 47, 55, 60
Oak, Burr	*Quercus macrocarpa*	Intro
Pine sp.	*Pinus* sp.	58, 59, 60
Pine, Pinyon	*Pinus edulis*	48B, 54
Pine, Ponderosa	*Pinus ponderosa*	60
Pine, Rocky Mountain Bristlecone	*Pinus aristata*	54
Spruce, Colorado Blue	*Picea pungens*	I, 2, 30, 47, 48B, 51, 54, 56, 58

VEGETABLES — Days to maturity

VEGETABLES	Days to maturity	
Beans, bush, Bountiful	46	3
Beets		3, 7, 17, 19
Beets, Early Wonder	50	3
Beets, Golden Boy	65-70	3
Cabbage		3, 4, 6, 7, 17, 19
Cabbage, Red Express	63	3
Carrots, Parisian	55	3
Cucumber, Marketmore	60	3
Cucumber, Sweeter Yet	48	3
Eggplant		19, 30, 38, 39
Eggplant, Fairy Tale	50	3
Eggplant, Orient Express	58	3
Onions		19
Peppers, sweet, Lunch Box Red	55 (green)	3
Pumpkin, Atlantic Giant		21
Pumpkin, Autumn Gold		21
Pumpkin, Cinderella		21, 5, 7
Pumpkin, 'Jack Be Little'	90	21
Squash, summer, Yellow Crookneck	42	3
Tomato		Intro, 1, 3, 4, 5, 6, 7, 12, 15, 17, 19, 20
Tomato, Absinthe		20

Common Name	Botanical Name	Chapters
Tomato, Anna Maria's Heart		
Tomato, Early Girl	52	3
Tomato, First Lady, Shane's favorite early tomato	50	3
Tomato, Gold Nugget	55	3
Tomato, Silvery Fir	58	3

VINES
Annual

Morning Glory	*Ipomoea* sp.	50
Sweet Pea	*Lathyrus odoratus*	50

Perennial

Clematis	*Clematis* cultivars	50
Grape, American table	*Vitus labrusca* (Concord, Valiant, Reliance, Himrod, Swenson Reds)	50
Grape, Frontenac (wine)	*hybrid x Vitis riparia*	25
Honeysuckle, Trumpet	*Lonicera sempervirens*	50
Honeysuckle, 'Kintzley's Ghost'	*Lonicera reticulata* 'Kintzley's Ghost'	50
Hops	*Humulus lupulus*	50
Rose, Climbing	*Rosa* sp.	50
Silver Lace Vine	*Polygonum aubertii*	50
Sweet Pea	*Lathyrus latifolius*	50
Trumpet Vine	*Campsis radicans*	50
Virginia Creeper	*Parthenocissus quinquefolia*	50

WEEDS

Canada Thistle	*Cirsium arvense*	9, 11, 52B
Creeping Bellflower	*Campanula rapunculoides*	9, 11
Creeping Charlie	*Glechoma hederacea*	27
Dalmation Toadflax	*Linaria dalmatica*	11
Dandelion	*Taraxacum* sp.	11, 18, 52
Dead Nettle	Laminum amplexicaule	27
Field Bindweed	*Convolvulus arvensis*	9, 11
Horehound	*Marrubium vulgare*	27
Kochia	*Kochia scoparia*	11B2
Lanceleaf Sage	*Salvia reflexa*	27
Motherwort	*Leonurus cardiaca*	27
Plantain	*Plantago major*	11
Russian Olive	*Elaeagnus angustifolia*	48
Skeleton-leaf Bursage	*Ambrosia tomentosa*	37

Pictured in the Plant Gallery   **Native to Wyoming**

PLANT GALLERY

See the *Plant List* for the botanical name and particular chapters the plant is mentioned in.

Plants named in **bold** type are native to Wyoming, according to Robert Dorn.

BULBS
Chapters
5, 14, 29, 36,
47, 62

Allium, Gladiator

Crocus

Crocus, snow

Daffodil

Dwarf Iris

Glory of the Snow

Grape Hyacinth

Hyacinth

Species Tulip

Squill

Tulip

Sunflower, Annual

Cosmos

Marigold, Pot

Bee Plant, Rocky Mountain

Geranium, Zonal

Autumn Sage

Bee Balm, Monarda

Black-eyed Susan   Blanket Flower cultivar Blanket Flower

Blazing Star   Britton's Skullcap   Columbine, Western

Coneflower,   Coneflower, Prairie   Coneflower, Purple
Narrow-leaved Purple

Coyote Mint   Goldenrod   Hummingbird Mint

Maxmilian Sunflower

Milkweed, Butterfly

Milkweed, Showy

Missouri Evening Primrose

New England Aster

Obedient Plant

Penstemon, Rocky Mountain

Selfheal, Common

Sneezeweed, Common

Spiderwort

Tickseed variety

Yarrow, Common

Bearded Iris

Hardy Water Lily

Hollyhock

Pasqueflower, European

Sedum 'Autumn Joy'

Sweet William

Apple, Jonathon

Cherry, Nanking

Grapes, Frontenac

Plum, American

Strawberry, Fort Laramie

GRASSES

Chapters
36, 42, 45, 47,
48, 530

Blue Oat Grass

Bluegrass with white clover

Buffalograss

Feather Reed Grass 'Avalanche' summer

Feather Reed Grass 'Karl Foerster' fall

Little Bluestem

Switchgrass

GROUND COVERS

Chapters
34, 47, 51

Creeping Phlox

Periwinkle

Soapwort

Spotted Deadnettle

Sweet Woodruff

Turkish Veronica

Wild Geranium

HERBS

Chapters
16, 26, 27,
28, 47

Chives

Garden Sage

Lavender

Oregano

Parsley

Thyme

HOUSE-PLANTS

Chapters
34, 64

Jade Plant

Pothos

Spider Plant

SHRUBS

Chapters
22, 31, 32, 36,
41, 42, 45, 47,
48, 57, 59

Cherry, Nanking

Cinquefoil, Shrubby

Chokecherry

Currant, Golden

Dogwood, Redtwig

Rabbitbrush

Rose, Austrian Copper

Rose, David Austin 'Mary'

Rose, Harison's Yellow

Russian Sage

TREES

Chapters
Intro, 1, 2, 11, 23,
30, 45, 47, 48, 52,
53, 54, 55, 56, 58,
59, 60

Cottonwood, Plains

Cottonwood, Plains (branch)

Crabapple, Flowering

Crabapple, Flowering (flower)

Crabapple, Flowering (fruit)

Fir, White

Fir, White (branch)

Juniper, Rocky Mountain

Juniper, Rocky Mountain (branch)

Linden, American

Linden, American (branch)

Locust, Honey

Locust, Honey (branch)

Mountain-ash, European

Mountain-ash, European (bloom)

Mountain-ash, European (fruit)

Oak, Burr

Oak, Burr (branch)

Pine, Pinyon

Pine, Pinyon (branch)

Pine, Ponderosa

Pine, Ponderosa
(branch)

Pine, Rocky Mountain
Bristlecone

Pine, Rocky Mountain
Bristlecone (branch)

Spruce, Colorado Blue

Spruce, Colorado Blue
(branch)

VEGETABLES

Chapters
Intro, 3, 4, 5, 6,
7, 12, 15, 17, 19,
20, 21, 30, 38

Beets, Early Wonder

Beets, Golden Boy

Cabbage

Carrot, Parisian

Eggplant, Orient
Express

Onions

Peppers, sweet,
Lunch Box Red

Pumpkin, Cinderella

Tomato, Anna Marie's
Heart

Tomato, Gold Nugget

Tomato, Silvery Fir Tree

VINES

Chapters
25, 50

Clematis

Honeysuckle,
Kintzley's Ghost

Morning Glory

Silver Lace Vine

Virginia Creeper

WEEDS

Chapters
9, 11, 18, 27,
37, 48, 52

Canada Thistle

Creeping Bellflower

Dalmation Toadflax

Dandelion

Field Bindweed

Plaintain

ACKNOWLEDGEMENTS

First, I must thank my husband, Mark, vegetable gardener, who graciously allowed me to try my hand at growing our tomatoes back in 2012. He gives up garden space for my flowers and helps me enlarge the beds.

More than 100 people have contributed to my gardening knowledge, to my Wyoming Tribune Eagle garden columns and to the process of making this book. Thank you, everyone.

Wyoming Tribune Eagle

At the Wyoming Tribune Eagle, former Features Editor Jodi Rogstad championed the idea of a monthly garden column back in 2011. Michael Smith and other former WTE photographers accompanied me to gardener interviews in the early days. Feature editors since Jodi have continued to support the column, including Niki Kottmann today, and so has managing editor Brian Martin.

Editing and Design

This is the second book Niki has edited for me and she was willing to tweak Associated Press style to accommodate standard botanical nomenclature. And she allowed the Garden Gossips to be referred to by their first names on second reference — I'm not one of those people who calls their friends by their last names.

Chris Hoffmeister, gardener and Western Sky Design owner, and I first collaborated on *Cheyenne Birds by the Month*. We are getting more efficient at the book-making process. She always has great ideas for making books more attractive and readable.

Laramie County Master Gardeners

This book is based on the principles exemplified by the Wyoming Master Gardener mission statement:

"The Master Gardener Program within the University of Wyoming Extension exists to extend the University to the people of Wyoming via volunteer service in horticulture. The program provides research-based, horticulturally sound information to the public to solve problems in growing plants, determining the causes of problems with plants, and recommends procedures to follow for solving plant problems. The emphasis is on environmentally sound methods of growing plants utilizing the principles of Integrated Pest Management and Sustainable Agriculture and Horticulture."

Laramie County Master Gardeners are generous with their time and knowledge. Kathy Shreve, Michelle Bohanan, and University of Wyoming Laramie County Extension horticulturist and Master Gardener coordinator, Catherine Wissner, have been my most frequent sources of information. Chris Hilgert, state Master Gardener coordinator, has also been an important source. The list of "Gossips" below includes the many other Laramie County Master Gardeners who contributed to chapters.

Not all the garden columns I've written fit in this book, and so I'd like to thank these Laramie County Master Gardeners that contributed to those: Carolyn Elliott, Riley Elliot, Bob Janssen, Judy Kowrach, Kathryn Lex, Marie Madison, Timi Saville, Scott and Jackie Taylor, Jennifer Wolfe (and her sister Gina John) and Chris Wright.

You too can be a Laramie County Master Gardener, acquiring gardening expertise through hands-on training. Call the University of Wyoming Extension Laramie County office or the office in the county where you live.

Cheyenne Botanic Gardens

Director Tina Worthman is enthusiastic about this project and all of the staff are cheerfully supportive. Thanks to the Friends of the Cheyenne Botanic Gardens also, for financial support of this book.

Reviewers

As I compiled the columns, interviewees from as far back as 2012 were happy to review what I'd written to see if corrections and updates were needed. Then I asked three knowledgeable gardening friends to be reviewers. Each has their own area of expertise.

Susan Carlson is a 20-year member of Laramie County Master Gardeners. She started gardening when she was just a kid in West Virginia, where the climate was so salubrious and fertile, she didn't have to do anything but put the seeds in the ground to make them grow. She's been gardening in the Mountain West since 1965, including 11 years in commercial carnation greenhouses in Fort Collins and 10 years in retail garden centers. She's been gardening in Cheyenne for 34 years. Susan has served as the floriculture judge at the Laramie County Fair. She says, "Every garden season is another experiment," such as trying the straw bale technique (Chapter 39). She also contributed to the chapters on herbs (Chapter 26), trellis and vine (Chapter 50) and groundcovers (Chapter 51).

Jane Dorn, a Rawlins, Wyoming, native, has been gardening since childhood. "All my mother's family were gardeners and I learned early what it meant to garden at 8,000 feet (her grandparents' ranch) and deal with cool summers, short growing seasons, winds and frost and snows any time of the year." Her degrees in wildlife management (bachelors and masters from the University of Wyoming) included botany courses. Her husband, Robert (doctorate in botany also from UW) took her further into the plant world. Her artwork illustrated his books and professional articles on the native floras of Wyoming, Montana and the Black Hills. She co-authored with him *Growing*

Native Plants of the Rocky Mountains.
Research for it took them throughout
the Rocky Mountains and northern
plains to see and evaluate native
plants in their natural habitats.
Jane has been a frequent speaker on
the topic of using native plants in
landscaping as she did at her home
in Cheyenne and does at her current
home near Lingle. She has added to
this book's information on strawberries (Chapter 24), wild mints (Chapter 27), hoop house cooling (Chapter
40) and has suggested plants for
wildscaping (Chapter 48).

Jessica Friis, a Cheyenne native,
pursued her horticultural career
when she determined that spending
the winter months in a greenhouse
would cure her annual winter blues.
She received her horticulture degree in landscape management from
Brigham Young University. She
served as an intern at the Children's
Village at the Cheyenne Botanic Gardens and then was hired by
them. After three years, she left for
eight to follow her husband in his
educational pursuits, experiencing
gardening and gardens in Arizona
and Pennsylvania. She returned to
the Children's Village in 2020. She
likes to grow bonsai and to grow annuals from seed. Her new interest is
learning to grow native plants. Jessica
contributed to the chapters on seed
starting (Chapter 4), seedling transplanting (Chapter 5), spring bulbs
(Chapter 29) and wrote Chapter 57
on shrub pruning.

When I asked Shane Smith, the
founder and now retired director of
the Cheyenne Botanic Gardens, if
he would like to write the foreword,
he read through the manuscript
and offered additional nuggets of
wisdom, highlighted in the text,
that only a trained horticulturist, gardening in one place for 40
years, can accumulate.

The "Garden Gossips"

*Numbers indicate chapter(s) to which
each person contributed.*

Jutta Arkan, Garden Gallery,
Laramie County Master Gardener

Tyler Berry, 63, agriculture
teacher, Central High, retired

Michelle Bohanan, 6, 20,
26, 29, 35, 45, 45B, Laramie
County Master Gardener

Verena Booth, 4, gardener
and beekeeper

Marti Bressler, 38,
container gardener

Larry Bressler, 38, container gardener

Rusty Brinkman, 19, 30, heirloom
vegetable gardener and chef

Florence Brown, 13,
Cheyenne gardener

Susan Carlson, 26, 39, 50, 51,
Laramie County Master Gardener

Mitchell Chapman, Garden
Gallery, Cheyenne gardener

Katie Collins, 45, program manager,
Fort Collins Water-Wise Landscape

Tava Collins, 51, Garden Gallery,
Laramie County Master Gardener

Andy Corbin, 21, giant pumpkin grower

Linnie Cough, 26, 51, Laramie County Master Gardener

Sandra Cox, 2, 45B, 13B Cheyenne gardener

Charlie Culp, 34, Cheyenne gardener

Bud Davis, 16, Garden Gallery, Laramie County Master Gardener

Claire Davis, Garden Gallery, Laramie County Master Gardener

Judy Day, 38, container gardener

Bea Dersham, Garden Gallery, Cheyenne gardener

Jane Dorn, 24, 27, 40, 48, co-author, *Growing Native Plants of the Rocky Mountain Area*

Robert Dorn, 27, Wyoming plant authority, co-author, *Growing Native Plants of the Rocky Mountain Area* and author, *Vascular Plants of Wyoming*

Wendy Douglass, 7, 44, Laramie County Master Gardener

Nettie Eakes, 35, 36, head horticulturist, Cheyenne Botanic Gardens

Mark Ellison, 61, director, Cheyenne Urban Forestry Division

Charlette Felte, 33, co-owner, C & T Iris Patch

Tim Felte, 33, co-owner, C & T Iris Patch

Richard Franz, 21, Laramie County Master Gardener

Sylvia Franz, 21, Pumpkin Cookie baker

Jessica Friis, 4, 5, 29, 57, horticulturist, Cheyenne Botanic Gardens

Jeff Geyer, 48, 53b, water specialist, Laramie County Conservation District

Marty Gill, 49, homeowner, Granite Springs Retreat

Pam Glick, 25, Laramie County Master Gardener

Danny Glick, 25, grape grower

Ron Godin, 8, Colorado extension agronomist, retired

Vally Gollogly, 19, 30, 64, market gardener

Carlos Gonzales, 9B2, Cheyenne Boys and Girls Club

Mark Gorges, 2, 4, 9, 12, 13, 15, 23, 37, 55, Laramie County Master Gardener

Salli Halpern, 16, Laramie County Master Gardener

Rhea Halstead, 31, rose gardener

Gary Halstead, 31, rose gardener's helper

Bonnie Harper, Garden Gallery, Laramie County Master Gardener

Tom Heald, 55, former agent,
Natrona County Extension

Mike Heath, 16, 24, Laramie
County Master Gardener

Susie Heller, 9 Laramie
County Master Gardener

John Heller, 9, Laramie
County Master Gardener

Devon Henry, 10, Laramie
County Master Gardener

Chris Hilgert, 24, 25, coordinator,
Wyoming Master Gardeners

Ron Hoffman, 21, giant
pumpkin grower in Riverton

Lila Howell, 43, Garden Gallery,
Laramie County Master Gardener

Garry Howell, 43, water
garden co-builder

Susan Jones, 16, Laramie
County Master Gardener

Christine Johnson, 23, Laramie
County Master Gardener

Steve Johnson, 23, Laramie
County Master Gardener

Mary Ann Kamla, 51, Laramie
County Master Gardener

Bruce Keating, 50, Laramie
County Master Gardener

Carla Keating, 50, Laramie
County Master Gardener

Panayoti Kelaidis, 44B, 45, senior
curator and director of outreach,
Denver Botanic Gardens

Mike Kintgen, 44B, curator of alpine
plants, Denver Botanic Gardens

Dennis Knight, 59b, professor
emeritus, University of Wyoming

Phillipa Lack, 38,
Cheyenne gardener

Brent Lathrop, 53, 53B,
buffalograss grower

Bob Lick, 49, homeowner,
Granite Springs Retreat

Nancy Loomis, 42, 42B, 48,
Laramie County Master Gardener

Pam Loomis, 42, rain
garden gardener

Stephanie Lowe, 61,
Historic Cheyenne

Jonathan Magby, 23, graduate
student, University of Wyoming

Wanda Manley, 16, 45, Laramie
County Master Gardener

Rebecca Marcy, 64, owner,
Yellowstone Animal Health Center

Jacob Mares, 44B,
former horticulturist,
Cheyenne Botanic Gardens

Tyler Mason, 10, 40, former
horticulturist, Cheyenne
Botanic Gardens

Michael Smith, 56, tree owner

Jim Stallard, 16B, tool sharpener

Richard Steele, 16, 51, Laramie County Master Gardener

Amy Storey, 63, Bright Agrotech

Tiger Tree crew, 61

Mary Weinstein, 50, trellis gardener

Jeff Weinstein, 50, trellis gardener

Barb Werner, 49, homeowner, Granite Springs Retreat

Milt Werner, 49, homeowner, Granite Springs Retreat

Jeff White, 61, volunteer, Rooted in Cheyenne

Catherine Wissner, 3, 4, 7, 12, 13, 17, 22, 38, 41,45,51, 52, 52B, 53, 56, 58, 60, University of Wyoming Extension horticulturist and coordinator, Laramie County Master Gardeners

Patrick Zimmer, 25, co-owner, Table Mountain Winery

Authors and experts cited
Numbers indicate chapter(s) in which they are cited.

Patricia Coccoris, 62, author, *The Curious History of the Bulb Vase*

Elliot Coleman, 2, 40, author, *Four-Season Harvest*

Barbara Damrosch, 26, author, *The Garden Primer*

Evelyn Haddan, 47, author, *Beautiful No-Mow Yards*

Leslie F. Halleck, 4, author, *Gardening Under Lights*

Joel Karsten, 39, author, *Straw Bale Gardens*

Howard Dill, 21, grower, first giant pumpkin

George F. Harison, 32, discoverer, "Harison's Yellow" rose

Gene Howard, 24, last director, Cheyenne Horticultural Field Station

Joe Lamp'l, 4, author and TV host, www.joegardener.com

Jeff Lowenfels, 8, author, *Teeming with Microbes*

Suzanne McIntire, 30, author, *An American Cutting Garden, A Primer for Growing Cut Flowers*

William Prince, 32, first propagator, "Harison's Yellow" rose

Douglas Tallamy, 45, 48, author, *Bringing Nature Home*

Susan Tweit, 48, author, *The Rocky Mountain Garden Survival Guide*

PHOTO CREDITS

All photos were taken by Barb Gorges in Laramie County with these exceptions.

Photos taken by Barb elsewhere

Chapter 11, dandelions, Medicine Bow Range, Albany County

Chapter 33, field of iris, C & T Iris Patch, Weld County, Colorado

Chapter 44, natural rock garden, Albany County

Chapter 60, lodgepole pine with sap, Albany County

Grapes, Table Mountain Winery, Goshen County

Photos taken by others in Laramie County unless noted otherwise

Garden photo, her garden, Jutta Arkan

Garden photo, her garden, Lila Howell

Garden photo, her garden, Kim Parker

Chapter 8, rototilling, Getty Images, unknown location

Chapter 14, rabbits, Chris Hoffmeister

Chapter 24 and plant photos, Fort Laramie strawberries, Mike Heath

Chapter 24, Seascape strawberries, Chris Hilgert, Albany County

Chapter 27, Britton's Skullcap, Jane and Robert Dorn, Wyoming

Chapter 31, pink rose bush, Rhea Halstead

Chapter 43, water garden, Lila Howell

Chapter 51, walk lined with pink groundcover, Martha Mullikin

Chapter 61, Tiger Tree crew, Rooted in Cheyenne

Britton's Skullcap and Coyote Mint, Jane and Robert Dorn, Wyoming

Rose, 'David Austin,' Rhea Halstead

Soapwort, Mary Ann Kamla

Turkish Veronica, Mary Ann Kamla

BARB'S GARDEN BOOKSHELF

When reading any garden information, season all of it with what you learned in this book about gardening in Cheyenne using modern, sustainable methods.

ORGANIC GARDENING, SPECIFICALLY

2019   Margaret Roach, *A Way to Garden: A Hands-on Primer for Every Season*

2018   Eliot Coleman, *The New Organic Grower: A Master's Manual of Tools and Techniques for the Home and Market Gardener*

2012   Jane Shellenberger, *Organic Gardener's Companion: Growing Vegetables in the West*

2010   Jeff Lowenfels & Wayne Lewis, *Teeming with Microbes: The Organic Gardener's Guide to the Soil Food Web*

2009   Fern Marshall Bradley, Barbara W. Ellis and Ellen Phillips, editors, *Rodale's Ultimate Encyclopedia of Organic Gardening*

2008   Barbara Damrosch, *The Garden Primer: The Completely Revised Gardener's Bible, 100% Organic*

1999   Eliot Coleman, *Four-Season Harvest: Organic Vegetables from Your Home Garden All Year Long*

1961   Ruth Stout, *Gardening Without Work: For the Aging, the Busy & the Indolent*

HOW TO GARDEN

2016   Cheryl Moore-Gough and Robert Gough, *Rocky Mountain Vegetable Gardening Guide*

2015   Robert Kourik, *Understanding Roots…Discover How to Make Your Garden Flourish*

2015   Tovah Martin, *The Indestructible Houseplant: 200 Beautiful Plants That Everyone Can Grow*

2012   Willi Galloway, *Grow Cook Eat: A Food Lover's Guide to Vegetable Gardening*

2011   Lauren Springer Ogden, *The Undaunted Garden: Planting for Weather-Resilient Beauty*

2010   Linda Chalker-Scott, *The Informed Gardener Blooms Again*

2008   Linda Chalker-Scott, *The Informed Gardener*

2007   Jodi Torpey, *The Colorado Gardener's Companion: An Insider's Guide to Gardening in the Centennial State*

2007   John Cretti, *Month-By-Month: Gardening in Wyoming: What to Do Each Month to Have a Beautiful Garden All Year*

2000   Lauren Springer and Rob Proctor, *Passionate Gardening: Good Advice for Challenging Climates*

2000   Shane Smith, *Greenhouse Gardener's Companion: Growing Food & Flowers in Your Greenhouse or Sunspace*

1998   Patricia Lanza, *Lasagna Gardening: A New Layering System for Bountiful Gardens: No Digging, No Tilling, No Weeding, No Kidding!*

1993   Christopher Brickell and Elvin McDonald, editors, *The American Horticultural Society Encyclopedia of Gardening*

1992   Rhonda Massingham Hart, *Trellising: How to Grow Climbing Vegetables, Fruits, Flowers, Vines & Trees*

1985   Jeff and Marilyn Cox, *The Perennial Garden: Color Harmonies through the Seasons*

1984   Roger B. Yepsen, Jr., editor, *The Encyclopedia of Natural Insect & Disease Control*

1981   T. Jeff Williams, *How to Select, Use & Maintain Garden Equipment*

1967   George Kelly, *Rocky Mountain Horticulture: George Kelly's Garden Book*

GARDEN PLANT DESCRIPTIONS

2017   *Plant Select, Pretty Tough Plants: 135 Resilient, Water-Smart Choices for a Beautiful Garden*

2015   *Fort Collins Wholesale Nursery, Descriptive Guide* (to plants they sell)

2015   *Baker Creek Heirloom Seeds, The Whole Seed Catalog* (any year)

2014   Sarah Shaub and James Klett, Colorado State University Extension, *Dependable Landscape Trees from the Colorado State University Arboretum*

2014   Amy A. Fluet, Jennifer S. Thompson, Dorothy E. Tuthill, Brenna R. Marsicek, University of Wyoming Extension, *Plants with Altitude: Regionally Native Plants for Wyoming Gardens*

2007 Robert D. Dorn and Jane L. Dorn, *Growing Native Plants of the Rocky Mountain Area*

2006 Lance Hattatt, *Dictionary of Garden Plants*

1962 Peter Coats, *Roses: Pleasures and Treasures*

1939 Rosetta E. Clarkson, *Magic Gardens: A Modern Chronicle of Herbs and Savory Seeds*

GARDENING FOR CONSERVATION

2019 Douglas Tallamy, *Nature's Best Hope: A New Approach to Conservation That Starts in Your Yard*

2016 Larry Weaner and Thomas Christopher, *Garden Revolution: How Our Landscapes Can Be a Source of Environmental Change*

2015 Thomas Rainer and Claudia West, *Planting in a Post-Wild World: Designing Plant Communities for Resilient Landscapes*

2007 Douglas Tallamy, *Bringing Nature Home: How You Can Sustain Wildlife with Native Plants*

2005 Audubon Colorado (now Audubon Rockies), *Colorado Wildscapes: Bringing Conservation Home*

WILDLIFE

2018 Barb Gorges and Pete Arnold, *Cheyenne Birds by the Month: 104 Species of Southeastern Wyoming's Resident and Visiting Birds*

2016 David Allen Sibley, *The Sibley Field Guide to Birds of Western North America*

2011 Bill Thompson III & Connie Toops, *Hummingbirds and Butterflies [and gardening for them]*

2007 Eric R. Eaton and Kenn Kaufman, *Field Guide to the Insects of North America*

1994 George Adams, *Birdscaping Your Garden: A Practical Guide to Backyard Birds and the Plants That Attract Them*

1970 Donald J. Borror and Richard E. White, *Peterson Field Guides, A Field Guide to the Insects, America North of Mexico*

NATIVE PLANT IDENTIFICATION

2018 Denver Botanic Gardens, *Wildflowers of the Rocky Mountain Region*

2018 M. Walter Pesman and Dan Johnson, *Meet the Natives: A Field Guide to Rocky Mountain Wildflowers, Trees, and Shrubs*

2015 University of Wyoming Extension, *Rangeland Plants: Wyoming Tough, publication B-1265*

2015 Denver Botanic Gardens (Michael Bone, Dan Johnson, Panayoti Kelaidis, Mike Kintgen, Larry G. Vickerman), *Steppes: The Plants and Ecology of the World's Semi-arid Regions*

2014 Dennis H. Knight, George P. Jones, William A. Reiners, William H. Romme, *Mountains and Plains: The Ecology of Wyoming Landscapes*

2011 James Ells, *Rocky Mountain Flora*

2007 Robert D. Dorn and Jane L. Dorn, *Growing Native Plants of the Rocky Mountain Area*

2006 Brooklyn Botanic Garden, *Native Alternatives to Invasive Plants*

2001 Robert D. Dorn, *Vascular Plants of Wyoming*

2001 University of Wyoming, multiple authors, *Weeds of the West*

1998 Linda Kershaw, Andy MacKinnon, Jim Pojar, *Plants of the Rocky Mountains*

1992 Ruth Ashton Nelson, revised by Roger L. Williams, *A Guide to Rocky Mountain Plants, 5th edition*

1991 Bob Krumm, *The Rocky Mountain Berry Book*

1981 J. Stubbendieck, Stephan L. Hatch and Kathie J. Kjar, *North American Range Plants: 200 Descriptions as a Guide to Identification*

1976 William A. Weber, *Rocky Mountain Flora*

1963 John J. Craighead, Frank C. Craighead, Jr. and Ray J. Davis, *A Field Guide to Rocky Mountain Wildflowers*

1932 Per Axel Rydberg, *Flora of the Prairies and Plains of Central North America* (1965 facsimile)

GARDEN WRITING

2020 Jennifer Jewell, *The Earth in Her Hands: 75 Extraordinary Women Working in the World of Plants*

2019 Margaret Roach, *A Way to Garden: A Hands-on Primer for Every Season*

2018 Christopher Woods, *Gardenlust: A Botanical Tour of the World's Best New Gardens*

2016 Tim Richardson, *You Should Have Been Here Last Week: Sharp Cuttings from a Garden Writer*

2014 Bill Laws, *A History of the Garden in Fifty Tools*

2012 Thomas C. Cooper, editor, *The Roots of My Obsession: Thirty Great Gardeners Reveal Why They Garden*

2011 Vanessa Diffenbaugh, *The Language of Flowers* (novel)

2010 Robin Lane Fox, *Thoughtful Gardening*

2010 Anna Pavord, *The Curious Gardener: A Year in the Garden*

2009 Amy Stewart, *Wicked Plants: The Weed That Killed Lincoln's Mother & Other Botanical Atrocities*

1998 Susan Orlean, *The Orchid Thief: A True Story of Beauty and Obsession*

1991 Michael Pollan, *Second Nature: A Gardener's Education*

1991 Richard Goodman, *French Dirt: The Story of a Garden in the South of France*

1985 Jane Brown, *Vita's Other World: A Gardening Biography of V. Sackville-West*

1981 Eleanor Perenyi, *Green Thoughts: A Writer in the Garden* (newer editions available)

1981 Henry Mitchell, *The Essential Earthman: Henry Mitchell on Gardening*

1973 Thalassa Cruso, *To Everything There is a Season: The Gardening Year with Thalassa Cruso*

1968 Ruth Fouts Pochmann, *Triple Ridge Farm*

1963 Janet Gillespie, *The Joy of a Small Garden*

1936 Dorothy Biddle and Dorothea Blom, *Garden Gossip: Chronicles of Sycamore Valley*

RESOURCES

These are resources mentioned in the text.

The author continues to post garden columns written for the Wyoming Tribune Eagle at cheyennegardengossip.wordpress.com/.

FREE, LOCAL, PROFESSIONAL PLANT-RELATED ADVICE

Cheyenne Botanic Gardens, www.botanic.org

Cheyenne Urban Forestry Division, www.cheyennetrees.com

Laramie County Conservation District, www.lccdnet.org

Laramie County Extension Office, wyoextension.org/laramiecounty

Laramie County Master Gardeners, www.lcmg.org/

University of Wyoming Extension, wyoextension.org

University of Wyoming Extension publications,
www.wyoextension.org/publications

OTHER AGENCIES

Call Before You Dig, call811.com/before-you-dig

City of Cheyenne Compost Facility, www.cheyennecity.org/
Your-Government/Departments/Public-Works/Compost-Facility

PLANT GROWING INFORMATION

Alfalfa seed sprouting, Wikihow, www.wikihow.com/Grow-Alfalfa-Sprouts

Amaryllis, Amaryllis Man, stores.ebay.com/amaryllisman

Apples, Wyoming Apple Project, www.uwyo.edu/barnbackyard/_files/
documents/magazine/2014/winter/010114bbwyappleproject.pdf

Flowers, Slow Flowers Society, slowflowerssociety.com

Flowers, Slow Flowers, www.slowflowers.com/

General, Colorado State University Extension, PlantTalk,
planttalk.colostate.edu

Grapes, Table Mountain Winery, wyowine.wixsite.com/

Grapes, University of Wyoming Extension, Wyoming Grape Guide,
    www.wyoextension.org/agpubs/pubs/B-1341-grapes-for-web.pdf

Grapes, University of Minnesota, grapes, www.grapes.umn.edu

Grass, Buffalograss, "Buffalograss Lawns,"
    www.ext.colostate.edu/mg/Gardennotes/565.html.

Grass, Buffalograss, Stock Seed Farms, Murdock, Nebraska,
    www.stockseed.com

Grass, "Landscaping: Turf in Wyoming,"
    www.wyoextension.org/agpubs/pubs/B1129.pdf.

Grass, "Low-Maintenance Grasses for Revegetating Disturbed Areas and
    Lawns," www.wyoextension.org/agpubs/pubs/B1070.pdf.

Lavender, Lavender Association of Colorado, coloradolavender.org/

Microbiome, Jeff Lowenfels, www.jefflowenfels.com/

Noxious weeds, U.S. Department of Agriculture Plant Database, noxious
    weeds, plants.sc.egov.usda.gov/

Orchids, Fantasy Orchids, www.fantasyorchids.com

Orchids, Denver Orchid Society, denverorchidsociety.org

Organic farming, Eliot Coleman, fourseasonfarm.com/

Plant Finder, Missouri Botanic Garden,
    www.missouribotanicalgarden.org/plantfinder/

Plant hardiness, U.S. Department of Agriculture Plant Hardiness Zone Map,
    plants.sc.egov.usda.gov/hardiness.html

Poisonous to pets plants, ASPCA,
    www.aspca.org/pet-care/animal-poison-control

Poisonous to pets plants, Animal Poison Control, 1-888-426-4435

Regenerative gardening and agriculture, Soil Food Web School,
    www.soilfoodweb.com

Roses, planting, Wikihow, www.wikihow.com/Plant-Roses

Roses, hardy roses, High Country Roses, www.highcountryroses.com/

Soil testing, Colorado State University Soil, Water and Plant Testing
    Laboratory, www.soiltestinglab.colostate.edu/

Trees, Arbor Day Foundation,
    www.arborday.org/trees/whattree/fullonline.cfm

Trees, Cheyenne Botanic Gardens, www.botanic.org/about/arboretum/

Trees, Cheyenne Urban Forestry Division, www.cheyennetrees.com/

Trees, Don't Move Firewood.org, www.dontmovefirewood.org

Trees, Emerald Ash Borer Information Network, www.emeraldashborer.info

Trees, iTree landscape design tools, www.itreetools.org/

Trees, Rooted in Cheyenne, www.RootedinCheyenne.com

Trees, Wyoming State Forestry Division - Community (Urban) Forestry, wsfd.wyo.gov/forestry-assistance-programs/community-forestry

Winter sowing, Trudi Davidoff, www.wintersown.org/

POLLINATORS, WILDLIFE, WILDSCAPING, WATER-WISE GARDENING

Bumble Bees, "Bumble Bees of Western United States," search for the title at www.fs.fed.us/wildflowers

Douglas Tallamy, "Bringing Nature Home," www.bringingnaturehome.net

Douglas Tallamy, "Homegrown National Park," homegrownnationalpark.org/

Habitat Hero, Audubon Rockies, rockies.audubon.org/habitat-hero

Habitat Hero, demonstration garden, Cheyenne Board of Public Utilities, www.cheyennebopu.org/Home

Insect i.d., Bug Guide, Iowa State University, www.bugguide.net

Monarchs, University of Wyoming Biodiversity Institute, Monarchs and Milkweeds, www.wyobiodiversity.org

Monarchs, Monarch Joint Venture (government agencies, non-profits, academics), monarchjointventure.org

Native plants, "Plants with Altitude" by Fluet, Thompson, Tuthill and Marsicek, available through the University of Wyoming Extension

Pollinators, The Xerces Society, www.xerces.org/pollinators-mountain-region

Water-wise, Fort Collins Water-Wise Landscape program, www.fcgov.com/utilities/residential/conserve/water-efficiency/xeriscape

SEED AND PLANT COMPANIES

Alplains, Rocky Mountain native plant seeds, Kiowa, Colorado, www.alplains.com

Applewood Seed Company, native bulk seed, Arvada, Colorado, www.applewoodseed.com

Arkansas Valley Seed, Denver, Colorado, www.avseeds.com

Atlantic Giants Genetics Cooperative, giant pumpkins, www.aggc.org

Baker Creek Heirloom Seeds, Missouri, www.rareseeds.com

Bath Garden Center and Nursery, Fort Collins, Colorado, www.bathgardencenter.com

Beauty Beyond Belief Wildflower Seed, Boulder, Colorado, www.bbbseed.com

Botanical Interests, Broomfield, Colorado, www.botanicalinterests.com

C and T Iris Patch, Eaton, Colorado, www.candtirispatch.com

Fantasy Orchids, Louisville, Colorado, www.fantasyorchids.com

Ft. Collins Nursery, Fort Collins, Colorado, fortcollinsnursery.com

Ft. Collins Wholesale Nursery (look for list of retailers), www.ftcollinswholesalenursery.com

High Country Gardens, natives, Plant Select, seeds and plants, New Mexico, www.highcountrygardens.com

High Mowing Organic Seeds, Vermont, www.highmowingseeds.com

Johnny's Selected Seeds, cold climate, Maine, www.johnnyseeds.com

John Scheeper's, bulbs, Connecticut, www.JohnScheepers.com

Pine Tree Garden Seeds, cold climate, Maine, www.superseeds.com

Prairie Moon Nursery, native plants and seeds, Minnesota, www.prairiemoon.com

Richters Herbs, seeds and plants, Ontario, Canada, but ships to U.S. www.richters.com

Riverbend Nursery, Cheyenne, riverbendnurseryandstone.com

Sand Hill Preservation Center, heirloom seeds and poultry, Iowa, www.sandhillpreservation.com

Seed Savers Exchange Heirloom Seeds, Iowa, www.seedsavers.org

Seeds Trust, Denver, Colorado, www.seedstrust.com

Territorial Seed Company, Oregon, territorialseed.com

Western Native Seed, Coaldale, Colorado, www.westernnativeseed.com

Wind River Seed, Manderson, Wyoming, www.windriverseed.com

Wyoming Plant Company, Casper, Wyoming, www.wyomingplantcompany.com

GARDENING TOOLS AND SUPPLIES

Bath Garden Center and Nursery, Fort Collins, Colorado, www.bathgardencenter.com

Corona gardening tools, www.coronatoolsusa.com

Espoma Plant-tone, www.espoma.com

Felco pruners and other tools, www.felco.com

Fiskars gardening tools, www.fiskars.com/en-us/gardening-and-yard-care/products

Ft. Collins Nursery, Fort Collins, Colorado, fortcollinsnursery.com

Garrett Wade gardening tools, www.garrettwade.com/gardening.html

J & M Industries, Solarig High Tech Woven Plastic Sheeting for hoop houses, www.jm-ind.com

Lee Valley Tools, www.LeeValley.com

Northern Greenhouse Sales, www.NorthernGreenhouse.com

Riverbend Nursery, Cheyenne, riverbendnurseryandstone.com

Wyoming Worm Wrangler, www.facebook.com/wyomingwormwrangler

HOW TO BUILD

Firewise landscape

Laramie County Firewise information, www.lcfd10.org/firewise

University of Wyoming Extension, "Living with Wildfire in Wyoming," www.uwyo.edu/barnbackyard/_files/documents/resources/wildfire2013/wildfire_web.pdf

Firewise Natrona County, plant list, www.firewisewyoming.com/

Colorado State University Extension, Firewise Plant Materials, www.ext.colostate.edu/pubs/natres/06305.html

National Fire Protection Association, Firewise Communities, firewise.org

Hypertufa containers

www.finegardening.com/how-to/articles/make-hypertufa-trough.aspx

www.finegardening.com/article/make-your-own-hypertufa-container

Hoop houses

Wyoming Hoop House Information Network, www.wyomingextension.org/whhin

Rain gardens

Historic Sunrise Rain Gardens Project, educational demonstration, 2311 Reed Ave.

Jeff Geyer, water specialist, Laramie County Conservation District, 772-2600

Rain Garden Design Site and Selection Guide, University of Nebraska-Lincoln Extension, an interactive guide, www.extension.unl.edu/web/extension/publicationsandapps

Wyoming Department of Environmental Quality, non-point source water pollution, deq.wyoming.gov/wqd/non-point-source/

Rock gardens

Kenton Seth, www.paintbrushgardens.com

North American Rock Garden Society, www.nargs.org

Artificial rock making, www.artificialrock.com.au/

Water gardens

www.pondliner.com

Vertical gardens

Vertical Harvest, Jackson Hole, Wyoming, www.verticalharvestjackson.com

Plenty, www.plenty.ag

ZipGrow towers for hobby, school and commercial use, zipgrow.com

PUBLIC GARDENS

There is no entrance fee for Cheyenne Botanic Gardens. However, it has a reciprocal agreement with the other two gardens listed below (and hundreds more nationwide) that do charge, so its membership card will often get you into those and other gardens free.

Cheyenne Botanic Gardens, www.botanic.org

Denver Botanic Gardens, www.botanicgardens.org

Gardens on Spring Creek, Fort Collins, Colorado, www.fcgov.com/gardens

KEY WORD INDEX

Numbers indicate chapter, not page. "0" indicates Introduction.
Search these key words online for more information.